KIYO'S STORY

KIYO'S

For Aleine Enstein — with gratitude for your dedication to our children —

Kiyo Sato
1/21/20

KIYO SATO

STORY

A JAPANESE-AMERICAN FAMILY'S QUEST
FOR THE AMERICAN DREAM

Published by
Soho Press, Inc.
227 W 17th Street
New York, NY 10011

Library of Congress Cataloging-in-Publication Data
Sato, Kiyo, 1923–
[Dandelion through the crack]
Kiyo's story : a Japanese American family's quest for the American dream / Kiyo Sato.

Previously published as: Dandelion through the crack.

ISBN 978-1-56947-866-0
eISBN 978-1-56947-714-4

1. Sato family.   2. Sato, Kiyo, 1923–3.   Japanese Americans—Biography.
4. Japanese Americans—Evacuation and relocation, 1942–1945.   I. Title.
CS71.S2585 2009
929'.20973—dc22
2008040711

Printed in the United States of America

10 9 8 7 6 5

To my parents and their Issei generation, who navigated the treacherous waters of the Depression, racial prejudice and internment, and delivered us, the Nisei generation, to safe shores, for which we are eternally grateful.

With non-violence and the safety of their children foremost, they coped with a most humiliating civil disaster and helped our country move forward toward a better America.

Mary Tomomi Sato

John Shinji Sato

The Sato family's first home

The Sato family

· CONTENTS ·

· AUTHOR'S NOTE ·

I owe so much to my father, Tochan, John Shinji Sato, the great story-teller and educator, whose Japanese legends, Bible stories, poems of Longfellow, made-up anecdotes of Kuzu, made my dishwashing for our family of eleven a pleasure. And to Mama, whose love continues to flow through each one of us and out to everyone else.

My brother, Sanji Don, married Trudy Mayeda, who translated the *haiku* poetry written by Tochan, which we found after his death scribbled in a notebook. The translation does not attempt to follow the classic form of the *haiku*. They express the thoughts of the poet as closely as possible in another language.

· 1 ·

THE TERROR
OF DECEMBER 7TH

Hai ide te
Mishin ni hikareshi
Kawazu kana

– JOHN SHINJI SATO

It crawled out
Then crushed by a car
A frog

– TRUDY SATO, TRANSLATION

MAY 17, 1942. SACRAMENTO, CALIFORNIA.

WITH A START, I notice a police car following me. As I glance in my rearview mirror, peering through the pile of old suitcases in the back seat, I quickly figure I must be at least three miles outside of my legal five-mile radius. My hands begin to sweat.

Will the cops take me to jail? What will they do with the suitcases? My brothers and sisters need them to pack up for the "trip." If I don't get home by curfew time, what will Mama and *Tochan* ("Daddy") do? At eighteen, I am the oldest, and the only one who drives besides Tochan. My brother Seiji is close to my age, but he volunteered for the US Army after the Pearl Harbor attack and is stationed at Fort Leonard Wood.

What if the police think I'm a spy?

Mr. Saiki, our neighbor, flashes through my mind. He is in prison somewhere, and his family doesn't know where he has been taken. People say there is a special prison in Missoula, Montana for spies. His son Mickey quit school to take over the farm.

FBI agents showed up at a farm, and not finding Mr. Mizukami at home, agents went to Elk Grove High School and demanded that his son tell them the whereabouts of his father. They found Mr. Mizukami pruning pear trees in Courtland, and took him in. The next morning, much to the embarrassment of his family, their father's picture appeared in the *Sacramento Bee*, branded as a spy.

If the FBI thinks a good man like Mr. Saiki is a spy, there is no telling what they will do to me. If I were to be picked up now, what would my family do? Would my parents be notified? I must write down somewhere that my name is Kiyo Sato and that my parents are Shinji and Tomomi Sato at Route 2, Box 2917, in Sacramento, California. What will they do with my Studebaker? Dear God, please, please, not now!

I slow down. The police car slows down. My steering wheel becomes wet and slippery. He follows me steadily. I reach the town of Perkins, almost within the legal radius of five miles. I pass Bradshaw Road and he is still right behind me. I hold my body erect to keep from crumbling. My spine stiffens from fear. My foot can hardly control the pressure on the gas pedal and I try hard not to jerk or spurt forward.

I wish desperately now that I had taken the time to get that permit, but just to get it I have to go to Sacramento, which is over the five-mile radius. Besides, my *Nisei* Japanese-American friends tell me that it takes hours of waiting, that no one seems to know what they are doing. Right now, traveling eastward, out of town, I can't tell the officer that I'm on my way to get it. The steering wheel begins to slip.

I had planned to make one more stop for vegetables at the Chinese truck farm on the north side of Folsom Boulevard, but decide to turn right and head straight for home.

Explicitly following the law, I signal a right hand turn with my left arm at a right angle out of my window, allowing plenty of time. My right foot falls heavily as I try to step lightly on the brakes to slow down. I try with every ounce of energy in my body not to provoke the police car behind me.

A simple right turn takes all my effort to turn my steering wheel and maneuver over the slope of the railroad tracks. It is not until after the descent that I notice that the police car is no longer in my rearview mirror. I let my car roll down the incline, and my body goes limp. My leg is too weak to step on the brakes. When, finally, my Studebaker comes to a rolling halt, I fall over the steering wheel.

It is a long while before I feel the flow of blood into my blanched hands and feet.

I lift my head and see the chilling reminders down the road—huge 18" x 24" public notices nailed onto the fence posts:

INSTRUCTIONS TO ALL

PERSONS OF JAPANESE ANCESTRY

I didn't want to stop when I first saw them. I didn't want the world to know that I was "one of them" and have them see me jump the ditch, hold on to the barbed wire fence while I read the instructions. The small print would seal our fate. I checked my rear view mirror for oncoming cars. Up ahead I saw more posters. I drove on. It got easier to pass by another one. Rarely traveled, quiet, one-mile-long Routier Road appeared violated by black and white public notices indiscriminately nailed its whole length. With only five mailboxes on the road, why didn't they send five letters? Actually, only four letters. Mr. McDonald is Caucasian.

Like a huge, ominous wave, the dreaded day creeps up the state, ridding it of anyone with more than one-sixteenth Japanese blood, which goes back five generations, guaranteeing that not a single drop of Japanese blood will be left to "contaminate" the state. Herded into fairgrounds, horse stalls and temporary assembly centers, men, women and children await the construction of permanent concentration camps.

It's like going to a Boy Scout summer camp, the authorities tell us. Now that concentration camps are a reality, we are advised that they are not to be called "concentration camps." They are now to be referred to as "relocation centers." Imagine! We are to be kindly relocated to a relocation center!

News reaches us from those incarcerated at the Santa Anita racetrack. "Our family has a horse stall. No amount of scrubbing takes the smell away. We find old planks to cover the muddy front. I hope you don't come here. It's terrible!"

Feeling braver and needing the vegetables for supper, I decide to turn around and scoot across Folsom Boulevard.

I spot Mr. Yuen working at the far end of the truck farm, picking lettuce. I drive slowly along the edges of the plots to avoid raising dust. When he sees my Studebaker coming, he leaves his row to meet me. I tell him about my close shave with the law.

"Next time, if they stop you," he tells me, "you call me. I come get you. I tell them you my daughter."

He will never know how much it means to me to have someone who is not Japanese stand up for me, especially when more and more Chinese are wearing "I am Chinese" buttons. Driving home, I feel that a bit of sun is shining through the threatening, dark clouds. I don't tell my parents about the police. They've got enough to worry about.

· 2 ·

"Don't Come Back Here, Shinji"

Oya-dori no

Nure-te asaru e

Aki shigure

– JOHN SHINJI SATO

Mother hen, drenched

Searches for food

In the autumn rain

– TRUDY SATO, TRANSLATION

WITH SMALL, PIERCING eyes too weary for tears, she whispers barely audibly to her fourteen-year-old son, "Don't come back here, Shinji."

Her small body is bent as if it did not have time to straighten up from the long hours in the rice paddy, pressing the young plants one by one into the mud and water. Not knowing a moment's rest, she labors to feed her five children, only to have her meager earnings gambled away by her husband. When the children whine from hunger, she reminds them: "You will eat rice with sweet potatoes!" The thought of another mouthful of the *beta-beta*—the sticky, yellow mixture of a small portion of white rice extended with mashed sweet potatoes—tightens Shinji's throat and he swallows to soften a gag reflex. With his father's gambling habits, there is often no money left for food.

Around the gambling table there is much talk.

"If you get to America," they say, "even streets are paved in gold."

"*Eh! Honto desu ka?*" Is that so?

"*Honto, honto.*" True, true.

"*Amerika made ittara kane wa nambo demo aru.*" If you get to America there is plenty of money. There are not enough workers for the fields of California, they say.

Desperate, penniless, and on the verge of losing their plot of land and house, Shinji's father, having no other recourse, signs up at the village government house to go with a contingent of laborers to America, with a promise that he will send home enough money to pay his debts and save the family plot. This is not new to him. Five years ago he had gone to the plantations of Hawaii and returned home, not rich, but with enough money to pay off debts. America should be better, he decides. This time he will come home a rich man.

As tradition dictates, it is understood that Ichiji, the first son, barely eighteen, will stay home to be the head of the household.

With a bedroll over his shoulder and an old reed suitcase of clothes, Shinji, the youngest son, takes leave, bowing reverently to his mother. His mother does not lift her head until Shinji turns and follows his father, walking around the curve and down the dirt path along the rice paddy. When they reach the first mountain road, Shinji looks back and sees the four small figures in the distance, still standing as he had left them. It is a long walk around the base of three mountains to the Onjuku station. This was where his father often related how he would encounter the wily fox at night, which led him on the wrong path. Leaving Onjuku and his friends, Shinji hopes his father's gambling habits will change.

As the train clacks northward through villages and fields already foreign to him, he wonders what lies ahead. His mother's last words tug at his chest. He remembers helping his mother pick the edible weeds by the creek for supper when there were no vegetables in the garden and no money to buy *tofu* bean curd or fish.

Gazing out the train window, he becomes suddenly conscious of his feet being imprisoned in his brother's shoes, the only pair in his family, worn only on special occasions. He slips them off and changes to the more comfortable *zori* that his mother had woven from rice straw. In his bare feet, he remembers how lithely he could climb the giant gingko tree in the front yard and how cool they felt chasing the tiny fish in the creek by their plot of land.

His father dozes across the aisle, his head leaning against the window.

Shinji unties the *furoshiki* of lunch his mother has prepared. The rice balls with the salted, red *umeboshi* plum make his mouth water. The black strip of *nori*, dried seaweed, keeps his fingers from sticking. There are pickled vegetables and two small rounds of *manju*, sweet pastry, which are served only on special occasions. When did his mother get to Onjuku to buy them, he wonders? And where did she get the money? He remembers his father emptying the old stained teapot with the chipped spout where his mother kept the coins. He will never forget his mother's head bent over the open fire on the bare ground of the cooking area, staring into the embers for a long while. Shinji swallows a lump in his throat. He promises himself that he will not disappoint his mother.

It is a long day's train ride from Onjuku in Chiba-ken to the harbor city of Yokohama, where they meet a group of contract laborers coming from different parts of Honshu, the main island of Japan. The largest contingent comes from Hiroshima in southern Japan. They greet each other with a polite bow. Shinji notices that all the men wear hats. He is the youngest and without a hat. The contract boss of each group leads the men onto the ship and down into the bottom deck, the hole.

Shinji tosses his bedroll on the upper bunk above his father's. Even before the ship gets underway, there is the sound of money and boisterous exchange of talk in a dialect unfamiliar to him.

"*Sato-san, doka?*" How about it? they urge.

His father joins them with the money which is to last them until they reach their destination. Shinji turns on his back, resigning himself, and studies the only book he has, a small Japanese-English pocket dictionary.

The words are strange and difficult. *Mizu* is translated as "water" and pronounced "wa-ta." The word for *boshi* is "hatto," and spelled h-a-t.

"I'd better learn how to say *arigatoh*," he decides. "Thank you." The spelling makes no sense but he learns that one says "sahn-kyu." He repeats to himself, over and over "sahn-kyu, sahn-kyu."

The sea is rough and the voyage is long. At least they will be fed on the journey. Day after day, the men gather around a crate from morning until late at night. When they disembark, a few will be rich and the rest penniless. Shinji worries that his father will be among the penniless.

A small group of laborers go to the McClintock Farm, fifty miles north of San Francisco in the rolling hills of the Napa valley.

Almost as tall as the short Japanese men, Shinji works with all the energy and determination in his five-foot-five body to keep up with the adult men. Not a stranger to hard work, having helped his mother with planting and harvesting rice, he learns quickly. With some difficulty, he gains control over his fourteen-foot ladder, carries it from tree to tree, and stands it upright. Soon he sprints up and down with agility, emptying his bucket of peaches as quickly as the adult workers. At the top he pauses, drinking in the vastness and the beauty of the orchard. He finds it hard to believe that this whole orchard belongs to only one man, Mr. McClintock.

Shinji's father Sanzo, a responsible man when not gambling, works as the foreman of the ranch. During the busy season, he hires more workers. In the winter, a skeleton crew is maintained for the pruning of the trees. Others go south or to the Japanese boarding house in San Francisco, which serves as a way station where friends meet and exchange news. Work is plentiful and the honest and hardworking Japanese immigrant laborers are in constant demand. In the hot Imperial Valley in southern California, the melon harvest needs workers. It is 110 degrees but the pay is good. The husband and wife managers of the boarding house feed the men well and direct them to sources of work up and down the productive California valley.

"Yangu. Yoh-yaru na." You surely do well, one of the men comments, impressed with Shinji's seriousness. *Yangu*, a Japanized English word for "young man," denotes any younger male.

Around the packing shed, Mrs. McClintock notices the young boy picking up pieces of paper. He carefully folds a torn box label and stuffs it into his back pocket. Sometimes it is a whole page of an old newspaper. For the outhouse, perhaps. But it doesn't make sense, as there is always a pile of neatly cut square pieces of newspapers and an old Sears Roebuck catalog in the outhouse.

"What do you do with those pieces of paper, Shinji?" she finally asks, pointing to his pockets.

Pulling out a piece from a label, he points to a word. Orchard. With his hands he tries to explain to her that he opens his dictionary and looks up "orchard." Impressed with his eagerness to learn, she decides to help him.

"You come tonight and I will teach you English," she says. Noting that he does not understand, she explains in elaborate sign language, walks her fingers from his chest to the house, opens both palms for a book and says "seven."

Seven, she repeats and puts up seven fingers.

"Yes, yes! *Wakarimashita, wakarimashita*," he blurts out. "I understand, I understand. Sahnkyu, sahnkyu," he says bowing up and down.

"Shinji, say 'thank you.' Put your tongue between your teeth like this. Th . . . th . . ."

The afternoon goes by quickly. "Thank you, thank you," he keeps repeating quietly, pushing his tongue against his front teeth, as he stacks the fruit boxes. The lisp does not come easily. There is no word in the Japanese language with the sound of "th." Back home, he would be considered odd or retarded if he were to speak with his tongue showing.

There is a new spring in his steps as Shinji returns to his cabin to prepare for his first lesson. He lays out his clean clothes, his well-worn pocket dictionary and notebook. He carefully sharpens his pencil with his pocketknife.

At exactly seven o'clock, he knocks on the back door of the McClintock's big house.

Mrs. McClintock opens the screen door. "Come in, come in," she says.

She leads him through the screened-in porch to the spacious, bright kitchen.

"Sit here, Shinji." She beckons to the large, oilcloth-covered table upon which is a copy of an old book, a few sheets of notepaper and a pencil.

"My name is Mrs. McClintock," she says pointing to her chest. "What is your name?" She points to him. "Say, my name is Shinji Sato."

She takes his hand and points to Shinji's chest and repeats slowly "My name is Shinji Sato."

"My name is Shinji Sato," he repeats.

"Perfect!"

"This is a table. Table," she repeats, tapping the tabletop.

"Tayburu," he says.

"Table. Look at my tongue. Ta-ble." With her mouth wide open, she shows him how the tongue rests lightly on the roof of her mouth. It takes him by surprise that a lady would allow him to see the inside of her mouth.

Mrs. McClintock walks to the sink. "Water," she says as she turns on the faucet.

"Watah," he repeats. There is no sound of "er" in the Japanese language.

"Wa-ter."

With difficulty he imitates the pronunciation "water."

"Very good!" exclaims Mrs. McClintock. She is excited by her pupil's quick learning.

"Come this way, Shinji," she says signaling down the hall.

This is his first time inside an American house. How do they live, he had wondered? Curious, he glances into the rooms. It is true, he notices, that American beds are on stilts. That is because, he was told, Americans wear shoes inside their houses. Why do they need such a big house, he wonders? His whole house back home could fit inside the McClintock kitchen.

They enter a room full of books.

"This is our library," Mrs. McClintock explains. She pulls out a large volume. "Japan," she reads. Shinji cannot understand why Americans insist on calling his country "Japan." *Nihon* sounds nothing like Japan.

On the inside cover, he finds a map of Japan and points to the city of Tokyo. In sign language he indicates that his home is near the tip of Tokyo Bay. His teacher is delighted.

"Well, let's get down to business," she says, pulling out a copy of the *McGuffey Reader*. "Sit down." She reads the sentences slowly, knowing that much of it will not be understood.

"Study these words at the end," she advises. "Come next week at seven."

"Thank you," he says properly, conscious of the placement of his tongue.

The evening ends much too soon for Shinji. He feels that a whole new world has opened up and he returns to his cabin filled with dreams in this new country. He can hardly contain the thought of being able to read the newspaper. He will know what is going on around him. He will know what is happening in America. He will be able to read the books in the McClintocks' library. Forgetting the weariness of the day, he studies the

McGuffey Reader way into the night, laboriously looking up the meaning of each word in his dog-eared Japanese-English dictionary.

Tomorrow when he sends the money order to his mother, he will tell her of his good fortune. Will she be pleased to know that he is learning to read and speak English?

· 3 ·

SHINJI'S DREAM

Kaze nagi te

Ami amu kumo no

Yoh mijikashi

— JOHN SHINJI SATO

The wind has calmed

But for the spider to spin his web

The night is much too short

—TRUDY SATO, TRANSLATION

A DISTURBING LETTER arrives from Japan.

Riichi, the second son, is not well. After one year as an apprentice at a shipyard, he has returned home, thin and frail, unable to earn his keep.

He is again working, the letter states, at a shirt factory, where the job is indoors and less strenuous.

"I will write a letter tonight and tell them to send Riichi here."

Shinji's father, who is not one to discuss his thoughts with his young son, talks to himself for a stamp of approval. He does not ask for Ichiji, the first-born son, whose responsibilities are carved through the centuries as the caretaker of his family.

Riichi arrives, looking much thinner, though taller. In contrast to his younger brother, who is suntanned and sturdy, Riichi is pale and wan and a serious young man. He no longer is the brother with whom Shinji had climbed trees, or who entertained their sisters with a puppet show.

Work had been hard at the shipyard, he tells Shinji.

"I was sick and there were days when I couldn't get out of my *futon*."

"How was it at the shirt factory?" Shinji asks.

"Better. We worked indoors, and they fed us regularly."

Shinji listens. He remembers his mother's last words as she stood with her four children at her side, "Don't come back here, Shinji."

What thoughts went through her mind, he wonders, as his mother saw him, perhaps for the last time. He begins to understand the depth of anguish in her words, "*Koko e kaette kuru na, Shinji*," telling her young son never to return home.

As he listens to his brother, Shinji realizes how little thought he has given to feeding himself since coming to America.

Much to Shinji's relief, Riichi likes America. The two brothers work steadily with the crew of *Issei* men, stopping only for lunch. The day ends with a robust meal prepared by the camp cook. Each month, without fail, they send money to their mother, so their brother and sisters will eat adequately.

With renewed hope for the future, Shinji works to save money for an education. At fourteen he has not completed grammar school. If he had stayed in Japan, his chances of attending high school would have been slim. Like his brother Riichi, he would have had to go to work. Respect grows for his oldest brother Ichiji, who through the worst of times must share the family's burden.

By the time he is fifteen Shinji has learned to speak the English language and now he can read the newspaper. Bookkeeping, he decides, is what he must know to survive. Then he must learn to type. If he can get to Heald College in San Francisco, he can take whatever course he chooses. In America he can work and dream and plan with hope.

He finds that a bicycle is no longer adequate if he is to achieve his goals. The ferryboat from Napa to San Francisco is adequate only when he has a whole day at his disposal.

To buy an automobile is out of the question. With money saved, he buys an old motorcycle. With the cold wind blowing through the newspapers padding his jacket, dodging potholes in the asphalt road, Shinji reaches Heald College. It is another long ride home through Vallejo, the midway point. With his newly acquired books tied to the rear rack, he can hardly wait to reach his cabin to open them. A new and exciting world opens.

Their father, Sanzo, returns to Japan with money enough to save the family plot, and with pride restored.

⌒

"*Eh, bippin san da na!*" What a beauty, they exclaim, as they pass the photographs from one man to the next, while finishing their evening meal. Dressed in colorful Japanese kimonos, hair done in the classic pompadour, the women look young and pretty. All are arranged for by a *baishakunin*, a marriage broker.

"There is a young girl in my village," Seki-san from Katsuura City tells Riichi. "She is nineteen years old. I can arrange it for you."

With Seki-san acting as a *baishakunin*, arrangements are made and Riichi returns to Japan to marry Chieko.

Shinji travels to Seattle to meet the newly-married couple. He easily spots his brother and his wife in the crowd, as both are taller than the average Japanese. The petite Japanese women wear colorful kimonos. Apparently picture brides, they walk down the gangplank, taking mincing steps in their richly brocaded *zori*. Chieko follows her husband Riichi.

Shinji watches from a distance as the women approach with photographs in hand, anxiously scanning the waiting group of men of all sizes. One by one contact is made with much bowing on both sides.

"*Yoroshiku onegai itashi masu*," they repeat. "I thank you for your future care and concern." It is a salutation, more or less, as one would say in America, "How do you do."

One by one the matched couples disperse, with the women following their men at proper distances. A short man not five feet tall remains.

"*Komatta-na*," Shinji says to himself. This is a worry. He empathizes with the pretty, young woman standing alone. The two approach each other and bow respectfully. If she is disappointed, she shows no sign of it. He takes her suitcase and leads the way.

"I am not doing it this way," Shinji decides, as he walks to the end of the dock to join his brother and his wife. He likes what he sees in America. He likes the way Americans choose their own wives. "But how do I find a wife here?" he wonders. "And under California law, I can't marry anyone but a Japanese."

He dismisses the problem. He has plenty of time.

1922. OAK PARK DISTRICT, SACRAMENTO, CALIFORNIA.

Shinji drops in for a visit and finds Riichi and Chieko talking animatedly, having received news from home. It is always good to hear that their mother is doing fine and is in good health, but the topic of their conversation today concerns him, not the family.

"Shinji, you need to think about getting a wife," his brother suggests. Barely twenty-four, Shinji is in no hurry to get married.

"Chieko's cousin would like to come to America. How about it?"

So that is it. Shinji hesitates. He does not know how to answer his older brother, whom he was taught to respect and defer to.

Riichi continues. To his dismay, Shinji realizes that arrangements have already been made. A *baishakunin* has been engaged and all that Shinji has to do now is go to Japan and marry her.

"I don't want to marry someone I don't know," Shinji tells his brother. Riichi is aghast that his younger brother does not gratefully accept his plans.

"She comes from a good background. There are no bad illnesses in the family. Everything has been carefully checked out by the *baishakunin*. You have nothing to worry about," Riichi tells his younger brother. "Besides, they are in good circumstances."

"I would like to wait, until next year perhaps," Shinji replies.

"But it will be too late. With the Oriental Exclusion Act, you won't be able to bring anyone."

His hands holding his downcast head in exasperation, Riichi exclaims: "*Komatta-na,*" Now, what am I going to do? All the extensive plans that he and his wife have made for his brother come crashing down. He knows he is responsible for his younger brother's welfare. He had not expected that Shinji would defy him, the *niisan*, the respected older brother.

To make matters worse, a steamship ticket has already been purchased with a set date of departure. Trapped, Shinji responds that he will go to Japan only to meet the person, but will not promise to bring her back as his wife.

Riichi concedes. He is confident that once in Japan his brother will have to follow Japanese tradition and the plans he and Chieko and the *baishakunin* have arranged for him.

Even before he sets sail, Shinji is determined that his wife will be of his own choice. If they can do that in America, why can't he, he argues with himself. However, he has promised his brother that he will at least consider the arrangement. The thought weighs heavily on his mind.

⁓

Tokyo is a busy, bustling city. In this big city, surely there is a wife for me, he feels.

At the *ryokan* where he plans to stay a few days before heading for Onjuku, news spreads that a handsome young man from America is visiting. Women workers appear constantly, bowing politely and offering their services.

A petite young woman rushes past him in the hallway, barely acknowledging his presence with a slight bow. It is early in the morning. She slides the front *shoji* screen and disappears. Late at night he notices her again, the crispness gone from her white clothes, her dark hair held back with a white scarf. She sits alone at the far corner of the dining room, away from the din of noisy guests. He surmises that she is not one of the workers of the *ryokan*.

A Japanese woman does not eat alone in public. Who is she? What is she doing?

"She comes from the north," the owner relates, "and works in a hospital for tuberculosis patients down the street." After she lost her brother in a tragic drowning accident, she left Aizu to drown her own sorrow, they say, and immersed herself totally in nursing. She is twenty-seven years old and has turned down all offers of marriage. Now, they say, she is beyond marriageable age. Her name, they tell him, is Tomomi.

Nonetheless, something about Tomomi impresses Shinji. Is it because she walks with confidence? Her quick steps seem to know exactly where they are going. He has seen this kind of independence in American women. Mrs. McClintock taught him English without first asking her husband's permission. That would not happen in Japan.

He must follow proper protocol. Shinji asks several of his friends to make contact, to act as *baishakunin*. They agree that Tomomi will be a good wife for Shinji. She comes from a family of moderate means. Without hesitation, Tomomi agrees to marry him. She has heard much about America. American women are like American men, they say. With the date of his departure imminent, whirlwind arrangements are made. Legal papers are signed, and he makes a quick trip to Onjuku to see his mother and introduce his new bride to his family and friends. To avoid conscription into the Japanese army, they must leave Japan's shores within the month.

Tomomi follows her husband, walking for miles on the rough, hilly country roads of Onjuku, winning the admiration of those she meets. His promise to his older brother to meet his wife's relative is pushed to the inner recesses of his mind. Occasionally, it surfaces with a twinge of guilt, but he knows that new arrangements will be made for her by the *baishakunin*. He will have to face his brother's disappointment later.

1922. SAN FRANCISCO, CALIFORNIA.

"She's like a Japanese doll!" someone remarks as the young couple disembarks in San Francisco. Even after a long and arduous voyage plagued with seasickness, Tomomi, dressed in her bright *kimono*, walks down the gangplank with a sprightly step to where Shinji's old friend Yoshioka-san awaits with his automobile. A pharmacist and owner of a drug store, Yoshioka-san is one of the few successful immigrants to own a car and a business.

"You need to get her some American clothes," his friend suggests.

"I don't have any money left," Shinji confesses.

"Don't worry about it. I know where to go."

The small department store, owned by an immigrant couple, carries all manner of items to meet the needs of the Japanese population.

After introductions, Tomomi is led to the back of the store by the woman proprietor, who appears to have done this many times before.

Time passes by quickly for the two friends, who have not seen each other for several years. Conversation stops abruptly when Tomomi walks down the aisle wearing a black dress draped loosely below the waist and a deep, black hat with a small brim smartly tilted to one side. With purse, shoes and silk stockings, she looks like a picture from the Sears Roebuck catalog.

"*Suteki da na!*" How elegant, both men exclaim, thoroughly impressed.

"This is a basic style and can be worn anywhere, to church and to funerals," the proprietor explains.

Yoshioka-san pays the bill.

"*Omedetoh.*" Congratulations, he says as he hands his friend fifty dollars. "You did very well."

⁓

The road into the McClintock farm seems never ending, flanked on both sides by rows of fruit trees. What will I be doing here? Tomomi wonders.

They drive into a deserted packing yard. Much to Shinji's relief, the workers are out in the orchard picking peaches. Tomomi follows her husband to their cabin, beyond the bachelors' barrack. Mrs. McClintock has been in, he notices. She has placed an extra cot and blankets in the room and covered the table with a red and white patterned oilcloth.

"*Tai hen desu ne?*" It is not easy, is it? Tanaka-san, the cook, greets Tomomi in the women's shower cabin.

"*Onegai itashimasu.*" I beg your assistance, she acknowledges politely. America is not as she had expected. They live in a small cabin, not a big house. The bathroom is a distance away. An outhouse. And the shower room is far from the luxurious *ofuro* bath she had access to at the Tokyo inn.

"Do you have any work clothes?" Tanaka-san asks.

"Only my hospital uniform," Tomomi answers.

Later, there is a knock on the cabin door. It is Tanaka-san.

"You might be able to fit into these pants and shirt. I am sorry I don't have extra shoes. Did you bring a pair of *zori?*" she asks. "That will be all right for now in the shed."

The pretty, new, knee-length black dress and the high-heeled shoes are carefully put away in her suitcase and pushed under her iron cot. She washes out the silk stockings and hangs them up to dry. What tomorrow will bring, she does not know, but she will put on her pants and shirt, which are much too large for her, and do what is expected of her.

Assigned to the packing shed, she learns quickly to pack fruit according to size and quality. Having been an efficient nurse, she does not waste motion and rapidly stacks boxes of uniform, snugly packed peaches at her station. The carrier is impressed.

"*Hayai desu ne!*" How fast you are, he says, hustling back and forth to the loading dock with the boxes.

When a truckload of peaches comes in from the orchard, the workers carefully empty the contents onto the conveyor belt. Quick hands pluck the culls off the moving belt, a task Tomomi does easily and naturally; but when others comment on her speed, she slows down, not wanting them to feel that she is better. Already she senses that her way of speaking does not fit. Working with a crew of laborers from another *ken*—province—she becomes conscious of her Tokyo dialect and speaks sparingly for fear of being labeled "uppity."

By day's end, her back is stiff and the calves of her legs ache from the constant standing. At the trough in the washroom, she splashes cold water on her face and neck and feels better.

"*Tai hen desu ne*," Tanaka-san says sympathetically, watching Tomomi from the next faucet. "You will get used to it."

Tanaka-san feeds the crew well. A hearty curry stew over rice; a side of boiled, cold spinach; always accompanied with pickled *tsukemono* of *nappa,* or cabbage, and plenty of hot green tea. Tomomi helps the cook serve the seven men and then they both sit down to eat.

The men linger over cups of hot tea, talking.

"Riichi is doing well growing strawberries in Oak Park," Shinji tells them. "Many Japanese are settling there. Land is cheap. The soil is not too good but the Oregon Plum strawberries do well."

"How can you farm when we can't own land?" they ask.

"If you have children old enough, they are American citizens so you can buy property in their names."

"Yamamoto got five acres."

"How did he do it? Orientals can't buy property in California."

"I hear he 'borrowed' the name of a *Nisei*."

"If you know any *hakujin* Caucasian, they can buy it for you. Of course, they will own it until you can legally buy it back."

"Under the Alien Land Law, I don't think Japanese are allowed to lease land, either."

Sentiment towards the Chinese and Japanese is not only bad, it is dangerous. Six hundred Chinese workers were drowned, one says, when the floodgates were opened up before payday. Only *they* know that it was no accident.

One by one the men leave and head for the shower. Several prefer the small, wooden *furo* tub they have built against the side of the washroom. The walls are barely the height of the men, with open space between the top and the lean-to roof.

"Tomomi-san, you go and rest. I can finish this alone," the older woman urges the young woman, whose smooth tender hands are stained and scratched.

"*Arigatoh*," She thanks Tanaka-san, relieved to leave and soak the aches of her body in the hot *furo* bath.

"*Oyasumi na sai*." Rest well, they tell each other.

She walks to her cabin to fetch her *yukata* cotton robe and returns to the bathhouse. By now, she figures, it should be empty. Culture dictates that men bathe first. Just as she is about to pull the latch, she hears the sound of a body moving in the water. Quietly, she withdraws. Her cabin seems so far away. She rests her exhausted body on a tree stump set alongside the bathhouse wall where the men often sit and smoke. Her head nods against the wall and is still. Insects hum in the cool night air.

"*Ara! Sumanai-na*." The bather emerges, surprised to see Tomomi dozing. He apologizes and quickly disappears. Dazed, awakened from a deep sleep, she walks inside, feeling the welcome warmth of the enclosure. She hangs her *yukata* and sash on one of the large nails on the wall and then removes her soiled work clothes and undergarments and places them in a pile beside her on the wooden lattice platform. With buckets of hot water scooped from the tub, she washes her clothes one by one, scrubbing her work pants until no stains are left. Pouring a bucket of water over her long, black hair and body, she washes and then rinses herself until no sign of soap is left. With both hands on the edge of the redwood tub, she lifts her petite body over the side and slowly sinks into the *ofuro*, her black hair flowing on the surface around her.

Sitting on the lattice rack on the bottom of the tub, she feels the comfortable warmth generated by the last of the embers beneath. Water comes just above her breasts. To cover her tight, sore shoulders, she moves her body forward, bracing her feet against the opposite side of the four-by-four-foot tub and closes her eyes. The hot water caresses and releases all the tightness in her weary body. She falls asleep.

She awakens with a start. How long she has slept she does not know but the water feels cool. She hurriedly dries and puts on her *yukata,* worried that Tanaka-san may have been waiting. Outside, she stokes the dying fire, and leaves only when she is sure that there is enough fire to reheat the water. Carrying her wet, clean clothes, she heads towards her cabin.

1922. SOUTH SACRAMENTO, CALIFORNIA.

"Where you going? Wanna ride?"

A car stops to offer Shinji a lift as he walks to his brother's new house in Sacramento.

"Where you from?" he asks.

"Napa," Shinji answers.

"I mean, what country you come from?"

"Japan," Shinji answers.

"You interested in farming?"

Shinji tells him that he is working at an orchard and would one day like to have a place of his own.

"I have five acres not too far from here. Been lying fallow for several years," the man tells him. "The soil is not too good, clay, but there is an irrigation pump," he says. "You can have it for reasonable."

"He must know that I can't lease land," Shinji thinks. "After all, he is Negro, and he is willing to lease his land to me."

"I'll drive by it and show you the property."

They drive past his brother's house on Franklin Boulevard. Much of the land lies low and the last rain left an expanse of water on half of the property. Mr. Jackson drives down the long, dirt road. Tall weeds surround a small, unpainted cabin and a barn. Down the road, he tells him, a Japanese man grows strawberries. Shinji notices a small plot of neatly growing rows of strawberry plants to the west.

"I would like to look around," Shinji tells Mr. Jackson.

"If you decide to take it, leave a message with Oshima," he says as he drives off. The Oshima Grocery Store is where the Japanese immigrants trade.

Shinji walks through the high weeds to a fenced-in enclosure. Down below in the center of a dark hole, he sees the pump. It may take a little priming, Mr. Jackson had said. Weeds hang down the eroded edges. He takes note of the broken slats of a ladder at the far end.

Bermuda grass surrounds the cabin. In the back, a row of tall cottonwood trees shed blossoms like snow.

He decides to walk down the lane to check the strawberry patch and finds the farmer irrigating.

"My name is Sato Shinji," he introduces himself in the Japanese way, giving his surname first.

"I'm Makino."

Makino-san is delighted to share his experiences. "The shallow clay works well for strawberries," he says.

"My berries ripen much sooner than the others so they are the first on the market," he continues. "Half of that land is too shallow and holds water but you need only one or two acres for strawberries," he advises Shinji.

Shinji had heard from other immigrants that strawberry growing is hard work but profitable and that there is no competition.

He thanks Makino-san as he leaves.

"By the way," Mr. Makino offers, "I built a *furo* bath. You and your wife are welcome to use it any time."

The day's shadows are long as the young couple drive down the dirt road towards the old barn and cabin. The rent is paid for the month; he left money for Mr. Jackson at the Oshima Grocery Store on Franklin Boulevard. "You can move in anytime you want," Mr. Jackson has told him.

The old Chevrolet truck carries all that they own, held in on both sides by black, lattice racks—blankets, two iron cots given to them by the McClintocks, suitcases with their special-occasion clothes, cardboard boxes with work clothes, tools and odds and ends acquired over the past year. A box of old books, an old Remington typewriter and textbooks from his Heald College night courses, canned foods, kitchen utensils, teacups, mismatched plates, forks, chopsticks and other useful items from the workers' kitchen, which Tanaka-san has thoughtfully shared, and pans scorched from years of use, including a cast-iron rice pot and a teakettle.

Tomomi alights from the high seat of the truck onto the soft carpet of Bermuda grass and quickly walks towards the small, unpainted, weather-beaten house. Choked by weeds, the screen door refuses to budge.

She returns to the truck.

"*Anata*, where is the *kama?*" Tomomi asks. The Japanese *kama*, an indispensable tool, is Shinji's constant working companion. Carried thrust through his belt, he uses it to cut weeds and chop off suckers from trunks of trees and vines wherever he encounters them.

In the back of the truck he finds the *kama* and cuts the weeds and the wiry Bermuda grass and pulls open the screen door. Tomomi steps in. To her dismay, tendrils of the Bermuda grass cover the earthen floor. Pale from lack of sunshine, they grow relentlessly in every direction.

She turns the doorknob to the kitchen and steps onto the tattered lino-leum floor. A small, oilcloth-covered table against the wall is brown with a thick layer of dust. On the opposite side, to her delight, a rusty hand pump stands above a long, shallow, chipped porcelain sink. No longer will she have to go to an outside faucet to wash the dishes.

She pulls down the handle of the pump . . . one, two, three, four, five, six, seven, eight, no water . . . nine, ten, no water . . . eleven, twelve . . . there is no water. No water to wipe the dirt off the table. No water to cook with. No water to wash her hands. Without water, she cannot exist, not in the hospital, not on the farm, not anywhere. To keep clean and healthy, one needs water.

She rushes to the barn, where she finds Shinji gathering discarded, bro-ken shovels and tools, placing them in the corner.

"*Anata!*" Tomomi calls from the barn door.

Seeing his wife's distressed look, he immediately leaves his work.

"There is no water!" she exclaims. "I pumped so many times!"

"I'm not surprised," Shinji tells his wife. "Mr. Jackson told me the main pump might need priming. I'll work on it first thing in the morning. We have enough water to drink in the truck."

He finds the gallon jug of water, hands it to Tomomi and leaves quickly to work in the barn again. Tomomi carefully wipes off the dusty table with a wet rag to set out the *obento* lunch that the camp cook has packed for them. She unties the *furoshiki* and leaves it spread out on the table. Eight large, round *onigiri* rice balls with sesame seeds, boiled green spinach neatly lined into stems and leaves and cut into two-inch lengths, and slices of fried corned beef are all neatly packed inside a well-worn, two-tiered lacquer box. A small jar of pickled *nappa* cabbage and a jar of *takuwan* radish pickles, even a small bottle of *shoyu* and several pairs of used chopsticks thoughtfully complete the meal. In the back of the truck Tomomi finds the cardboard box of glasses, teacups, rice bowls and plates, a pretty can of green tea and another of coffee. She pours two glasses of cold water from the teakettle, examines her table of food and goes to call her husband for supper.

At the long sink, she carefully pours water over Shinji's grimy hands and offers him the rice sack towel.

"*Yoku yatte kureru.*" You do so well for us, Shinji says with deep gratitude as he sits down in the clean high-backed chair, showing more wood than varnish. He reaches for the *onigiri*, and then without taking a bite, he puts it down.

"Wait a minute!" he exclaims. "Hand me that teakettle," he says and quickly disappears out the door. She follows him to the barn, as she will not eat without her husband. In the barn, Shinji places the teakettle over the hole on top of an old five-gallon oilcan he had found in the back of the barn.

"I fixed this to cook our rice tomorrow," he explains as he stuffs twigs into the cut-out front panel and starts a fire. "Tonight we can have hot tea."

Tomomi can see that the barn floor has been cleared. He has piled the broken boxes outside against the wall, and stacked the usable ones neatly inside.

"See this shovel? All it needs is sharpening," he says picking up an old shovel. "See this broken hoe? I will cut it down shorter for planting and weeding strawberries."

He is full of plans. Tomomi listens while the water heats. Digging in the dirt and planting strawberries is not what she had dreamed of America.

What is her mother thinking now, she wonders? Would she be saying "You should have listened to me and stayed in Aizu. You could have learned the business of wedding preparations." She sees her father paying no attention, sitting by the warm charcoal *hibachi*, reading.

To spend the rest of her life in her mother's business, catering weddings, was not what she had wanted to do. She had wanted to get to the big city. She had wanted to become a nurse, to do something important. She had wanted nothing to do with the *baishakunin* who constantly brought up the subject of marriage. She was tired of being reminded that she was passing beyond marriageable age.

She had left Aizu on the pretense of visiting her cousin near Tokyo. Tuberculosis hospitals were constantly in need of help, she had heard, and offered training in patient care. That was where she met Shinji several years later, in the inn near the hospital where she worked.

At twenty-six, she was happy to be useful seeing to the care of a segment of the population that society shunned. Nobody would marry anyone discharged from the tuberculosis hospital, even though the disease was no longer active, nor would anyone marry members of a patient's family. Tomomi, too, would not be considered suitable for marriage, after having been exposed to the dreaded disease. It did not concern her.

The teakettle steams, just perfect for steeping the green tea leaves. As they walk back to the small, weather-beaten cabin, the sun, over the horizon, casts long shadows of the barn in their path.

⁓

Up before dawn, cooking rice in the chilly barn, Tomomi feels the warmth of the fire on her thighs as she squats, feeding the firewood into the oilcan stove. The cover of the rice pot begins to jiggle and white foam dribbles down the sides of the pot, emitting a comforting aroma of home. Twenty more minutes and the rice will be done. Then she will heat some water for *misoshiru* soybean paste soup cooked with the leftover spinach from last night.

"I will work on the pump today. By tonight you should have water coming to the kitchen," Shinji tells her.

Tall grass held back by bent and rusted chicken wire surrounds the well. Down below, in the dark, cavernous pit, the pump and belt are barely visible. Shinji finds the crudely built ladder hanging along the dirt wall. The slats are loose in spots. Carefully he descends to the bottom. It is dark, like a dungeon, except for a ray of morning sunlight hitting the upper wall of the well.

At the base of the pump he finds the switch and flips it over. He turns the large flywheel with difficulty. It is frozen from disuse. Expecting trouble, his pockets bulge with small tools. He uses an oil dispenser with a long spout to reach the crevices of the flywheel. It turns halfway. More oiling. With both hands tightly gripping the wheel he turns it with all his strength. The engine sputters and stops. He repeats this again and again until his arms ache. With a noisy clatter of metal hitting metal, the motor finally turns. He waits. There is no water.

He climbs back up the ladder.

"How much water do we have left?" he asks Tomomi.

"There's one more bottle in the truck," Tomomi replies.

Shinji pours the contents into a bucket, leaving just enough in the bottom of the bottle for their hot tea. With care, he carries the bucket down the ladder and into the hole.

Sunlight now filters closer to the dirt floor. He starts the motor. He knows that he has only one chance, one bucket of water to prime the pump, and that he must do it right the first time.

He turns off the motor and allows the noises to settle down completely. For once, he finds the birdcalls to be an interference, and wishes that they would go away. When there is silence, he dumps the contents of the bucket into the opening, places his ear against the pipe and listens intently as the glob of water drops downward, occasionally splashing along the sides. Just as he visualizes the water at the opening on the other end of the long pipe shaft, he turns the flywheel with all his strength. It starts with a muffled sound. The glob of water is caught; it slowly climbs back up, coaxed by the old motor, and gathers behind it water that had been resting for years deep in the earth's vein. He holds his breath, hoping that the motor will not die.

The clatter from the empty shaft diminishes. The end of the pipe emits a loud forceful sputter. Then another, then another, like an upset stomach vomiting its foul, brown contents.

Shinji climbs up the well and walks around to the front of the pipe. Through the weeds he sees dirt and water gushing forth like a caged animal let loose. He watches with deep satisfaction as the water gradually turns clear, and, like tentacles, spreads out in all directions.

The dry, dormant ground awakens.

· 4 ·

STRAWBERRY FIELD

Shita tari ya
Ichigo toru te no
Ya ya hiete

−JOHN SHINJI SATO

Dripping morning dew
Chilling
Berry picking hands

−TRUDY SATO, TRANSLATION

1923.

HER SMALL BODY moves with difficulty. It is her ninth month of pregnancy. Squatting while moving from plant to plant, like a praying mantis with bent knees, she derives a certain comfort in having her swelling abdomen protruding safely between her thighs, though at times she must stretch over it to reach the strawberries growing along the ditches.

The warm, bright sun hurries the color of the strawberries. Pale green berries are plump and red by the next morning. As if pursued by the thousands of big, juicy Oregon Plum strawberries, Tomomi moves her fingers non-stop from plant to plant, twisting each stem half an inch from the base and cradling it gently in the palm of her hand to protect the soft, ripe fruit from bruising. Then she places each handful quickly and carefully in the baskets. Her carrier, holding one crate with twenty-four baskets, becomes progressively heavy.

"*Yoku yarimasu ne.*" You do so well, Hada-san, the hired hand says, impressed by young Tomomi's steady work.

"*Eh,*" she acknowledges, as she places her filled crate on the bed of the truck. She examines the berries, moves a few to smooth the craters and turns over the green crowns. Unlike the others, Tomomi's crates appear as if they should be on display. Satisfied, she nails on the cover, takes an empty crate and goes back to her carrier. This is the only time her body has a chance to straighten up.

According to the "*sanba-san,*" the traveling midwife, the baby should arrive any day now. Being heavy with child these last nine months has not stopped Tomomi from working every day in the fields along with her husband, as she has always done, beginning with the planting and then the weeding and then the *koike*, the planting of young runners. It is now time to reap the fruits of their labors—their first crop and their first child.

⌒

It is late afternoon. Tomomi feels her child becoming restless as she moves her carrier. There is a tug and another tug. She takes her half-filled crate to the truck and calls Shinji. He quickly leaves his row, giving instructions to Hada-san to fill his crate, and hurries with his wife to the farmhouse.

"I will go to Oshima's grocery store and phone Yamaura-san right away," Shinji assures his wife, hoping that the midwife will not be at another home delivery. He hurries to his truck, unloads several empty boxes, and drives it, still loaded with the pickings of the day, to Oshima's store one mile down Franklin Boulevard. The *sanba-san* is available.

"I will come right away to pick you up," he tells her. It is another five miles to 1410 Fourth Street in Sacramento.

Tomomi busily readies herself before Shinji returns with Yamaura-san. She places big pots of water on the kerosene stove to heat. She carefully lines the foot of their bed with newspapers and covers them with a double-folded sheet. Towels, baby shirts and diapers are stacked neatly on the old bureau.

Shinji leaves Yamaura-san with Tomomi and returns to the strawberry field, where he finds that Hada-san has filled both crates and piled them at the side of the road.

⌒

On the eighth day of May in 1923, a girl is born. Not a son, but it does not matter in America. She is named Kiyo.

"Tomomi-san, you must rest for twenty-one days," the *sanba-san* scolds, as Tomomi busies herself with the duties of motherhood. "I will come every morning to take care of you and your baby."

Yamaura-san takes over Tomomi's household chores, not only bathing the baby but also cooking and cleaning. She sees to every need of mother and baby.

To have to stay in bed one week is like a sentence to Tomomi. Her husband is busy; the berries are at the peak of their crop. According to her *sanba-san*, she can begin to do light tasks after a week. In twenty-one days she can go back to work in the strawberry field. Sitting in her bed with her baby bathed and dressed in her arms, she rocks and sings softly:

Hato poppo
Hato poppo
Omame o yaru kara
Tonde koi

Come, pigeons, come.
I will give you some beans,
so come flying to me.

The *sanba-san* comes daily. She removes Tomomi's bindings from her breasts and abdomen and takes them out to wash. While they hang out to dry in the midmorning sun, she bathes the mother.

She has been very busy delivering babies out on the farms, she tells Tomomi. When it is too far from town, she refers them to other Japanese midwives. She will soon be able to drive, she says, so that it will be easier for everybody.

"You must drink plenty of water," she advises. "Would you like some tea?"

"*Hai. Arigatoh,*" Yes, thank you, Tomomi answers. Always having been the one to see to the needs of others, she finds the pampering both comforting and uncomfortable.

With yards of smoothly ironed muslin binding strips draped over her left arm, the *sanba-san* returns. Tomomi lies on her back as the midwife firmly wraps the wide piece several times around her small, firm breasts and secures it with safety pins. She takes another strip and binds it smoothly around the lower abdomen, alternating diagonally to lift and encourage the sagging muscles to tighten around the cavity left by the infant.

On the third day, Tomomi has a plan. She knows that Shinji and Hada-san cannot keep up with the rapidly ripening strawberries. With the loss of her help, each day one third of the crop is not picked.

"I think I will hire another picker," Shinji mentions at breakfast. "I will ask at Oshima's. He may know of someone looking for work."

It is the fourth day. When Yamaura-san finally takes leave, Tomomi hurriedly steps out of her bedroom, picks up an empty strawberry crate from the entryway, and then returns to the bedroom. She lays a *zabuton*, a flat chair pillow, on the bottom and covers it with a soft baby blanket. She then gently places her sleeping baby in the crate and covers her lightly with a clean diaper.

She changes into her work pants and long-sleeved shirt, puts on her wide-brimmed straw hat and her hand protectors sewn from rice sacking, and walks with short, determined steps to the field, carrying the crate under her arm.

She places her baby on the shady side of the old Chevrolet truck, picks up her carrier with the empty box and starts in the line next to Hada-san, her fingers moving rapidly through the plants. She works as if her body has not missed a beat.

With her first filled crate deposited on the truck, she hurriedly checks her baby. "*O-chichi?*" Breast milk, she whispers, gently picking up the tiny, pink-faced, sleeping baby stretching her arms and legs as she is lifted from the crate. Sitting on the ground, Tomomi leans against the running board of the truck. She unbuttons her shirt and pulls down the muslin cover from her breast to feed her child. The baby suckles contentedly with her tiny, fleshy lips and after extracting sustenance from her mother's breast, falls asleep. Tomomi holds her baby tenderly, humming "*Hato poppo*" and swaying softly to its rhythm.

An occasional gentle breeze caresses mother and child.

I don't know when I became aware of the world around me. I slip off my *zori* straw slippers and feel the soft spring grass under my feet. Sometimes I wander away from the strawberry field to the puddles in the neighboring property to pick tiny pink flowers. The strawberry crates are my playthings; they become a house, a table or a chair. I have one kewpie doll about as tall as my glass of milk. Mama puts the doll in her lunch crate along with a gallon of water every morning before we walk to the strawberry field. She also has a snack for me, like a box of cheese crackers, and on cold mornings, a bottle of hot chocolate wrapped up in a dish towel.

My father takes me everywhere: to the gasoline pumps, to the grocery store or to visit friends. My favorite place to go with Tochan is to the Gomez Grocery Store on Franklin Boulevard. Mr. Gomez and my father like to talk for a long while but Mr. Gomez always stoops down and talks to me first. Then he reaches into the big jar on top of the tall glassed-in meat counter and hands me a lollipop. I say, "Thank you."

In the kitchen, Mama is teaching me a dance about a butterfly that flits from flower to flower when Mrs. Kodama from the Baptist Mission stops by.

"I'd like to have her dance for our church ladies' meeting," Mrs. Kodama tells Mama.

"When will that be?" Mama asks.

"The meeting is today, this afternoon."

"I'm afraid we can't send her today," Mama says. "She doesn't have a pair of good shoes."

"I would be delighted to take her shopping with me to Walnut Grove," Mrs. Kodama tells Mama.

That is how I got the prettiest black patent leather shoes with a strap across the top. The ladies are happy with my singing and dancing and exclaim so many times: "*Ma-ah, kawaii desu ne!*" How cute she is, they say.

But it is my shiny, brand new pair of shoes that makes me happy.

I don't know how it happened but suddenly, in the middle of summer, Mama comes home with a little baby wearing a knitted white hat and wrapped up in a soft white blanket.

I forget all about my kewpie doll while Mama bathes the baby and changes his diapers. After feeding him, she puts him on a baby blanket in the middle of their big bed, and then leaves to work in the field. The windows are wide open. It is August, much too hot even in the truck's shade for my little brother. I go with Mama and play with the boxes while she picks strawberries.

"Kiyo-chan," Mama calls me after a while. "Will you go to the house and see if your little brother is awake or crying?"

I feel like an important big sister and trot seriously towards our little farmhouse. The blanket is crumpled up as if Seiji has been moving around. His tiny arms and legs are going every which way, and he smells.

I report to Mama. She takes off her hat and places it on top of her half-filled crate to protect the strawberries from the hot sun. She removes her half-gloves and places them on the handle of her carrier.

I follow Mama back to the house. In the kitchen, under the hand pump, she scrubs her hands and then with her soapy palms she washes mine. Another couple of pumps of water and both our hands are clean.

I hold my brother's tiny, soft hand while Mama changes his diaper. Actually, he holds my finger tightly and won't let go.

"Look, Mama," I say, lifting my arm. Mama looks and smiles, and continues talking and singing in Japanese as she cleans the mess.

I wish that he would hurry and grow up so we can play.

—

"Look! Look!" I yell at the top of my voice. Mama is cooking on the kerosene stove with her back turned. Tochan is just coming in for supper, hanging his straw hat in the dirt floor entryway.

"Look everybody!" I say again. "He's standing up!" Seiji is upright, holding onto the kitchen chair. We clap so loudly, one would have thought no one had ever done that before. He pays no attention and goes on to the next chair.

Once he starts to walk, he doesn't stop and gets into everything. Mama says Seiji never stayed inside the crate like I did out in the strawberry field.

Mama gets so exasperated sometimes. Seiji won't lie still for diaper changing. He turns over and scoots away so fast and Mama can barely grab him by his feet and drag him back. She gently smacks his bottom. Surprised, he lies still. I am surprised, too, because Mama never does things like that.

DECEMBER, 1926.

Then one day it all happens again. Mama and Tochan rush back from the field before quitting time.

"Get in the truck," Tochan tells us after he goes in the house for a small bag. Mama is already seated in the front seat.

It is a cold day in December. The Chevrolet truck has one long, narrow leather-covered hard seat and no doors. Mama braces herself with both hands on the seat with elbows stiffened. She looks as if she could easily roll off onto the road.

Seiji and I sit in the back on the bench seats, he on one side and I on the opposite. The high sideracks are in place. When the truck is moving, Seiji thinks it's fun to run from one side to the other. I scold him and tell him to sit down. Through the rack I can see that we just passed the Gomez Grocery Store. I've never seen Tochan drive so fast.

When we get there, Tochan tells us, "Stay in the truck" and helps Mama up the stairs. Is Mama sick, I wonder? We go home without Mama.

For the next few days, Tochan takes care of us. We wash in the *ofuro* bath every night but he doesn't much care if I wear the same dress the next day, whereas Mama washes everything we take off. I find our clean underwear in the old bureau drawer. Overalls are folded and stacked on top.

It is the third day that Mama has been gone. Tochan fixes oatmeal mush every morning. I help dress my brother.

"We'll go to Oshima's to make a phone call," Tochan announces. "Maybe Mama can come home." Suddenly everything seems fine. I like my father but he is not like Mama.

"Mama's coming home, Seiji," I tell him. He follows a cricket along the floorboard and ignores me.

After a stop at the Oshima Grocery Store to telephone, Tochan drives into town to where we left Mama. Carrying a big white bundle in her arms, Mama descends the stairs looking so pretty in her church dress. She comes to the back of the truck and lifts the corner of her bundle and peeping at us are two small bright eyes.

"This is Sanji. He is your new baby brother," Mama tells us.

Except for the first few days, Mama decides she would rather not have the services of the *sanba-san* this time. She does the work of the midwife herself every morning. After she cooks breakfast for the family, she sees that we are dressed and then we watch her bathe Sanji on the kitchen table. In the little metal tub half filled with water, she pours boiling water from the kettle, adds cold water and carefully tests the temperature with her elbow.

Rice cooks for lunch, filling the small kitchen with its warm, comfortable aroma. Before she goes out into the strawberry field, Mama loosens the rice with the bamboo spatula, then wraps the big, heavy Guardian Ware pot, *furoshiki* style, in the rice-sacking towel, and places it under a heavy comforter on my bed to keep it warm until lunchtime. When all her morning chores are done, she bundles up Seiji and Sanji in layers of removable clothing. She picks up her hoe and her crate of necessities and heads for the field. The boys follow her. In the crate are a box of Graham crackers, a Mason jar of hot chocolate wrapped in a towel, and a jug of water. She keeps neatly folded clean rags in the corner of her crate for wiping dirty hands and faces and blowing noses.

With a fourteen-inch metal file, Mama sharpens her short-handled hoe until a blade of grass can be split cleanly in two. She runs her expert finger lightly over the edge and gives the hoe a few more strokes from the inside.

"Mine, too," says Seiji, handing Mama his short hoe, its blade worn down almost to the handle. Mama gives it a few cursory strokes along the worn and rounded edge.

"Mine, too," says Sanji. Mama does the same. Satisfied, the two brothers happily dig nearby.

It is already February and the *koike* must be done in the new field. "*Ko*" means child and "*ike*" means to plant. The runners with the baby plants on the ends are properly spaced and planted to form four straight rows on the bed with the center area left for the picker's carrier and feet. Only when she reaches the end of the row does she stand up.

"Look, Mama!" The boys proudly point to their "mountain" upon which a twig pole stands with a leaf flag. Hands, faces and even their hair are brown with dirt. Having been flat on their abdomens, their coveralls are more brown than blue.

She pours water from the jug and wipes their hands. After crackers and warm chocolate, they go back to their mountain while Mama continues the *koike*.

MAY, 1928.

And then it happens again. Aizo is born—a pretty baby, not at all wrinkled. That is when Tochan decides to teach me English. All summer long, he reads from books he buys at a used book store. I start first grade at Pacific School in the fall, which is a half mile walk through an open field. Mama knits me a red lunch carrier with a matching holder for my hot chocolate in a Coca Cola bottle. I don't ever remember drinking Coca Cola. On rainy days Tochan carries me piggyback through the field. Leaning against my father's warm back, I like the sound of rain falling on my hat. When we reach the schoolyard, I want to slide off and walk but Tochan goes straight to the school's stone steps and deposits me where the steps are dry. When Mrs. Bacon, the eighth grade teacher, walks by and gives my father an approving smile, my embarrassment melts away.

A dream is within reach. After six years of hard work on leased land, my father decides to take the big step and buy his own farm. By now a few *Issei* have learned of ways to circumvent the Alien Land Law and are farming on their own land. If one's child is not old enough, the name of an eligible citizen is "borrowed."

Mr. Coyle owns the property that Tochan is interested in. "We might have some trouble. He's an attorney," I hear my father tell Mama.

California law prohibits any immigrant from Asia from owning land.

"If we do, we can 'borrow' the name of a *Nisei*," that is, a name of someone of the second generation who is an American citizen over twenty-one years of age.

"Do you think Mr. Coyle will agree to that?" Mama worries.

"If only I could become a citizen," Tochan says ruefully. Seventeen years had gone by since he had set foot on America. "Caucasian immigrants can apply in five years but we are not even allowed to apply," he adds. "Only white people can become naturalized citizens."

America is now home to my father and my uncle. The brothers continue to send money to their mother.

⌐⌐

1929. MAYHEW AREA, SACRAMENTO, CALIFORNIA.

Near an abandoned airfield, land is cheap. Marginal soils lie fallow. Flat land extends to the horizon in all directions, interrupted only by a dry, unattended almond orchard. To the southeast and across the rusted railroad tracks, overgrown weeds surround huge slabs of cement, the only remnants of what was once Mather Air Field. On our new twenty-acre parcel, a creek runs through the middle, creating a deep swale. Tall cattails grow where water settles.

Finally, their dream begins to unfold. Mama listens. They will first dig a well and start an irrigation system, Tochan explains. Then he will build a small garage and a barn to shelter the family while working on the farm.

"A barn? Not a house?" Mama questions.

"Not yet. We need a barn first," Tochan says. Mama's dreams of a house with running water and a nice stove are shattered. It is hard for her to grasp the thought of living in a garage or barn with their five small children.

"With Riichi and Okamura's help, it won't take long. We will partition three small rooms on the south side of the barn. Each room will have a door to the outside and a window."

"And the floor?"

Mama did not want the dirt floor of the barn.

"It will be wood where we sleep," Tochan assures her. "Half of the barn will be our kitchen and a place to eat. The other half will be for box-making and storage for the shooks."

Whatever disappointment might be lurking in her, Mama does not say. Her hands and feet keep constantly moving as if their dream depended upon it.

Moonlight bathes the flat land. Leaning on his shovel, Shinji watches the irrigation water flow evenly from ditch to ditch with the same deep satisfaction as an artist admiring his work.

An eighty-acre parcel now belongs to the two brothers and Abe-san, who has a forty-acre almond orchard. The brothers divide the remaining forty acres, with the front twenty-acre parcel going to Riichi and the back portion to Shinji.

It takes many months to level two acres of land in preparation for strawberry planting. First, it is plowed to soften the soil, then the soil is moved to the lower parts on a large, flat homemade sled pulled by a horse borrowed from Mr. McDonald, who lives down the road. At the end of the day, it seems an interminable task to tame the marginal land, cut through the middle by a meandering creek filled with cattails. Much of the property is high and rocky and the rest is low and wet. After many weeks, two acres along the slope are leveled so that water will flow and stay in the ditches at an even level.

This is their land. Now everything is possible.

Next they will build the barn.

At the crack of dawn, Mama prepares breakfast and then helps Tochan load the old Chevrolet truck with his tools to work on the new farm. On the front seat she places their lunch of warm rice balls made earlier. Slices of canned corned beef and salted *nappa* cabbage in a three-tiered, red and black lacquer box, a thermos of hot green tea and chopsticks are all tied up neatly with a clean, rice-sack *furoshiki*. She places two boxes of Cracker

Jack inside the *furoshiki* and peanut butter and jelly sandwiches wrapped in waxed paper on top of the lunch box.

With Seiji and Sanji beside him, Tochan drives to the new farm. Seiji stands, his face almost against the windshield.

"Look! Look!" He points, seeing a jackrabbit hop across the road.

"You will see lots of jackrabbits on our farm," Tochan tells the boys, "and snakes and frogs."

"And fish?" Sanji asks.

"Maybe," Tochan answers. "You might find some in the creek."

Cows graze along the roadside. A snake lies dead, run over by a car. The fifteen-mile trip to the new farm ends much too quickly.

They ride a sled hitched to a horse when Tochan levels the ground along the creek. They come home so dirty that Mama has to rinse them off at the outside faucet before they come in the house for supper.

Inside his overall pocket, Sanji takes out the tiny car he found in the box of Cracker Jack. He pushes it along the edge of the oilcloth-covered table.

"Let me try it," Aizo asks.

"Here," says Sanji, handing it over before rushing outside.

He returns with a can. Proudly he places it on the table. Inside the can, the water is wriggly black with hundreds of polliwogs, some with tiny legs.

"No, no!" Mama exclaims. "Take that outside!"

She could see the can spilling on the table and floor. And how do you clean up polliwogs squirming all over the floor? The two obediently walk outside with their treasure.

⁓

"Mama, sit down here," Tochan coaxes as he reads with me at the small kitchen table Mama had just cleared.

Reluctantly Mama wipes her hands on the corner of her rice-sacking apron, steps around the boys and sits beside me.

"You have to learn to speak English, Mama," Tochan encourages her. She agrees, but each time she sits down her head begins to nod from the weariness of the day.

But it is from Mama that I learn to talk and sing and dance in Japanese.

"Run, Jane, run. Run, Spot, run." I know all those words now, but I don't think Mama does.

Tochan helps me to read *The Little Red Hen*, which is more fun than "Run, Jane, run." There is Foxey Loxey and Goosey Lucy. Mama listens to me read.

"American stories are bad for children," she says thoughtfully. "They teach children selfishness. Nobody helps Little Red Hen and in the end, she eats the bread all by herself. She does not share a morsel."

Hansel and Gretel is a most terrible story, she tells Tochan. "A little boy and a little girl push a woman into an oven to burn. It does not matter that she is a witch."

Tochan does not say a word. He is deep in thought. That's when he starts the nightly story times, telling us his own stories, which I like better than my first grade books.

The long day of cleaning the ditches to ready them for irrigation ends later than Tochan expected. At dusk, finally, Tochan switches on the pump. The boys follow with glee the strong gush of water coursing down the main ditch. Seeing the water traveling evenly into each branching ditch, Tochan calls his sons to eat. It is good that Mama has packed enough for leftovers. Sitting on old boxes, the boys devour the stale rice balls and eat the peanut butter and jelly sandwiches with relish while their father drinks the still warm green tea.

"See those three stars close together?"

"I see it!" the boys exclaim. "Right there!"

"That is called the *mitsu-boshi*. *Mitsu* means three and *boshi* means stars."

"That moon," continues Tochan, "is seen by everybody. Mama sees the same moon at home, and the same *mitsu-boshi*."

The three of them walk toward the end of the field to check the progress of the irrigation. They follow the water flowing slowly into each ditch, pausing as it curves around the bend, curling around clods of dirt. It will take past midnight, Tochan figures, for the whole field to be irrigated, longer than he had planned.

"When the water reaches the end of this last ditch, Seiji, I want you to turn the pump off," Tochan says.

"All right," Seiji replies without hesitation. He feels important. He has turned the pump off and on many times before.

"I will take your brother home and come back early in the morning."

"I want to stay, too," Sanji says.

As the two leave, Seiji picks up his father's shovel and moves to the next ditch. He sits down to watch as the water shimmers down the long length of the ditch. By the pump house, a frog croaks, and then another. With the bright moonlight, the night is like muted day. The moonlight spreads a friendly layer of calm over the field. Large clods of dirt cast weird shadows on the ground. He throws a small clod into the ditch and watches with fascination as the water quickly flows around it.

Several hours pass. The last ditch is filled. He shoulders his father's shovel and walks along the field with its long straight rows of silver water.

As he walks toward the pump house, he picks up a clod of dirt to see how far he can throw it . . . then another.

At the pump house, in the semi-darkness, he finds the small black switch and pushes it to the right. The powerful engine stops and he hears the water drop deep down into the earth, occasionally splashing along the sides of the long metal shaft. In the cement holding tank outside, he rinses his hands and splashes his face with water. Filling his cupped hands with water he drinks, swirls it in his mouth, and spits it out onto the weeds as he has seen his father do.

At the three-walled shed, he leans his shovel against the wall of the garage, takes off his shoes and lies on his cot with his head facing so he can see outside the door-less garage. Arms under his head, he looks up at the vast sky filled with millions of stars. He finds the *mitsu-boshi*. His eyelids droop to the song of the frogs.

⁓

"Where's Seiji?" Mama asks, worried when Tochan returns with only Sanji.

"I left him at the farm to turn off the irrigation pump."

Mama looks at him seriously, with almost a frown, but she does not say a word and goes about reheating the cold supper.

"Sanji may not be hungry. The boys ate the leftovers."

⁓

I ask Seiji the next day: "Weren't you scared to stay out there all by yourself?"

"No-o," he answers, with a lilt on the "o" like it was fun.

"Was it dark?"

"I could see everything in the moonlight almost like daytime."

"Did you find any frogs?"

"When I stay real quiet, they get big like a balloon and croak," he explains as he spreads his arms to show me. I wish that I could see it myself.

Then, he says, he went to lie down on the cot and watched the falling stars. "I saw lots of them."

Seiji tells me that Tochan was already out in the field when he woke up and he found a bag with a fried egg sandwich and a bottle of milk by his cot.

"The irrigation went well," Tochan reports to Mama. "The strawberry plants we put in the other day are now upright, having soaked up all that water."

I hear him tell Mama, "As soon as the barn is built, we can move."

· 5 ·

THE DEPRESSION AND
REARING NINE CHILDREN

Fuji wa fuji de rippa na

Fuji ni ookiku shite

Age na kereba

– JOHN SHINJI SATO

Wisteria as a wisteria,

we need to help it to grow

into the best wisteria

– TRUDY SATO, TRANSLATION

HELD IN BY side racks and loaded to the top with iron beds, cartons of pots and pans, dishes, blankets and clothes are all securely tied down. The old Chevrolet truck moves almost reluctantly, leaving behind a small, empty skeleton of a house, its soul extracted. No longer will the sounds of five happy children reverberate within its flimsy walls.

My brothers, bathed and in their pajamas, and I ride in Okamura san's Model A Ford. We follow the truck up ahead. I see parts of clothing flapping between the ropes and hope that nothing will fly out. We pass an occasional lit up farmhouse. Kozo, not two yet, falls asleep, his head bumping against my shoulder as we travel on the rough asphalt road, our headlights the only ones on Fruitridge Road.

Finally, at the end of the long, bumpy, dirt road, we reach our new home. Tochan drives right up to the barn door, directing the headlights inside. Okamura-san parks alongside and does the same.

"Let's get the beds first," Mama suggests, "so the children can go to sleep."

They place our beds along the south wall of the barn on the dirt floor. Tomorrow, in the daylight, Tochan says, we can move into the side rooms with the wood floors. Mama unrolls the blankets and fixes each bed. My brothers claim theirs, sitting cross-legged, happily chatting.

Mama doesn't walk as fast as she helps unload. She is getting rounder again.

"Can we sleep upstairs?" Sanji asks, hanging onto the top rung of the slats, poking his head into the attic.

"We'll see," replies Tochan.

After unloading the heavy beds and boxes, Okamura-san leaves.

"I will come by early tomorrow morning," he says.

I fall asleep listening to Mama and Tochan quietly walking back and forth, whispering occasionally. In the middle of the night, when I awaken for the toilet, they are still working. Mama sees me sit up and points to the white *omaru* chamber pot she had placed in the corner of the barn. I am glad that I don't have to walk in the dark to the outhouse a distance away. I try not to clink the lid. No one stirs.

After she washes the supper dishes under the outside faucet by the pump house, Mama fixes my school lunch on the long, wooden table in the barn Tochan made. It is where we eat and draw and color and read and cut vegetables and everything else. As darkness comes, the kerosene lamp in the middle of the table invites the children to gather around. A lone sixty-watt light bulb hangs over the box-making equipment.

Every night after supper, Tochan lights another lamp and walks down the long dirt path to work on the new house. It is still only a frame sitting on cement blocks. During the day, we run from room to room and stake out where we are going to sleep.

Each night Mama takes us to the *ofuro* bath, which Tochan built under the huge, elevated water tank. The square redwood tub is large enough to hold four children. It has a sheet metal bottom where the wood fire heats the water from below. It takes half the afternoon to heat the large tub of water. A wooden rack keeps our bodies off the hot metal. A small hole at the back of the tub drains the water each day.

The day ends with a happy family ritual of gathering on the wooden pallet around the tub to scrub each other's backs and to pour bucketfuls of warm water over one's head. Mama lifts each child into the tub after an inspection and final rinse. While they play with their washcloth bubbles, Mama fills a large washtub with warm water and launders everything the children take off, scrubbing vigorously on the metal washboard with Fels Naptha soap.

"Time to get out now," she says as she dumps the soapy water onto the cement floor, which drains through a pipe leading to the outside. We dry

ourselves, put on our pajamas, put on our *zori* slippers and walk back to
the barn with Mama carrying Kozo.

"*Onen-ne*," "Go to sleep," she says as she tucks the blankets snugly
around our bodies and feet.

I hear her rinsing the clothes at the outside faucet, and then it is quiet
for a long while when she hangs the clothes with wooden clothespins on
the long wire lines.

A flicker of light awakens me. Mama relights the lamp on the table and
walks to the new house. I hear Mama and Tochan hammering way into
the night.

Driving down our lane at night on our way home from church, Mama
notices a window in our new house lit up in a weird sort of way, like huge
orange ribbons swaying.

"*Anata*, did you leave the lamp on in the new house?" Mama asks with
alarm in her voice.

"No. I took it back to the barn," Tochan answers.

Parking the truck by the barn, Tochan runs over to the house, looks
in the window and rushes back. He fills two buckets with water and runs
back, forces open the window, which was temporarily nailed down, and
throws the buckets of water inside.

"Get in the truck!" he yells as he runs back.

He quickly turns the Model T truck around, and as we drive off, an
angry young man appears, flailing his arms and yelling words we don't
understand.

When we reach our uncle's house, Tochan tells his brother that "the soldier" was about to be burned. He was only inches away from the fire he had
built inside the large wooden tool box in which Tochan keeps all his carpenter's tools. Mather Field has been reactivated, and since then, drunken young
men sometimes stray onto our farm. Once I found a man sleeping in a ditch.

"I threw the first bucket of water on him to wake him up," Tochan
explains, "and the second one inside the tool box. It was a good thing I
could pry the window open."

Ojisan (Uncle) goes back with us. The angry man is nowhere in sight.

Inside, they find that the fire has burned through the bottom of the tool chest and even through the new floor, creating a huge crater in the middle of the bedroom. We stand around it, scared and awed about what a fire can do. They put out the smoldering fire with more buckets of water.

Tochan carefully lifts the metal parts of his tools from the still hot ashes. The hammer is reusable, though a part of the handle burned. The measurements on the large, heavy metal square are scorched beyond reading. He notes that the saw needs replacement, along with the level. Half the floor can be salvaged, he estimates, if he carefully saves the periphery.

"*Yokatta na!*" How lucky it was, Tochan remarks, that the young man did not catch on fire. If we had stayed at church longer, our house would have burned to the ground with the young man. He sighs with relief that the soldier is safe somewhere.

The Great Day!

"Everybody, carry what you can!" Tochan announces.

Mama and Tochan load the iron cots onto the Model T truck, which Tochan bought for loading and unloading strawberry crates. The children trudge along the dirt road to the new house with their arms full of their belongings, overalls dragging the ground.

Sun shines into my little room from the east and south windows. Two orange crates hold my sweater and underwear. My small, red diary and pencil go on top. I like the smell of the new lumber and the clean walls and floor. My four brothers scramble for their positions in the big room, dumping their clothes on their beds. The middle-sized room for Mama and Tochan has a closet with three huge drawers for blankets and things. We have a bathroom with only a sink and the white *omaru* chamber pot in the corner. Later a flush toilet and a bathtub would be installed.

In the parlor, a cylindrical kerosene heater surrounded by a protective wooden railing stands, with a long, curved metal chimney extending through the wall. The heavy door to the kitchen swings either way, which the boys think is great fun.

"Be careful, boys. Be sure there's nobody on the other side when you open the door," Tochan advises. So far there are no mashed noses.

We have a brand new white cooking stove with two butane tanks on the outside wall. The long, rectangular, white porcelain sink with water running from the faucet above solves most of Mama's problems. Maybe because she trained as a nurse, there is nothing Mama can't take care of with water, soap, Clorox and *tawashi*, the round Japanese porcupine-like brush she keeps at every faucet inside and outside the house. Each *tawashi* has its own specific duties, one for dishes, another for scrubbing boots outside, and a large one for the outhouse.

The never-empty, large kettle always sits on the stove next to the sink for hot water.

It is a two-and-a-half-mile walk to Edward Kelley School. Miss Mary Aline Cox has almost sixty children in the one-room schoolhouse, which was built in 1869. To call the children indoors, she pulls on a long heavy rope, at least an inch thick, which connects to the bell in the belfry tower.

At the next farm, my cousin Chiyo, who is in the second grade, joins me. I carry my lard can lunch pail in which I have a peanut butter and strawberry jam sandwich wrapped in waxed paper and an apple. Sometimes I find a few pieces of Hershey Kisses in the bottom.

With every new school book I bring home, Tochan buys a used copy from Beers bookstore and reads to me every night.

"Don't teach her to read, Mr. Sato," Miss Cox tells Tochan one rainy day when he drives us to school. "She is picking up your accent. She'll do just fine," she assures him.

Tochan no longer takes me with him to his bookstore. I don't mind. He takes so long. I worry that I might lose him in the stacks of old books that go up clear to the ceiling.

"Seiji, let's go! You'll be late for school!" He squats by a pothole in the middle of the asphalt road and pays no attention to me.

It is 8:30 in the morning. He keeps stirring the puddle forever. We've come only a mile.

I go back a few times to get him but he refuses to move. Exasperated, I give up and go on with the rest of our friends from the neighboring farms. School starts at nine and we have two more miles to go.

On Old Placerville Road, from the farm lane where the *Issei* parents grow strawberries, the children from the Toguchi, Higashi, Sakuma, Matsumoto, Furuike and Kitada families join us. As automobiles rarely come by, we take up the whole road. Sometimes Yukio Yamasaki stops his Ford coupe and allows a few of us to ride in his rumble seat.

Fire roars in the huge black stove in the back of the schoolroom, a warm welcome to chilled hands and faces. Miss Cox assigns the older boys to come early to carry the wood from the outside shed and start the fire.

I keep looking towards the front door for Seiji. It is past ten o'clock when he finally saunters in, not even looking embarrassed.

Miss Cox sees him from the blackboard where she has a group of us sitting on the edge of the stage for our arithmetic lesson. She stops, smiles and recites:

A diller, a dollar, a ten o'clock scholar
What makes you come so soon?
You used to come at ten o'clock
But now you come at noon.

I squirm with embarrassment, but she seems to understand. For some reason I can't understand, she calls him her "Bismarck," maybe because he goes by his own time.

Miss Cox is our music instructor, our drama director and our umpire for all sixty pupils. Miss Cox knows everything. We sing "Home to Our Mountains" from the opera *Il Trovatore* as though it were an ordinary second grade song. She teaches democracy with fervor and gets all of us excited about campaigning. We are supposed to be voting for our own candidate but none of us dares to oppose Miss Cox, who has her own favorite.

The whole community looks forward to our Christmas production, with everyone participating in the program. Ted Kobata, a short seventh grader who can barely reach the pedals, drives his family's farm truck to gather a load of green ivy to decorate all around the stage. For weeks we make our costumes and practice.

On the night of the performance, the one-room schoolhouse buzzes with activity, filled with parents, grandparents and people from all around the area. As they crowd along the walls, the schoolhouse has no standing room left.

Four first graders—my brother Kozo, Yuki Toguchi, Ben Mayeda and Isamu Furuike—all dressed up like a clock and wearing tall hats, march onto the stage. Tony Yamamoto, a seventh grader, advises them behind the curtain: "If your hat falls off, don't worry about it." They sing "Hickory, Dickory, Dock," their hats swaying to the rhythm. Midway through the song, Kozo's hat drops to the floor. He continues swaying his head to the rhythm, remembering Tony's advice. Yuki stoops over, picks up Kozo's hat and tries to put it back on his head. Kozo, following Tony's advice, knocks it off. Yuki picks it up again and tries to place it on his head. The song ends. The three march off, leaving the hat on the floor. Isamu stands alone, mesmerized by the crowd of people clapping and laughing.

"Pssst! Isamu," Kozo whispers from the side curtain. Isamu doesn't move. Kozo calls again, louder. Isamu stands immobilized. Exasperated, Kozo, with arms swinging, walks onto the stage and drags Isamu off, touching off a round of applause and merriment.

The harmonica band, which is almost all of us in school, plays "O, Susanna." Miss Cox plays the harmonica better than the piano. She plunks the piano notes only to teach us the pitch of the notes.

At the climax of the evening, Santa Claus bounces in from the side door, carrying a big white bag filled with candies and nuts for all the excited children.

And Miss Cox receives a tall, elegant Japanese vase.

⁓

Plentiful water flows into leveled ditches. Strawberries grow and produce abundantly with steady, hard work. Knowing that strawberries thrive in this marginal soil, Tochan decides to experiment with a variety of berries—loganberries, youngberries and raspberries. He requests information from the Department of Agriculture at the University of California at Davis. A new variety of bush berry on the market called the boysenberry causes quite a stir. Its large, dark, sweet fruit rapidly replaces the youngberry. Tochan plants a half a dozen rows. After a season of successful harvesting, he pulls out all the youngberries and replaces them with boysenberries.

Raspberries, too, thrive. Little hands pluck them as the children listen to Tochan's stories. The faster pickers help the slower ones so everyone can keep within listening distance. Tochan is like our radio. Mama goes way ahead, filling crates twice as fast.

"We got a special order from Canada for two crates of raspberries, Mr. Sato. Will you be picking tomorrow?" the hauler asks.

"Canada?"

Berries are shipped to Oregon and Washington and sometimes eastward but never to Canada.

"I hear that the King and Queen of England are traveling across Canada, and this order is for their banquet table," the driver tells Tochan. "And you grow the biggest raspberries."

For the King and Queen? It's like a storybook!

We each carry the small, shallow, wooden baskets and go from bush to bush, picking the biggest and the reddest berries for the King and Queen. Mama carefully and very gently packs the finest two crates. She places a cluster of three vibrant green leaves in the lower corner of each crate. We crane our necks to get one close look before the covers are nailed. Tomorrow the King and Queen will eat the raspberries we picked for them!

Several days later, another order arrives for two more crates! We know then that the King and Queen liked our raspberries.

Strange equipment appears on the adjacent property where we go mushroom hunting with our lard cans. Friendly hoboes who camp out under the cluster of eucalyptus trees disappear. Big bulldozers and dump trucks, lined up along the fence, appear ready for the charge.

A tremendous, rumbling noise shatters the early morning quiet. We open the front door and watch in fascination as the heavy machines roll across the terrain, tearing up everything in their path, digging up huge rocks. In no time, a long wide trench forms as bulldozers dump the dirt at each end.

Soon, huge brown clouds of dust relentlessly well up from the cavernous hole. Bulldozers drone down below and, like fish coming up for air, appear at the rim of the pit, dump, turn around quickly and disappear into the dust.

It is still early morning and already the air does not smell good. Shouldering his shovel, which he keeps leaning against the porch pillar, Tochan walks toward the strawberry field. On the other side of the barbed wire fence, the Teichert Gravel Company mines for gravel. It is rumored that because it is only three miles from a gold dredger, they will find plenty of gold.

Each day the pit grows larger and the dust increases. With no wind, yesterday's dust stays suspended in the air, leaving a permanent thin brown layer along the horizon.

A slight shift in the wind moves a huge, brown cloud northward, turning the morning sun into a red fireball. It is not good. Tochan knows that there is nothing he can do but to hope for a change in the direction of the wind. That, too, is not hopeful. The prevailing wind comes from the southwest and only a miracle would change it to the north and blow the dust away from his new plants.

The young raspberry plants just planted in the new field soak up the irrigation water and spread out their small, serrated leaves, no longer limp on their upright wiry stems. Water has not yet touched a few plants. By noon, they, too, will come alive. But will the young plants survive the onslaught of dust from above? Dust covers the established rows of berries in the adjoining field.

The sky darkens. The breeze shifts the dust clouds northward and the sun peers like a half-moon from behind the ominous dust.

Suddenly the land turns an eerie red-brown color. Large clods of dirt cast shadows like a flat painting on the ground. The wall of dust clouds head northwards.

The bulldozers relentlessly gouge into the earth with no respect for its surroundings. The topsoil, made pregnant through thousands of years, dissipates into nothingness. Seeds that carpeted the field a golden orange each spring with California poppies vanish into the inert pit, never to bloom again.

Tomorrow is Saturday. The Teichert Gravel Company does not work on weekends. For a short while, the dust will not settle on the leaves and sap their energy.

Dust seeps through every seam into the farmhouse. My brothers think the windowsills are places to draw and leave handprints. With a vengeance, Mama wipes up the dust every day. After every mealtime, she attacks the sills and countertops in the kitchen. She reminds us that the bathroom and kitchen must always be clean enough to be able to eat off the floors.

The rice sack rags are thin from rubbing and washing and bleaching. Like the cutting board, which is smooth and concave from use, the wooden surfaces around the kitchen sink appear as if they had been sanded. Even the stove has a dull patina from Mama's constant rubbing.

As if it had not done enough damage, the dust now attacks Mama's nose. She sneezes and blows constantly. When she works out in the field, she wears a mask, which she sews from several layers of rice sacking. Every day she irrigates her nasal passages with warm salt water. The children are in awe of Mama, who can swallow water up into her nose without drowning, and spit it out.

"If this keeps up," Tochan says after supper, "we need to make some changes."

Mama agrees.

Moving is out of the question. This is home.

"Because of the dust, the raspberry plants are totally infested with red spiders. We need to plant something that is resistant to them," Tochan tells Mama. "The only thing I can do now is to write to Mr. Teichert and see if he will pay us for the cost of the two thousand new plants and replace the field with another crop."

"Grapes seem to do all right in this area. There are Tokays south of here and wine grapes along Folsom Boulevard."

I listen while Mama and I finish the dishes. I want to say "Muscats" but I know better than to interrupt. The Yamasakis grow Muscats. We crawl under their fence sometimes and pick a bunch. How sweet those grapes are! We know we are stealing and we know they know. Even so, when we get there Mrs. Yamasaki invites us for fried noodles, crispy on the outside and drizzled with soy sauce and vinegar. We never have it like that.

Tochan continues: "We can start the grape canes now in the strawberry field where they will be watered along with the strawberry plants. How about Ribiers?" He tells Mama that he had seen the big, dark blue grapes at the wholesale house. The market is flooded with Tokays, he says, and something like a good table grape might be better.

"Where the bush berries are growing, we will plant walnuts." Tochan doesn't ask for Mama's opinion. He talks as if he has thought this out for a long while and now needs to have a nod of approval, which he always gets from Mama.

The next day, I ride with Tochan in the front seat of our Model T truck, and my three brothers sit on the back flatbed, leaning against the cab. I worry that they might fall off. We go to Mr. Buckley's Ranch on Coloma Road to ask him if we can pick up a sackful of black walnuts along the roadside.

Mr. Buckley and Tochan stand talking for a long time, while the four of us gather the nuts. Seiji finds two rocks and finally cracks open a nut. The shell is so thick and the nutmeat so small that we decide it's not worth the trouble.

Mr. Buckley talks all the time and Tochan listens. Mr. Buckley tells him how deep to plant the walnuts. He tells him about all the different kinds of English walnuts there are.

"Come in the early spring and I will show you how to graft."

"How long will it be before I can graft my trees?"

"Not for four or five years," he tells Tochan. "By the way, do you know of anyone who wants the job pruning my vineyard?"

"I can do it for you," Tochan says. He seems glad for the offer, especially since the dust has ruined the berry crop.

1932.

In the newspaper we see pictures of long lines of people waiting to get food. People are starving everywhere. I am nine years old, and I can't understand why they are standing in line to get a loaf of bread. Everybody talks about "the Depression," which I don't exactly understand. I wonder why children don't get enough to eat when we have tomatoes, cucumbers and all sorts of food growing and even rotting in our garden. When summer is over we have *nappa* cabbage, carrots and *sato-imo* potatoes. Mama fixes the long, white *daikon* radish in a million different ways. Shriveled *daikon* becomes *takuwan*, the smelly, tasty pickles. I like the *umani*, a stew of every kind of root vegetable we dig up and chickens, which run around the barn. Then there are our *tororo-imo* suppers, when we take turns grinding the long, succulent root inside the *suribachi* mortar, a large ceramic bowl which works like rough sandpaper. Mama dribbles the hot *misoshiru* slowly along the edge as we take turns grinding and stirring. We can hardly wait for Tochan to finish saying grace so we can have our scoop of *tororo-imo* over a hot bowl of rice to slurp down.

Why don't they plant carrots and stuff in their yards, I wonder? Then the children won't be hungry.

Okamura-san's Model A Ford drives up into our yard early Saturday morning. Their stately olive green automobile is the envy of all of us. Mr. and Mrs. Okamura usually ride in front and Setsuko and Tsuneo in the back. But today Okamura-san comes alone. We touch the shiny front bumpers just to let ourselves know that we were that close.

Tochan and Okamura-san take off in our Chevrolet truck. They return after several hours, and back up the truck to the front porch to unload.

"A piano!" Seiji yells. We know what a piano is, as there is one at Edward Kelley School.

I can hardly believe that we are getting a piano. They untie it from the back of the truck and roll it along 1x12 boards onto the porch and push it uphill through the front door.

"Mama!" Tochan calls. "Where do you want to put the piano?"

There is no choice, really. The small parlor has doors going into every room, with a stove near one wall.

"Right here," Mama says, pointing to the east wall with barely enough room between two doors. My brothers crowd around, hardly able to wait to touch the keys. They discover that the stool swivels.

"My turn," Aizo demands. Seiji gets off, seeing that the piano is in place and he can play it.

"You had it a long time," Kozo complains. "My turn."

"Next week you will start piano lessons," Tochan tells me.

"Me!" I exclaim in disbelief.

"You and Seiji. You will go after school on Thursdays to Mrs. Fairbairn's house.

The Fairbairn brothers are well known and respected in the area. Jack Fairbairn owns a large vineyard and his wife gives private piano lessons in their big, white house on the hill. The lessons cost seventy-five cents an hour.

⁓

I can tell that Seiji hates to practice. He sits at the piano and plunks at any note. He spends more time swiveling on his stool than practicing. I don't like my études much, either, but I practice half an hour every day. Just when I think that Seiji will be allowed to quit, I hear a familiar tune. Pushing the swinging door of the kitchen, I poke my head into the parlor and yell.

"Hey! That was 'Turkey in the Straw!'"

He drops his hands and glances at me sideways as if to say: "Oh, it's nothing."

I am so proud of my brother.

⁓

When springtime comes, keeping the weeds down around the farmhouse and in the fields never ends. Under the growing walnut trees, wild spinach grows, spreading like tiny, green doilies. I cut them with a paring knife at the base of the stem. It takes hundreds of them for a meal. Because they grow after the rainy season, the long, slender leaves have to be rinsed many times to wash out the dirt. I blanch them quickly in boiling water and then dip them into cold water. Then I squeeze out the water and cut them into one-inch pieces. Mama toasts and then grinds black sesame seeds in the *suribachi* and adds sugar. Then she pours in soy sauce, stirs and dribbles the mixture onto the platter of spinach. There never seems to be enough of this first taste of spring.

It is Mama who first notices the wild mustard growing in the field of tall, dry weeds in the vineyard, and brings in a bucketful for our supper. She blanches the tender greens for a few minutes and then cools them in tap water. She lines them all up by the stems, squeezes the water out and slices them into two-inch lengths, all the same size, and sprinkles them with soy sauce.

"*Hatsu mono.*" First of the season, Tochan says, with relish. I would almost expect him to start a *haiku* with *hatsu mono ya* . . .

Mama even harvests the young leaves from our little mulberry tree, dries them and makes tea.

"It's healthy for you," she tells us. "I wish I could find some alfalfa. Alfalfa tea is also very good."

I wonder how Mama knows all this.

While we weed at the back of the house, Mama cuts a handful of the broad leaf plantain with her *kama*.

"Kazu-chan, will you bring me the salt shaker from the stove?" she asks.

"Are you going to eat that, Mama?" I ask incredulously. She smiles.

She wets the largest leaf under the corner faucet, cuts off the stem and pours a generous amount of salt on it. She rubs it carefully until the leaf is limp and almost translucent.

"I will need a piece of thread and scissors," she says. Kazu knows exactly where to find Mama's sewing stuff, kept in a large, oval sardine can in their bedroom. By now all of us are curious. If not to eat, then what?

She rinses the leaf, gathers the edges of the limp leaf and ties it securely, forming a tiny balloon. Then she trims off the excess. Mama carefully cuts a small, round hole at the opposite end.

"What is it, Mama?" Kozo asks. By now all the children gather around her.

She puts the whole thing in her mouth. She is going to eat it!

Croak! The younger children look around for a frog. The rest of us erupt in laughter as we watch Mama squeeze her mouth on the marble-sized, leaf-balloon emitting a loud croak.

Weeding is forgotten but the plantain gets harvested as everyone tries to make a frog-croaker.

⁓

We walk through the dark saloon. My three little brothers follow me, looking neat and clean and wearing shoes. Coming in from the bright sunlight, I have trouble seeing. Three men seated at the bar turn to see who has opened the door and, as quickly, return to their mugs of beer.

The front door of the Mills Station Grocery Store is closed on Sundays. Sometimes when a farmer needs gasoline, Mr. Studarus unlocks the gasoline pump by the hitching post for the horses. Mr. Studarus allows us to go in through the saloon to get our usual bologna and bread for our week's school lunches. He is inside his post office "cage," wearing his green visor, busy with bookkeeping. When he sees us enter, he leaves his work and goes over to the high, glassed-in meat counter to slice and weigh two pounds of bologna. I buy three loaves of bread. Sometimes I buy stamps for Tochan.

My brothers squeeze the bread too hard under their arms, so I carry it myself. There is no way I can get the loaves back into shape for sandwiches after they are squeezed. Mama mixes the squeezed parts in *okazu* juice left from cooking meat and vegetables and feeds them to Molly and Dicky, our dogs. They lap it up like it's the best thing ever.

We walk to the far corner of the old store where the county has several shelves of books. Sitting on the floor, my brothers look at the books with pictures. I find *Windows on Henry Street* and decide to take it home. I like Jane Addams. Mr. Studarus lets us stay as long as we want.

We walk back along the railroad tracks, almost two miles to our farm.

My brothers rush back, anxious to jump into the empty railroad cars by the side of our property.

⁓

The smell of supper wafts through the screen door of our house. It is not the usual curry stew or tomato stew or *okazu* of meat and vegetables.

Aizo tilts his nose in the air and sniffs. "*Tem-pu-ra!*" he shouts and runs to the kitchen.

The children watch as the coated vegetables emerge nice and delicately brown, sizzling up from the bottom of the pan. A colorful array of sliced carrots, eggplant, sweet potatoes, okra, zucchini, and anything else from the garden, and shrimp on a large tray await cooking.

"*O-te-te,*" Mama reminds us gently. "Little hands" is all she has to say to have everybody wash their hands.

When Tochan comes into the kitchen, we are all seated. Kazu, Sanji, Aizo and Kozo sit on the bench against the wall. Seiji sits opposite me at the other end of the oilcloth-covered table and Naoshi is next to Tochan. Mama and I sit at the serving corner. Tomoko sits beside me. From the large rice pot behind me on the counter by the window, I fill the rice bowls with a bamboo spatula.

When Tochan bows his head, we do the same. He thanks *Kamisama*, God, for the good day and for our health. After the "Amen" we pass the food. Mama continues to cook the *tempura* until everybody is fed. Then she finally sits down to eat.

"Look! Mama's sleeping!" Kazu exclaims, seeing Mama's head nod with her chopsticks suspended halfway to her mouth. She jerks awake.

"*Gomen na sai ne,*" she apologizes.

Everybody talks. Around the table conversation flows non-stop.

Without warning, Kozo stands up on the bench. He commands total attention.

"Listen to me!" he demands, shaking his finger over the table. All eyes focus upwards on Kozo. Surprised by everyone's attention, he becomes tongue-tied. We wait with bated breath. Looking down on the sea of faces, he forgets what he was about to say. His arms droop with resignation and he meekly slides back down on the bench. Everybody breaks out in laughter.

Mama laughs so hard that tears flow down her cheeks, and we laugh even more because Mama can't stop laughing. When it finally subsides and quiet is restored, someone giggles and the outburst begins all over again.

When Tochan takes his last bite of food, puts his chopsticks down and places his warm teacup against his cheek, it is a signal for story time (and the vying for seats on Tochan's lap and legs) to begin.

Mama and I scrape and stack the dishes being passed to the end of the table.

"What will it be tonight?" Tochan asks. "Let's see."

Silence replaces the din of conversation. Tochan begins.

A carpenter lives in a small house in Japan. In the mornings he awakens to the song of the birds outside his window.

"What a beautiful day!" he says, pushing aside the shoji screen.

He cooks his breakfast of rice and misoshiru and packs onigiri rice balls for his lunch.

"And some bologna sandwiches?" Naoshi asks.

"Bologna? No . . . probably some dried fish."

"Like *iriko*, the tiny fishes?"

"That's right. The kind Mama toasts for us for snacks, sometimes," Tochan explains.

"Let him tell the story," Aizo impatiently complains.

Well, then, the carpenter picks up his tools and slings them over his shoulder. He stuffs his lunch in the pocket of his hakama, *his loose work pants.*

He sings as he walks along. The air is crisp, the grass is green, and the sun is bright. Wild flowers are beginning to bloom along the roadside.

The day passes quickly for the happy carpenter, building houses for the villagers.

He returns home whistling, feeling good to have done a day's job well, building houses for people.

Every day he looks forward to his work in the village.

One day on his way home, he finds a small cloth bag in the road. To his surprise it is full of heavy gold pieces. He looks around to see who might have dropped it, and seeing no one, he puts the bag in his hakama *pants.*

In his rush to get home, he does not notice that the sky is a beautiful pink and blue and that the sun is just sinking into the horizon.

"Where shall I hide it?" he thinks, looking all around the house. In the teapot? No. Inside the cupboard? No. Under his futon blanket? No. Where?

"I know, I know! Under his pillow," Aizo suggests.

"I think, inside the tea can," says Sanji.

"He should put them inside his bag of tools and take them to work with him," adds Kozo.

"That's a good idea," says Tochan.

"He should keep them in his pocket."

"Well, let me tell you what he did."

There is silence, all eyes waiting for the wisest answer.

The carpenter is so busy looking for a hiding place that he forgets to fix supper. He quickly eats some cold, leftover misoshiru *soup and keeps looking in every corner of his small house for a good place to hide his gold pieces.*

"That's it!" he says. "I will hide the gold pieces under the tatami *mat." He pulls back a corner of the mat and carefully slides the gold pieces one by one in a single layer so that when the* tatami *is pulled down, there are no bumps. He pats down the mat, and to be safe, he places a* zabuton *sitting pillow over the spot.*

"No one will know the gold pieces are under the zabuton," *he thinks.*

When he is satisfied, it is too late to take his furo *bath, his nightly ritual of relaxing in his small wooden tub, soaking away the weariness of the day.*

He sleeps fitfully, tossing from side to side. When daylight awakens him, he jumps out of his futon *and goes to the edge of the* tatami *and lifts it up.*

"At-ta! At-ta!" he exclaims. It's here! It's here! Relieved, he squats on the floor.

The aroma of the cooking rice fills the room but he does not notice. He sips the misoshiru, *worrying about the safety of the gold pieces while he is away at work.*

Carrying his tools over his shoulder, he does not hear the birds singing along the road, so worried is he about his new riches. At work he is no longer friendly with his companions. He can hardly wait until the end of the day.

He rushes home, lifts up the tatami *and exclaims with relief, "At-ta! At-ta!" It's here! It's here! He sits down and carefully counts the gold pieces. Relieved, he hides them back under the* tatami *mat.*

Day after day, he rushes back to his little house. No longer does he see the beautiful sunset. No longer does he feel the air and hear the song of the birds. No longer does he listen to the conversation around him at work. His friends avoid him but that does not worry him. His only concern is the gold pieces.

He rushes home. He no longer whistles. When he reaches his house, he lifts the tatami.

"Eh?" he exclaims incredulously. "Not here!?"

Furiously he rips the tatami mat further. Gone! The gold pieces are all gone!

Dejected, he squats on the floor and stays there for a long while.

Numbly he gets up, washes his rice to cook, starts to heat the furo, and fixes his supper and eats. He goes to bed.

He sleeps soundly and awakens with the sun shining through the screen. The birds are singing. The rice left over from the night before and the heated misoshiru taste good.

"Ahhhh . . . ," he sighs with satisfaction as he sips his hot tea.

He slings his tools over his shoulder and, with a spring in his steps, leaves for work, whistling as he walks along, enjoying the crisp morning air.

⌒

The hot, midsummer sun scorches the farm. Eight-year-old Kazu and her little brother, Naoshi, barefooted, rush to the first puddle of water on the long, dusty road. Two grateful bodies stand still in the shallow clear water leaking down from the main irrigation ditch along the loganberry patch. If Tochan were here he would shore up the break immediately. I find a large clod of dirt and throw it in place to stop the water from escaping onto the road. The two run ahead, eyeing the next cool puddle.

Halfway down to the mailbox, where the road dips and the irrigation water collects clear across it, the water reaches almost to their knees. There, our Model T truck gets stuck in the mud often, and we have to push it out.

With glee, brother and sister run around in circles, feeling the cool mud squishing through their toes.

Tomoko catches up, followed by Molly, our collie, and Dicky, her son. They are Tomoko's constant companions. Wherever Tomoko wanders, the dogs follow like self-appointed guardians. Where the collie came from we don't know. She just appeared one day and adopted us, and we called her Molly from one of our schoolbooks.

Kazu takes Tomoko's hand and carefully leads her across the muddy road and onto dry land on the other side. She knows that one fall could mean trouble. The dogs and I take a wide path into the adjacent field. We meet the threesome walking down the road, hopping onto rust-colored weeds, which are soft and flat like doilies, to keep from burning their feet.

We finally reach Routier Road, where Tochan has the breadbox nailed high enough on the fencepost so that raccoons and dogs can't reach it, and so that the bread man doesn't have to drive down the long dirt road to our house.

"There's nothing in here," Naoshi says, barely lifting the lid of the box.

"You sure?" Kazu checks. "Nope. I guess we have to wait."

They hop about tippy-toes on the burning, gray asphalt road. In the distance the rising water vapor, from the heated asphalt, distorts straight Routier Road, causing it to look like ribbons swaying in the breeze.

Naoshi lies flat on his abdomen in the middle of the road with one ear pressed against the asphalt and listens.

"I hear it! I hear it!" he yells.

All three of them press their ears to the road and listen with Molly and Dicky standing guard.

"Naw," Kazu says sitting up.

"It's coming! I hear it! I hear it!" Naoshi insists.

All eyes look north towards Folsom Boulevard. Half a mile down the road, the bread truck appears, dips out of sight and then reappears.

"Hi!" the friendly bread man says, handing them the three loaves of bread, hardly stopping to do so. He continues on to Old Placerville Road.

Each one hands me a loaf of bread, one already squeezed out of shape, and runs down the dirt road to a cool water puddle. I get the *Sacramento Union* from the mailbox and follow them. The dogs trot back and forth like sheepdogs, bringing up the rear, as if guiding the children back to the farmhouse.

Suddenly, Dicky dashes off the porch and barks, following a truck, which drives toward the front yard. Molly wags her tail, knowing that it is a friendly intruder. Kitagawa-san and his sons come often from the other side of Folsom Boulevard to bring us vegetables that did not sell at the farmers' market. Today they have a quarter of a load of watermelons in their large truck.

"Can you use these leftover melons?" he asks Tochan. He knows, of course, that Sato-san's large family will eat them, but he politely inquires.

"Thank you," Tochan says.

The Kitagawa boys, Fred, Sam and George, all tall for *Niseis*, and to whom work is no stranger, carry two and three watermelons at a time and pile them into our small, dark, basement.

"Wow! One hundred watermelons!" exclaims Kazu.

"Naw. I think there are two hundred," quips Aizo.

"We can eat watermelons for a hundred days!" Kazu says.

Delighted children follow the men back and forth, with Molly and Dicky darting in and out, getting in the way. Tochan places the biggest watermelon on the corner of the porch.

"Wow! Are we going to eat this one?" Aizo asks, trying to lift it.

"After supper," Tochan answers, as he continues to help with the unloading.

Never have the children seen so many watermelons! They fill up half of the basement. The Kitagawas leave quickly, eager to get home to dinner after a long day's work. Their day on the truck farm starts before daylight and ends way after dark. They must still load up tonight for tomorrow's market.

Supper is done. The dishes are cleared. Mama wipes the biggest watermelon. Tochan places it on a wooden cutting board on the table. Mama hands him her longest knife. Eager little bodies stretch across the table. Tochan places the knife carefully across the center, and like a samurai warrior, lifts up the knife and with a swift blow, splits the watermelon into two red, perfect halves. He cuts the halves into quarters and then into smaller, thick slices and places one on each of the eleven plates.

"Sit down, Mama," Tochan coaxes. He becomes irritated at times when Mama moves constantly, already washing dishes. She wipes her hands on the corner of her rice-sacking apron and dutifully sits.

I put away the food and wipe the dishes. In the crowded kitchen there is only room enough to walk between the table on one side and the sink and stove along the opposite wall.

Only seeds and rinds remain of the giant watermelon.

"Let's cut another one," Seiji suggests.

"Yah! Yah!" the children agree.

"No," says Tochan firmly. "Pass your plates to Mama."

Tomoko, as if on cue, quickly pushes her plate, scrambles off her chair and crawls under the table to reach Tochan's lap. She sits on his knees. Naoshi is not quite small enough and not quite big enough. Tochan stretches his legs onto Mama's chair for Naoshi to straddle on his legs.

"One story tonight," Tochan announces. After all day of cleaning the ditches of weeds and clods, he looks forward to a hot soak in the *ofuro* tub with his children.

"What happened to Jean Valjean?" Kozo asks.

Each night we hear a chapter from Victor Hugo's *Les Miserables*. Last night Jean hid from the police inside the huge sewer pipes.

Tonight, Tochan commands total attention as he weaves the story of Jean when he steals a pair of candelabra from a church.

"One more!"

"No," Tochan says firmly. "Get your pajamas."

"Oooo," they groan, disappointed.

Naoshi whines. No one can understand him. It sounds like "I want some more." Mama worries that he might be coming down with a cold. She feels his forehead.

"Leave him here. I will wash him and put him to bed," Mama says.

He continues to whine. Between mumblings she only understands "more, more."

With a bucket of warm water and a washcloth, Mama gently cleans the day's grime from Naoshi's body, meticulously getting into the grooves of his ears.

She feels his forehead once more, then puts the unhappy Naoshi to bed and goes to the basement. In the dim light she picks out the smallest watermelon. She wipes it with a damp cloth and wraps it in a soft, clean diaper.

She lifts the corner of Naoshi's quilt and places the watermelon beside him. Little arms enfold the small melon and the whimpering ceases. Mama quietly closes the door behind her.

Kozo tears the cardboard from the back of his school tablet and lays it on the living room floor. He steps on it and meticulously traces his one foot and then the other with a pencil, and then carefully cuts them out. After many trimmings of the edges, the pieces finally fit inside his old, worn-out shoes, covering the holes in the soles. Satisfied, he takes his shoes to the bedroom.

Tochan notices. There is no money right now for a new pair of shoes. It is early April and the strawberry crop is just beginning to come in. Tonight he must nail together another seventy-five boxes for the pickers tomorrow.

After the children are bedded, Tochan takes Kozo's shoes with him to the barn. He slices two thin pieces of rubber from an old tire with his trusty pocketknife that he keeps sharpened with a small pocket sanding stone. He keeps them both in his back pocket. Whenever he has time, he spits on the black stone and sharpens the blade.

In the poorly lit barn, a sixty-watt bulb hangs over the sturdy home-made table on which he works. Onto the cast iron shoe form, ordered from Sears & Roebuck, he places one of Kozo's shoes. Then he places a piece of the sliced rubber onto the sole and marks around it from below. Carefully, he carves around the pattern of the shoe sole. He repeats the same for the other shoe. He then brushes the soles of the shoes and the slices from the tire with rubber cement and allows them to dry until slightly tacky. He presses the pieces of tire onto the soles and while they dry, he moves over to his box-making stand.

From the wooden keg, he grabs a handful of three-penny nails and scatters them into the nail feeder, tilting it gently back and forth until all the long parallel slots are filled with rows of nails. They line up like tiny soldiers marching in one direction. A quick upward tilt discards the excess nails to the back of the nail feeder. With one last gentle movement forward, the nails are all ready to be drawn, eight to ten at a time, between his thumb and forefinger. He lifts up the front gate, allowing the rows of nails to easily slide out between his fingers.

From my open bedroom window, the rhythm of the rapid hammering lulls me to sleep. I can almost count the number of boxes nailed. Tap-tap-tap-tap-pause. With each single stroke he pounds a three-penny nail level with the shook. Tap-tap-tap-tap-pause. Tap-tap-tap-tap-pause. The bottom of the box is done. Tap-tap-pause; tap-tap-pause. One side slat is secured. Tap-tap-pause; tap-tap-pause. The other side slat is nailed down. Another longer pause means another box is piled up and ready. Several hours of the skillful, rhythmic, non-stop hammering continue.

After the last box is carefully placed atop the swaying pile, he picks up one of Kozo's shoes and fits it onto the Sears & Roebuck shoe form. With his coarse, metal file, he smoothes the edges to match the original shoe, then hammers small shoe nails along the edges.

It is after midnight when he pulls the chain on the light bulb and with Kozo's shoes in hand, walks down the dirt road to the farmhouse. He finds Mama still working in the kitchen.

Quietly he places the shoes by Kozo's bed.

In the morning, oblivious to the chill in the unheated bedroom, Kozo sits on the edge of his cot, elbows propped on his knees, his head cupped in his hands, looking at his neatly lined shoes between his feet. From above he can see the jagged edges around the thick soles. A sensitive boy, who would rather give a marble away than to fight over it, he sits for a long while with his head and body drooped, staring downward.

Finally, as if awakened by the cold, he reaches for his clean school clothes at the foot of his bed. His stiff cold overalls send an involuntary chill through his body. His white socks, permanently dirt-colored on the bottoms from the holes in his shoes even after many Cloroxed washings, feel stiff.

Mama uses Clorox on everything. Sheets wear out before they get tattletale gray. She saves worn out sheets for our kite tails and uses the unworn sections as protectors along the tops of our comforters. Whenever one gets soiled, she replaces it with another, basting it on with a big needle and string saved from the rice sacks.

Kozo unrolls his socks, wishing that he had his holey shoes with the cardboard in them. His shoes feel heavy. Conscious of each step, he walks awkwardly out the door, into the living room, and quickly turns into the kitchen door, avoiding his brothers and sisters warming up their school clothes around the stove.

Mama pours a ladle of pancake batter into the hot skillet as soon as Kozo seats himself on the bench against the wall. He dutifully eats the pancake drizzled with butter and Log Cabin maple syrup and drinks the hot chocolate. His feet are heavy under the table, as if every part of him has drained down to the bottom.

Noticing that Kozo is not eating well, Mama feels his forehead with the back of her hand. No fever.

"Let me see your tongue."

She sees that it is pink and healthy.

She hands him his lunch pail, a lard can with a peanut butter and jelly sandwich wrapped in waxed paper, several Graham crackers, a carrot, and four Hershey Kisses inside. Friends often bring us two-pound boxes of Hershey Kisses to thank our parents for something or other.

If we could cut straight across the wheat fields, our walk would be much less than three miles, but Mr. Robinson doesn't like it, even though we walk right along the fence. The Inouyes work as tenant farmers on the large Robinson property. They live at the edge on old Placerville Road. On hot days, when we walk home from school, Mrs. Inouye invites us in for ice cold glasses of Kool-Aid.

Sometimes we run into trouble with the big kids. "Get out of the way!" they yell at us. I try to steer us clear of them. We walk fast if they are behind us and slow down when they're in front. I think they like to pick on me because I'm sort of in the middle, not too big for them and not too little to be of any consequence.

Just as the bell rings, we reach the school and hurry to the back to warm up by the big black stove. Kozo walks in slowly, as if every step is heavy. I notice that he curls his feet against the step of the platform during his arithmetic lesson.

Dismissed for lunch, Kozo and his buddy Stanley walk past my desk. Overhearing Stanley, I cringe.

"Your shoes look like tractor wheels," he tells Kozo.

Kozo says nothing.

That night I ask Kozo, "How was school?"

"I had bologna sandwich."

"Oh?"

"Stanley really likes my peanut butter and quince jam sandwich, so we trade every day. He doesn't like bologna sandwiches."

Mama buys peanut butter in five-gallon cans. I try to vary the peanut butter sandwiches with strawberry jam, loganberry jam, fig jam or quince jam. Sometimes I mix the peanut butter with honey.

"I made a home run today," he announces proudly. Anything that goes over the fence and into the farm is a homer.

"Good for you!" I tell him.

He walks like he's forgotten all about his shoes.

"Tell us about the General," Kozo asks when supper is over.

"General?" Tochan looks quizzically.

"Yeah. Remember about the General and the soldier?"

"Oh, yes, yes!"

In a small village in Japan, a young boy receives a letter to serve his country as a soldier.

"You have no shoes," his mother laments.

"That's all right, Mother. These zoris are fine." The sandals are worn and ragged around the edges.

"I will weave you a new pair," his mother says and squats on the dirt floor by the hibachi charcoal warmer. The rice straw is still fresh and pliable. Her weathered, gnarled fingers work way into the night. She wishes she could finish the pair with a roll of fine, silk cloth for the straps to hold her son's toes. She cuts the hem from her cotton kimono and sews together several layers to make a soft roll.

Before sunrise, she places the new pair of zori beside her sleeping son. She pauses a moment, wondering when her little boy had grown up into a fine young man old enough to be a soldier to serve his country.

"Okaasan, arigatoh," thank you, Mother, he says, bowing respectfully upon seeing the new pair of zori.

She hands him his clothes, neatly folded inside her best furoshiki cloth. So that he will not be hungry on his journey, she tucks inside the package three large rice balls with salted, red umeboshi plum in the center of each one. She wraps the rice balls with rectangular sheets of nori seaweed to protect his fingers from the sticky rice.

She watches him walk toward the village town until she can no longer see him.

"I am doing fine," he writes home. "We are fed well. We have shoes and uniforms to wear. I hope the war will soon be over and I can return home."

For many months he does not write home. War is brutal. He survives with one leg gone.

A summons arrives from the General, inviting him to a banquet. He is to be awarded the highest medal for courage and bravery.

He finds himself seated next to the General at an elegant table, with crystal goblets and wine glasses, and a feast his eyes have never seen before.

The gracious General passes platters of food and fills his glass with wine.

He thanks the soldier for his faithful service.

Seeing that the General slices his piece of meat with a knife and fork, the soldier does the same. Japanese food is cut up into bite size pieces and picked up with chopsticks. There are no chopsticks on the table. To him it seems strange that one has to cut one's own piece of meat. This must be a European style banquet, he figures.

And why are there three glasses? There is a tall one with a skinny stem. There is a round, big one and a round short one. The soldier reaches for the glass closest to him and drinks from it. The kindly General seeing his soldier drinking from the finger bowl, picks up his own finger bowl and drinks the water and smiles approvingly.

"What's a finger bowl?" Kazu asks. "We don't have anything like that."

Tochan explains that if we are invited to the banquet table of the King and Queen of England, we will now know that one rinses the tips of one's fingers in the finger bowl and wipes them dry with one's napkin. How does Tochan know all that, I wonder?

⁓

The nights are cold in the small farmhouse. Little bodies curl up in their beds, trying to retain the lingering warmth of the *ofuro* bath. Late at night, I feel Mama raise the blanket at the foot of my bed and place a hot water bottle at my feet, a Mason jar wrapped in a towel. All the taut muscles in my body relax. I straighten my legs and curl the soles of my feet around the warm jar. Mama tucks the blankets snugly all around the sides of my body and feet.

Mama goes back and forth from the kitchen to the boys' bedroom. I hear muffled groans of gratitude as she places a warm jar at the feet of each of the children in the dark room.

I hear the click of the kitchen light and all is quiet in the house. Outside, in the creek, the symphony of the frogs lulls me to sleep.

"That's Tochan! Look!" Kazu exclaims, pointing to the three very tall men walking straight-legged towards us. Tochan wears long pants to hide the stilts. Mama cut off the legs of an old pair of pants and sewed them onto another pair of pants. The other two men walk along in unison on stilts two feet above ground.

It is the annual Picnic Day. Japanese immigrant families from miles around gather in an open field. There are races and prizes for all the children. Sack races, relay races, three-legged races. For the chopsticks and peas relay, each team starts with a bowl of ten peas and a pair of chopsticks. Grownups put on comedy skits. Mothers bring teriyaki chicken, sushi rice and *inarizushi* made of fried tofu skins filled with flavored rice. There are watermelons and sodas and lots of pencils and tablets and crayons for prizes.

That's when my brothers decide to make stilts. They nail small blocks for the feet on long poles they found in a pile of old lumber in the back of the barn. Soon they are playing "war," knocking each other down in the puddles of water by the barn.

Not challenged enough, Seiji nails the blocks for his feet almost as high as his shoulders.

"How you going to get on 'em?" Sanji asks.

"Boxes."

The pile of strawberry boxes falls. Seiji picks himself up and leans his stilts against the sloping barn roof. He disappears into the barn and appears on the roof. He slithers down to the low edge of the roof, grabs the stilts, carefully lowers his body, and places his feet onto the blocks. I watch with bated breath as he eases away from the roof. He lifts one stilt and steps forward. The other pole does not go forward. Then both poles sway precariously, and in another instant, Seiji and his stilts are on the ground. He picks himself up, picks up his stilts and places them against the roofline and disappears again into the barn.

Soon two brothers sit on the roof "boarding" their high stilts and walking triumphantly in the shallow water.

⁓

We like Saturdays and we don't like Saturdays.

We walk almost three miles to church school and Japanese school all in one morning. If we get there early, we get to play baseball in the cow pasture until Mrs. Igarashi, the pastor's wife, rings the brass bell.

Ted Kobata appears with an old taped-up bat as soon as he sees someone coming. He lives across the road. Sometimes there are enough players to fist the bat to the top to see who chooses first. Mostly, we divide evenly as we get there.

Short Ted runs fast. When he slides into base, the dried cow pie base flies off into the air. We don't need batboys; we need base-boys to bring the cow pies back into position.

Learning to read and write Japanese is a chore. We already know how to talk it.

⁓

In the parlor, the bottom halves of the curtains, where the windows open, change to a dirty brown color from the gravel pit dust. I have to wash them often, and they still look like two shades of tan. My little brothers still think that windowsills are places for finger-drawing in the thick layer of dust. Only when the air looks clear do we open the doors and windows, which is usually on weekends when the bulldozers rest. Beside the stove in the parlor, we have a small table where we do our homework, and six new straight-backed chairs. A "mysterious" young man gave us the chairs.

I ask Tochan why.

"I took him a gift to thank him for allowing us to use his name," he explains.

Tochan tells me that he had to "borrow" the young man's name in order to grow strawberries because it is against the law for Japanese immigrants to farm. The young man returned with six new chairs. Tochan never told me his name.

From pushing the chairs upside down and playing "train," the tips are worn to a slant and the wood floor has hundreds of streaks I can't mop away.

—

"Japan has frequent earthquakes," Tochan tells us, as he cuts a piece of bamboo from the back yard.

We play hide and seek in our bamboo grove, but it doesn't hide us too well as the growth is still thin. Mama sometimes breaks a young shoot appearing from the ground and slices it and puts it into the *misoshiru*.

"What is an earthquake?" Tochan asks.

The children shrug their shoulders.

"It is when the earth starts to shake. In Japan, where I grew up, the earth shakes almost every day. We don't pay any attention to them. When there is a serious earthquake, where do you think is the safest place to go?"

We wait for an answer.

"Outside?"

"See these roots?" Tochan says.

The roots are everywhere, like a webbed floor.

"Even when the earth cracks open, this will be a solid floor," Tochan explains.

Sometimes I think it would be fun to try it out and hold on to the tall swaying bamboo.

"Is that why you planted this bamboo, Tochan?" Sanji asks.

"No," he says. "Have we had earthquakes here? We planted the bamboo to knock the walnuts off our trees."

Right now he has another idea. He cuts the tallest spear and takes it to our front porch.

"What are you going to do with that, Tochan?" The boys are curious.

"Watch and see. Bring me some newspapers."

No one moves, not wanting to miss what is going to happen.

"Go get some," Seiji orders his little brother Naoshi. There is always a pile by the *ofuro* bath to start the fire.

Tochan goes to the kitchen, followed by curious little bodies. Into a small saucepan he scoops a cup of flour and mixes it with water. Then he heats it, stirring it constantly with a bamboo rice spatula, adding more water from the faucet as the mixture thickens. When the mixture is translucent and soft, he removes it from the stove.

"What's that for, Tochan?"

"Watch and see," he says. They follow him as he takes the saucepan to the porch.

He pulls out his pocketknife and skillfully slices the bamboo lengthwise into two long halves, and then slices a half into two thin quarter lengths.

"We need a piece of string."

We know exactly where Mama saves all the pieces of string from the rice sacks, wound up in a big ball. Kazu runs to the kitchen.

Tochan ties a cross with two bamboo pieces. Then he ties the string from one point to another, sequentially, forming the skeleton of a kite. He pastes two sheets of newspaper side by side with the flour paste, then lays the kite frame on top and folds the edges over the string.

"I need scissors," he says. The boys run into the house to Mama's mending can in the bedroom. Tochan carefully trims the edges. He lifts up the kite.

"Now we need a tail," he says. "Go ask Mama for an old sheet."

"Mama! Mama!" The boys run through the kitchen and into the back yard where they find her feeding leftovers to Molly and Dicky.

"*Chotto matte*," she says. Wait just a minute.

In the corner of their bedroom, Mama saves the worn out sheets, washed and folded neatly in an orange crate by the old Singer sewing machine.

Tochan rips a sheet right through the middle, and again tears a long two-inch wide piece from the center part and ties it to the lower end of the kite.

"Now! The string. We tie a piece to the top point and to the two side points and bring them together like this. Then all the ends are tied to the ball of string."

We hold our breath and watch.

"Is that going to really fly?" Aizo asks.

"I think we'd better dry it first. The wet paste might be a little heavy."

Holding the tail in one hand, he carefully carries the kite and lays it in the middle of the sunny yard. In awe, everybody stands around the kite and waits impatiently. Tochan picks up his shovel and leaves to check the irrigation level in the strawberry field.

"When I come back we will give it a try," he says.

The wait is interminable.

"I think it's dry," Sanji says.

"Let's try it," suggests Seiji, always ready to explore.

"Better not. We might break it," cautions Kozo.

The others watch on the sidelines waiting to see what their big brothers will do.

Other than straightening its long tail, the kite is treated with solemn respect. An occasional breeze lifts one end.

The children watch as if a dead body is about to come alive.

Finally Tochan returns. He picks up the kite and walks to the open field with seven children following excitedly.

"Seiji. You stand there and hold the kite this way. When I say 'Let go,' let it go. All right?"

"All right."

Tochan walks away, letting out the ball of string for about the length of our house.

"Let go!" he says, and gives several gentle tugs on the string. The kite surges upwards several times. And then he runs and the kite soars into the sky. All eyes look skyward, riveted to the kite climbing higher and higher.

"Yaaaay!" A chorus swells.

"Can I hold it, Tochan?"

"I wanna do it."

"Don't let it go. Hold it tightly." Naoshi grabs the string with both hands. He looks up at the kite and grins broadly. The others wait their turn. Sanji becomes tired of waiting.

"I'm going to make my own kite," he announces. He turns around and heads for the farmhouse. Aizo follows.

June brings the big event, the eighth grade graduation. Eight years of school and friends and baseball and Christmas programs come to an end and one feels thrust out into the world. Miss Cox prides herself in the fact that all her students leaving Edward Kelley School are well prepared for junior high school.

"Kiyo, you write a speech," Miss Cox tells me.

"Me?"

I had never made a speech before, but when Miss Cox tells you to do something, one doesn't say "I can't."

I try hard writing and re-writing. I go to bed thinking about my speech and I wake up wondering what to say. I jot down something about reaching for the stars.

"That's good," Miss Cox says the next day. "You might say 'hitch your wagon to a star.'"

So with gentle suggestions from Miss Cox, I finish writing my valedictorian speech.

We practice the program over and over until each student knows when to come on stage and what to say. The walk up the stage from the left seems interminable. I stop at the chalk mark on the floor, face the audience, deliver my memorized speech and walk off to the right.

"Why don't you put your knees together?" Tony tells me. He is the only child of the Yamamotos and gets pretty much what he wants.

"What do you mean?" I ask him, puzzled. I hadn't paid any attention to my legs before.

Am I bowlegged? I am devastated. Do I have *daikon-ashi*? Daikon is the long white Japanese radish, usually plump. Ashi means leg in Japanese. To be called *daikon-ashi* means one has ugly legs.

As I walk onto the stage, I am so conscious of my legs that they don't move naturally, one in front of the other. I try to hold my knees together, putting my weight on the inner sides of my feet. My knees become more important than what I am supposed to be saying. Walking off stage and trying to hold my knees together, I almost trip over myself.

Twelve of us graduate, girls in fancy white dresses with corsages and boys with white shirts and neckties and boutonnieres. The schoolhouse fills to the back wall with farming families from miles around. The majority of the children come from immigrant Japanese families who learned to speak English in first grade.

1938.

The first of the eight children graduates. My parents are faced with a new challenge, that of continuing my education twelve miles away. There are no buses going to Kit Carson Junior High School in Sacramento.

"She will have to drive to school," Tochan tells Mama.

"But will it be safe for her to drive to town?" Mama worries.

"There is no choice if she is to go to school," Tochan says. "And remember, next year Seiji will be going."

And so it happens that Tochan drives home a stately, greenish brown 1932 Studebaker for which he has paid $450. My brothers touch it; we sit in it; we pretend to drive it.

"Get in," he tells me. Seiji, Sanji, Aizo and Kozo rush into the back seat. The others stand by looking sad.

Tochan tells them he will be back to give them a ride.

He shows me how to start the automobile and how to engage the gear. It is different from the Model T truck, which has three pedals.

"Remember there are three gear speeds," Tochan explains.

I watch him closely as he drives down the long dirt road. When we reach Routier Road, he backs up and tells me to sit in the driver's seat.

With Tochan beside me, I feel confident.

"Step on the clutch," he tells. "Good. Now pull the gear forward. Good. Release the clutch slowly."

The Studebaker jerks forward. Four heads stretch into the front seat, silent and serious.

With confidence, I grind slowly into first gear, hardly aware of the potholes.

"Now step on the clutch," Tochan tells me. "Good. Pull the gear stick straight down. Good. Slowly release your foot on the clutch." The Studebaker jerks badly. The boys hold on to the back of the seat.

"That's all right," Tochan assures me. We drive on smoothly, much to my relief.

Then he instructs me to do what seems totally confusing: push the gear stick up half way and then push it to the right and push it up.

"Step on the clutch. Good."

He places his hand firmly over my right hand on the gear knob and guides it into second gear.

"Now let go of the clutch."

Silently I agonize: how am I ever going to drive this thing!

In second gear, I drive smoothly, relieved.

"Step on the clutch."

Not again, I groan silently.

"Pull the gear stick straight down."

"Let go of the clutch slowly."

The Studebaker moves forward smoothly and settles into a gentle speed, much to my relief.

My brothers settle back and talk amongst themselves.

We return home and turn at the elevated water tank. Tochan directs me to step on the brakes at the barn. I step on the brake pedal and the Studebaker comes to a sudden stop, totally jarring the passengers and killing the engine.

Tochan apologizes. "You need to step on the clutch to release the gear and then step on the brakes." How am I ever going to remember all this?

By now I am convinced that I will not be able to drive the Studebaker to town. I would rather get a job in town and do housework than drive this Studebaker.

I get my driver's license. As I am only fifteen, my parents have to sign for me. Mama worries but there is no choice.

My cousin Susumu and I take turns each week driving to school. My 1932 Studebaker has terrible brakes and I worry that I may not be able to stop in time, so I start pumping my brakes way before the intersections. I am so glad to get out of town and onto the long stretch of Folsom Boulevard. Every day Mama watches for the cloud of dust coming down the farm road.

"*Sorede anshin suru.*" She says that she has such a sense of relief seeing my Studebaker return.

⁓

"She's *eta*."

"What's *eta*?" I ask my Nisei classmate.

"You mean you don't know what that is?" She holds up four fingers.

"No," I reply feeling rather stupid. "What is it?"

"You don't talk to them." Without explaining any further, she walks away.

When I drive home, Tochan is working by the barn.

"What does *eta* mean, Tochan?" I ask.

He stops dead in his tracks, thrusts his shovel into the ground and looks at me seriously. I can almost hear him say "*Komat-ta na*, what a predicament." When he is faced with a problem and a solution is not forthcoming, that's what he says

"There are some things that should have been left in Japan," he says. "Mama and I did not want all of you to grow up with the old prejudices from Japan." He explains that there is class distinction in Japan. A long time ago, during the Samurai era, the rich and the elite subjugated a group of people for their convenience, much like slaves. These people learned to survive by performing jobs that no one wanted to do, like taking care of those who died, or working in slaughterhouses.

"What does four fingers mean?" I show him what my friend did.

"That means *shimin*."

As Tochan always does, in his very patient way, he explains that "*shi*" means four and "*min*" means people. *Shimin* means fourth class, the lowest of Japan's social scale, people who usually lived in the outskirts, isolated from the rest of the population. When one became of marriageable age, the *baishakunin*, a marriage broker, made certain that no *eta* blood would contaminate the family line.

"There are many ridiculous superstitions that should not be passed on. For instance," he tells me, "it is not proper in Japan to take camellias to the cemetery. Why? Because the head drops off," he chuckles. "And even now, beautiful roses are not used in funeral wreaths because there is some superstition about thorns. The Japanese seriously believe these things. It is best that we not pass such nonsense on to our children. That's why Mama and I never talk about such things."

"Is it true that you shouldn't marry into a family tainted with tuberculosis?" I ask. I had overheard some women tell about three daughters who will never be considered for marriage because a relative had tuberculosis, a dreaded disease.

"The lives of those three girls can be ruined forever by such gossip. Your mother was a nurse in a hospital where she took care of tuberculosis patients. With proper rest and care, they get well, like any other illness."

"What's *bakatare*, Tochan?" Naoshi asks.

Tochan tilts his head to one side and grows silent. We know that is when he is thinking.

"Tom said I was a *bakatare*."

"'*Baka*' means stupid," Tochan says reflectively, as if this was a subject for deep consideration. "'*Bakatare*' means someone who is not so smart."

"Always remember," Tochan continues, "it is the one who calls another *bakatare* who is the *baka*."

I begin to understand the significance of Tochan's stories about Kuzu. He is like the tenth child of our family. Story time is never complete without an episode about Kuzu. Kuzu is not very smart and people make fun of him, but we are very protective of him. In Japanese, *kuzu* means crumb or leftover. Sometimes when we do a stupid thing like touch a hot pan, Mama will say "*Obaka san da ne*," meaning "My little dumb person" while she dribbles soy sauce over the finger to soothe the pain.

Back to Kuzu.

Tochan weaves a story of a carpenter who takes many days to build his house.

The house is finally finished. Proudly he stands back to view it from all sides.

As his last task, he removes his tall ladder from the tatami *room where he had designed a* tokonoma, *a central and sacred spot in every Japanese home, for a scroll and a vase. The final touch.*

As he moves the ladder, a hammer he had forgotten slides off the top, hits the wall, and makes a gash in the clean, white wall.

The owner is beside himself.

"Ojisan," says Kuzu, "You can hang a picture over the hole."

"Yay!" the children exclaim in chorus. "That's a good idea!"

⁓

Succulent red strawberries hang crowded along the sides of the ditches. With sleeves wet to the elbows from the early morning dew, the pickers work as if pursued, straightening up only to carry a full crate to the truck parked along the edge of the field. Five bodies, hunched over like turtles, progress slowly down five rows. Mama is in the lead, always. Blood-red berries, too ripe for shipping, cover the bottom of the ditches. The picking is a day behind.

As pickers bring filled crates to the truck, they nail the covers on and stack them on the truck. The sound of the hammering reverberates into the clear blue sky. The months of May and June determine the outcome of a whole year's work, the fruition of the year's hard labor—which means for our family the stocking up of two thousand pounds of rice.

The one-hundred-pound sacks of rice piled almost to the ceiling in the boys' bedroom will become a smaller and smaller mountain to climb as the rice is consumed. Then the rice sacks become aprons, dish towels and strips of cloth to protect the edges of comforters, hand protectors for picking berries and even marble bags for us.

Between four-thirty and five o'clock, picking stops when Herb arrives for pickup. He skillfully maneuvers his truck backwards down the narrow road between the fields so that loading can be done across the two beds of the trucks.

"One hundred and ninety-nine crates. We did well," Tochan says.

"Let's make it two hundred, Mr. Sato!" Valentino Esguerra, one of the pickers, excitedly suggests, picking up his carrier to go back into the field. "It won't take us five minutes more." Juan Bautista and Ceriaco Esguerra follow suit.

"No, no. This is enough," Tochan tells them. "You did very well. Thank you."

Ours is the first stop for pickup, as our farm is the farthest north from the loading dock of the Berry Growers' Association in Florin. Mrs. Abe and her children work across the road and my uncle's farm lies to the west. Between our farm and the railroad docks, Herb picks up thousands of crates each day. Freight car loads ship out from Florin for Portland and Seattle and sometimes eastward. The sweet and juicy Oregon Plum variety does not do well on longer trips, he says, even in the refrigerated cars.

Valentino, Juan and Ceriaco, followed by the children, trudge back to the barn. They stoop to pick handfuls of wild morning glory leaves growing along the way.

"What are you going to do with that?" curious Kazu asks.

"Cook 'em," Valentino tells her.

"And eat 'em?"

"Yup. You want to taste it?"

The children help to gather more and place them in the workers' hands.

The workers live and cook in the side rooms in the barn, where we stayed before we moved into our new house. As Valentino prepares the meal, the others go to the *ofuro* and wash up like the Japanese, using the tub to soak away tired muscles. It is an understanding that the workers bathe first and we bathe after supper.

The children visit the workers' cabins as if it were home.

"Well," I ask Kazu, the Curious, "did you get a taste of the morning glories?"

"Yuk!" She wrinkles her nose. "It's slimy. I don't like it."

Kit Carson Junior High School has an orchestra.

"Anybody who has an instrument can be in the school's orchestra," I mention to my parents.

Mama and Tochan look at each other.

"What would you like to play?" Tochan asks.

I don't really know what an orchestra entails and violin is the only thing I can remember so I say "violin."

That weekend, Tochan brings home a violin "which cost fifteen dollars," I hear him tell Mama.

"Why did I even mention it?" I scold myself. Now I have to learn to play it.

———

"Lunch time!" I call from the top of our tallest tree.

Someone answers from the vineyard, where the farm truck is parked. I like the view from this maple tree. To the south and west of me lie the grape fields. To the north side of our house we have the walnut orchard, which Tochan started from Mr. Buckley's black walnuts, which he grafted into a variety of English walnuts—Franquettes, Paynes, Mayettes and others I don't remember. Tochan has become such an expert that Mr. Buckley now hires him to do his grafting. While the trees mature, he plants all varieties of bush berries from the house to the road. The orange grove stretches from behind the barn and to the northeast. Five acres of almond trees grow to the edge of the railroad tracks, which go to Mather Air Field, reactivated shortly before the war.

In the yard below me, I see the tops of two pomegranate trees, one red and the other pink, almost ready to be picked. Soon we will be able to crunch into our Fuyu persimmons, the first sign of fall. In the springtime, a red flowering peach blooms in the front yard and a snow-white peach blooms outside Mama and Tochan's bedroom window in the back.

The Wickson plums ripen before the Santa Rosas. All summer long we have something to pick and eat. No one pays any attention to the wild cherry plum trees and the quince, except the birds and Mama, who cooks them into jam for our lunches.

By the pump house, I see my favorite snacking tree, the Elberta peach, and next to it, spreading out in all directions, is my least favorite fig tree. Mama makes whole fig preserves, which make the best peanut butter and jam sandwiches.

The Japanese Black Pine grows outside my window. The wisteria at its foot stretches its tendrils from its arbor onto the pine tree. Roses and Mama's flowers bloom everywhere.

The oldest tree grows in front of the house—*ume-no-ki*, the flowering Japanese plum tree, which blooms in January. In Japan, Tochan says, poets write about the *ume* and artists paint it. It blooms in the snow. I wonder how it came to America and into our yard.

It is 1939. Masashi is my shadow. I take him everywhere.

The crops continue to do well. The long summer is busy, beginning with the harvest of the strawberries, then the raspberries and the boysenberries. In the fall, the Ribier grapes turn to a deep purple color. I order school clothes from the Montgomery Ward catalog. The hundred-pound sacks of rice neatly stacked in the boys' bedroom mean food for the coming year.

Tochan hands me a check. "Cash this check and buy a pair of shoes for Masashi," he tells me.

The last check from the Strawberry Growers Association, for over two hundred dollars, would buy shoes for all of us.

I drive the Studebaker with Masashi sitting beside me, combed and dressed for our trip fifteen miles into town. We stop at the Mills Station Grocery Store. Mr. Studarus cashes my father's check, handing me the cash.

As we drive down Folsom Boulevard, Masashi says, "I don't want Buster Brown shoes," I'm surprised that a three-and-a-half year old would make such a request.

"Oh?" I question. "What kind of shoes do you want?" I ask.

"I want Florsheim shoes," he states matter of factly.

Kozo's shoes flash through my mind. For his ninth child, Tochan does not have to repair his children's shoes by slicing rubber tires for soles.

· 6 ·

The Reign of Terror

Mi wa tsukare,
Wata no gotoku ni nari nure do
Tsuma-ko yasuki o
Kansha su yuhan

— JOHN SHINJI SATO

At our supper table,
Exhausted,
Strengthless like a wad of cotton
I thank God for the wellbeing
Of my wife and children.

— TRUDY SATO, TRANSLATION

IT IS NOT until Monday morning that I sense that something terribly wrong has happened over the weekend. Walking down the main hallway to my class at Sacramento Junior College, I notice that there is not the usual "Hi, Kiyo." Like the parting of the Red Sea, students turn their backs and walk to the side, leaving me the wide, dingy hallway. I catch a glimpse of a classmate from my French class and am about to greet her, but she pretends not to have seen me and joins her circle of friends against the wall.

The lonely walk down the old corridor seems interminable. I am conscious of my feet supporting my body, on which my head is held straight up. With a great sense of relief I turn the corner and see the open classroom door. Betty, who sits behind me, doesn't poke me asking to see my paper. I catch furtive, unsmiling glances, which quickly turn away when I smile. It's like I have done something hateful and the whole school has been advised of it. What have I done?

During break, I chat with a *Nisei* student.

"Didn't you know?" she asks incredulously, making me feel pretty dumb. "Japan bombed Pearl Harbor!"

"So?"

Why is that so important, I wonder? That's a foreign country. So what?

"Where's Pearl Harbor?" I ask.

"Hawaii. Don't you realize what might happen to us?"

"War?"

"No, to us. *Niseis*."

"Why us? I'm an American."

I now see what my short encounter in the hallway meant. A scary chill shoots through my body. Is this a sign of things to come? Are they all going to hate me? Mary approaches us, looking worried, her drooping eyebrows accentuating even more her look of constant doom.

"Are you going to quit school?" she asks. I am taken aback that anyone would even consider quitting. The gravity of the situation hits me.

"Didn't you listen to the radio? It's terrible!"

"I didn't want to come to school this morning."

Furtively, we look around to see if anyone is within listening distance.

"They're saying get rid of us."

"How?"

"They're even talking about putting us in concentration camps!"

Now I understand the looks of hate from my classmates, their cold shoulders.

I think back on yesterday. We had gone to Sunday School and church, and all afternoon I was busy ironing our week's school clothes. Mama and Tochan were burning the trimmings from the bush berries with everybody having a great time feeding the fire. None of us left our farm. I cooked stew and rice. We had story time, *ofuro* time and bed. It was a happy and peaceful day on our twenty-acre farm, while the world was raging around us.

Wherever I go I feel the daggers of hate—in looks, in newspapers and at school. It's as if *we* dropped the bomb on Pearl Harbor, and it has given license to every *hakujin*, Caucasian person, to spew out hatred, the worse the better. When Alberta Walker walks beside me in the hallway, in her quiet, unassuming way, I feel shielded. At lunch I seek out another *Nisei*, as do all the other *Niseis*, creating a small circle of safety. It keeps getting smaller as my friends leave to help their parents on their farms.

Hate escalates. It becomes the thing to do, the rallying cry.

"I hate Japs."

"You can't trust any of them."

"Get them out of here!"

"Once a Jap, always a Jap." General DeWitt of the Western Defense Command is quoted repeatedly.

"Throw them out in the desert and let them become like the skulls of cattle," writes Henry McClemore, the syndicated columnist.

"They planned this war by living near airfields." There was no airfield when Tochan bought this land, for heaven's sake!

"The fact that nothing has happened means that they are planning something," our Attorney General Earl Warren says, having no other good reason to give.

"They signal the enemy planes by the direction of their ditches." Imagine!

The word "Japs" reverberates throughout our state. I am so sick of reading about "Japs" this and "Japs" that, referring to us, that I avoid reading the newspapers, all filled with lies. The enemy is not Japan or Germany or Italy. It's us, the Japanese Americans! Me!

The *Issei*, they say, bought land near airfields years ago in preparation for this war. "Jap spies" stand ready to attack at any moment from the Japanese farms, they say. We plow the ditches in a certain direction to signal the Japanese enemy planes above, and at night we use our flashlights!

So they confiscate our flashlights and even long knives. A *Nisei* tells me that he hid the family's precious sashimi knife in their woodpile. It's scary. Nothing we do is right, even to drive to town! Who knows? Maybe it'll be okay to kill a Jap or two.

Will Tochan be next on the FBI list? Will he be gone when I get home? What will I do if he isn't at home? The scared, sick feeling doesn't go away. When they didn't find Mr. Mizukami at home, they went to Elk Grove High School and demanded to see his son. With every *hakujin* white person I encounter, my shoulders tighten. It is only when I turn onto our farm road and see Tochan working out in the field that I relax at the steering wheel of my '32 Studebaker.

JANUARY, 1942.

Hatred escalates. We are scared wherever we go. We are scared even to go to school. There are only two safe places for us, the Mills Station Grocery Store, where Mr. Studarus treats us as always, and Edward Kelley School, where Miss Cox protects her children like a feisty mother hen. *Nisei* students dread going to Sacramento High School and Sacramento Junior College, but we know we have to.

Kozo looks worried. "Mama's crying," he says.

Mama never cries. I might have thought that she was blowing her nose again from hay fever but I can see that her eyes are red.

Seiji quit school. He went to the US Army recruiting center to volunteer, and will soon be gone. He's not eighteen yet and needs only one more semester to finish high school. Mama could not dissuade him. She is devastated. Her one dream of seeing her children educated is shattered before it begins.

Tochan seems not as worried. He probably thinks that the Army is as safe a place as any right now. I have a feeling that Tochan is proud and wishes that he, too, could exercise such a privilege of citizenship.

It is a grim time to grow up as an American with "Japanese blood," to be eighteen and to be so hated, to no longer know who one's friends are. The only place one feels accepted is in the Japanese community. And to Seiji and his buddy Makoto, the Army may be a place to prove that they are Americans. They have volunteered to serve in the United States Army and leave on January 28th for Camp Robinson in Arkansas.

Curfew hits. By eight o'clock any people with "Japanese blood" must be in their homes. That means we can no longer attend evening church meetings or any meeting at night. We must stay in our houses until six in the morning. Will the next edict be to quit school? Jobs, maybe? What will happen to us if we can't go to school or not have jobs?

The minute I see Sam Kumagai at the noon dance, I know something terrible has happened. The usual friendly *Nisei* looks as if he has been hit by a ton of bricks.

"This is my last day," he tells me. "I just came to return my books."

We know that sooner or later all of us will have to quit.

"Why would you want to quit now, Sam? The semester will soon be over."

"I can't stay in school. The FBI took Dad. When I got home yesterday, Mom was crying and she wouldn't stop. I promised her I'd quit school and help on the farm. My sisters are young."

"I'm sorry," is all I can say to Sam.

I watch his defeated body go down the hallway and wonder if I will ever see him again.

I wonder if this is also going to be my fate. I look at him and see myself, both of us eighteen, both of us starting college with dreams of an exciting future—not only our dreams, but our parents' dreams of finally sending their first-born to college. Will they come for Tochan? What would I do if I had to be totally responsible for my family? I don't even want to think about it. I just wish I weren't the oldest but I wouldn't want to wish it on any of my brothers or sisters either. The thought of it pulls me into a dark place.

FEBRUARY 17, 1942.

When I turn the corner, a strange car parked in our yard causes me to jerk my Studebaker to a sudden halt. I freeze. My first thought is where is Tochan?

Am I about to become like Mickey Saiki, head of household for his whole family? Will Tochan be dragged away like Mr. Saiki, in his dirty working clothes with no time to say goodbye? They say the agents found a dead car battery behind Mr. Okazaki's orchard. Now Frank, his oldest son, has to take care of the family. What would I do with Tochan gone? Frightening realities crash in on me. How would I take my father's place?

Tochan is our pillar, our decision-maker and protector. Without him our household will collapse.

My hands tremble as I pull open the screen door. As feared, I encounter a somber scene. Mama sits stiff and straight, with the children crowded beside her, quiet and fearful. She motions to me to sit down, pointing her finger sternly to an empty chair.

I hear heavy footsteps above us up in the attic. It is not the sound of my brothers. Through the half-open door of my parents' bedroom, I see the back of a big Caucasian man wearing a hat. Methodically he opens each bureau drawer, dumps the contents on the bed and examines them carefully. He lifts the mattress from all sides; then he checks the closet.

My thoughts race frantically. Where is Tochan? Did they take him inside one of the rooms? Are they questioning him? Dear God, please, please, I plead from the depth of my soul.

I lean over to Mama and whisper: "*Tochan wa doko?*" "Where is Tochan?"

"*Mizu-ate.*" Irrigating, she answers barely audibly, looking straight ahead as if she had not said a word.

Please stay out there! Don't come in this house! Please, God, don't let him come near this house. I pray as if my words were shooting through a cannon right straight to the target.

I've got to go and warn him! The FBI agents are merciless.

When he irrigates, Tochan wears his high-top green rubber boots. His clothes smell sweaty. My mind is racing. When the agents clear out, I'll run into the bedroom and grab Tochan's Sunday shoes, which Mama keeps polished and ready for church. When they put Tochan into their car, I'll throw his shoes beside him so that he can take off his muddy boots.

The agents are absorbed, looking for things that aren't there, their backs turned. This is my chance. I'll get out the door and find him and warn him. I clench my hands and lift my bottom off my chair. How do I get past the squeaky screen door? One of them might get nervous when I open it, and shoot. I know they carry guns.

You'd better sit down, I tell myself.

Resigned, I lower my body back onto my chair. I look over to Mama. She sits quietly and seems to have no clue as to what I was about to do.

Another agent rummages in my bedroom. There is not much to search in my small room. I don't have a closet; my clothes hang behind the door. I can't see him checking my bureau drawers. He lifts up the mattress on my small bed and then sits down at my desk and opens all the drawers. To my horror, he finds my little red diary and begins to read it. Immediately, I stand up, ready to rush in and grab it away from him, but something stops me. If I did that, I might get all of us in trouble. Angry and frustrated, I sit down, totally embarrassed and humiliated. He'll get bored and put it down, I tell myself, but he reads it and slowly flips one agonizing page after the other, while I squirm in misery.

An agent comes down from the attic, says something about a radio up there and goes outside. He looks up and down the outside wall and disappears around the house. I remember the broken radio Seiji had in the attic before he left for the Army.

Finally, the three of them huddle together in the bedroom. I am trying so hard to hear every word that I have trouble making any sense of the mumble. Our future will be declared in a few minutes; my body feels wooden with fear. Every cell in my body screams "Tochan, stay away from this house!"

After what seems an interminable session, they disband, walking past us as if we were invisible. As the last agent passes by Mama sitting by the door, he pats her head.

"Good Christian family," he tells her, like she'd been a good little girl.

Mama hurries back to the kitchen as if she has more important things to do. My brothers and sisters run outside. I collapse against the straight-back chair, totally drained.

I go to my room and sit at my small maple desk, pull out my diary and flip its pages. What did it reveal? What did he find so interesting that he'd sit and read through the whole thing? Picking berries . . . sunny day . . . walking to Mills Station Grocery Store . . . reading *Windows on Henry Street* . . . washing and ironing . . . total number of crates of strawberries we picked . . . going to Mayhew Japanese Baptist Church . . . teaching Sunday School . . . That's it! Christian, he had said. My friends, whose fathers were taken away, belong to the Buddhist Church. Do they think all Buddhists are spies?

What do these families do with their fathers gone? How do my friends manage? Mickey had to quit school and now has to run the truck farm. The Okazaki family doesn't know where their father was taken. We hear that the prisoners are shuttled to a jail in another state right away. Rumors are that they are sent to a special prison for spies in Montana. We are spies, saboteurs, Japs, enemy aliens with buckteeth and slant eyes. It's the thing to do, to hate the Japs. If not for Mama and Tochan, who keep on doing what they have to do, I wouldn't know what to do. They don't waste their energy getting angry.

We have no place to go for help. We have only each other.

⁓

The scourge spreads throughout our farming community. We live in fear of where the FBI will hit next. They barge in, search from room to room and leave the house in shambles. People scramble to get rid of any incriminating evidence, even books and papers and photographs of relatives. They burn them or bury them, and even throw them down the outhouse. Treasured heirlooms are no longer important when one is about to lose a member of the family. Seeing how the agent methodically took apart Seiji's broken radio in the attic and then checked for wires around the house and even in the garden, I can see how important the agents think their jobs are. My cousin Chiyo tells me that her father, who is active in our church community, has a small suitcase packed and ready by their front door, just in case.

⁓

My classmate Masayoshi writes to me that the family is thinking of moving to Colorado, the only friendly state with the only friendly governor. Governor Ralph Carr looms like the Star of Bethlehem to all of us, but we must travel over a thousand miles of unfriendly territory to get there. "Remember the Pilgrims," he writes. "We can do it!" I wish we could move away, too, from this hate-filled world. I have to be careful about every step I take and every word I say.

Terror shatters our community when word reaches us that Mr. Iwasa committed suicide by drinking lye after harassment by the agents. Every farm has lye for curing olives. He had been recovering from a stroke and was lying in bed when the agents demanded that he get up so they could search under his mattress. Kaoru, only a few years older than I am, now must take care of her mother, her brothers and sisters and their twenty-acre farm. A terrible pall hangs over the farming families, and we are plunged into further depression. There is no place to go for help. No one cares, not even the churches, which profess Christian love. Only the small Mayhew Japanese Baptist Church on the corner of the Fairbairn's pastureland, gives some sense of comfort to the community. The future looks grim and hopeless.

As soon as darkness comes, I pull down my window shades, being careful that there are no seams through which a distant binocular can invade. Strange cars come and go and sometimes park for hours on Old Placerville Road between Mather Field and our property.

I could pass for Chinese, I suppose, and wear one of those "I am Chinese" buttons. The *hakujins* wouldn't know the difference. With each button the Chinese put on, my hiding place becomes smaller and smaller. My defenses weaken. What will happen when all the Chinese students wear them and we are then all alone?

A newspaper article advises people on how to tell the difference between the "Japs and the Chinese." We are supposed to be a "squat mongoloid with a flat, blob nose with less frequent double eyelids and a thick jaw bone." That's me? True, I am squat, five feet two inches, short by Caucasian standards, Mongoloid, according to textbooks. Blob nose, maybe. Hidden double eyelids, I think. A thick jawbone, Heavens!

It is May, almost the end of my first year in college. I try to stick it out, with the blessings of Mama and Tochan, but the frightening furor to be rid of us escalates.

There is no safe place to hide. It is like a government-condoned foxhunt. If we ran, surely we would all be shot. I worry all my waking hours, but Mama and Tochan keep right on working as they always have, and so do all their *Issei* friends. There is no other choice.

I pull down my bedroom shades. Moonlight shines through the sides. For three days now I remember a strange, dark car parked along Old Placerville Road, which goes to Mather Field. I wonder if the driver is still there peering with his binoculars through the sides of my shade. The only safe place is no longer safe. I pull the blankets over my head, wishing for some kind of comfort, for this terrible worry to go away. The moon does not shine through my open window, and the symphony of frogs no longer lulls me to sleep.

Ten days! On the tenth day by twelve noon, the public notice warns, we must be out of here, with only what we can carry. What do I pack? How do I manage carryable baggage for each one of us? Why did our good President sign such a terrible order, this "Executive Order 9066?" Doesn't he understand that we are loyal American citizens? Doesn't he know what he is doing to all of us? Our *Issei* parents keep right on working to make every minute count. There is no time to waste, no time to complain.

Wherever we go, public notices on buildings, power poles and fence posts blast to the world that all of us with more than 1/16 Japanese blood are to get out of here in ten days.

Our President was wise enough to become president. Maybe he will realize his mistake and rescind Executive Order 9066. Then we can all go back to our normal lives, and maybe hate will subside.

Seven days left. I've got to find more old suitcases. I've got to see to it that each one of us can carry something. Sanji, Aizo and Kozo can carry two and maybe Kazu can manage one middle-sized one, with smaller ones for Naoshi and Tomoko. Masashi is only three. I'll look for a tiny suitcase for him to carry. That means ten suitcases! I wish they'd tell us where we are being sent. I would know better what to pack. A heavy coat will fill up one suitcase. Maybe this will be a short trip. I hope.

Apparently, everybody's out there in the lower end of town scrounging around for used suitcases. They're not so easy to find. When I walk into a store, I feel as if they are eyeing me but so far I've had no confrontation. This part of town is used to seeing us, as Japantown is part of it.

Tochan and Mama leave all the preparations for "the trip" to me. They pick strawberries from early morning until the hauler arrives. With the next check, Tochan tells me, I can order clothes for the children from Montgomery Ward. Is there going to be enough time, I worry? Suppose the order comes a day late. Where would they forward our package? Will they send us south or north or to another country? Should I order warm clothes? Some people are saying they are going to wear all the clothes they can, even double sets of underwear.

"You know you're supposed to get a permit to travel over five miles," my worried neighbor reminds me.

"But you told me it took you two hours and I haven't got that kind of time," I tell him.

"Yeah, I know. They don't seem to know what they're doing."

Every minute counts. I must find more old suitcases.

Down the road, my aunt sees my car coming and flags me down.

"Will you pick up some suitcases for us?" she asks. I am feeling overwhelmed, with at least eight more to buy, but I promise her I'll look. Like us, they have nine children.

Two of my cousins drive, but they're scared. So am I. We're all scared. Chiyo got fired from her State job. So did everyone else with any "Japanese blood." How can they tell whether I have "Japanese blood" or "Chinese blood?"

Most of us stay close to home. We don't dare break the curfew from eight at night to six in the morning. Sometimes I wonder if Mama and Tochan worry about my safety. They don't seem afraid, or maybe they just don't show it. They make me feel a little braver. I come and go as I need to. Suppose the axle of my Studebaker breaks again and I'm outside the five-mile radius?

After a half a day of going in and out of second-hand stores in the lower end of town, I head for home. Suitcases of all sizes and shapes fill the back seat of my Studebaker, partially blocking the rear window. I try to decide which ones I will share with my aunt, maybe the large reed one and the smaller, old leather suitcase. I still don't have enough for our family and will have to go out tomorrow again to look for more.

It is a disastrous season for the strawberry growers. Farmers, forced to abandon their crops at the peak of the season, try desperately to salvage what they can. This couldn't have happened at a worse time. The Yamasakis and the Kitadas and the rest don't know how they will continue their mortgage payments on their twenty-acre farms. And no one cares. No one. With our own government putting us away, anything goes if it concerns "Japs."

I don't know how Tochan can keep so calm. I'm rushing and feeling so pursued, but Tochan goes from one task to another at a steady pace. What's he going to do with this farm? Is he going to sell it? What about all the stuff, the truck, the Studebaker, the tractor, the farm equipment, the piano, the stove, and all the beds? The "vultures" keep an eye on the properties, waiting on the sidelines to grab them at the right moment. They know that in ten days we will all be gone and it will be there for the taking. Why buy the stuff even for a few dollars? No one cares.

The sheriff has all our "contrabands" like cameras and radios and flashlights. Everybody's on the bandwagon to get rid of us, and our Attorney General, Earl Warren, pulls the wagon, wanting to be our next governor.

We have no one to go to for help. Not even a church. Anything goes, now that our President Roosevelt signed the order to get rid of us. How can he do this to his own citizens? No lawyer has the courage to defend us. Caucasian friends stay away for fear of being labeled "Jap lovers." There's not a more lonely feeling than to be banished by my own country. There's no place to go.

The Kitadas and a few other families store their things in the Mayhew Japanese Baptist Church on the Fairbairn property. I don't see how the things will be any safer there.

Lucky for us that the eighty-acre parcel that my father, my uncle and

Mr. Abe bought belongs to a good man, Mr. Coyle, an attorney. If they called him a Jap lover, I wouldn't be surprised. He probably will survive, being low-key.

Mama moves in high gear, non-stop, which is not unusual for her. She's the last to go to bed and the first to get up. Sometimes I wonder if she goes to bed at all. When we sit to eat, her head nods from fatigue, but Mama never complains.

———

At the supper table, the usual chatter fills the small kitchen. Only after our meal is over and story time is ended, the children bathed and bedded, do we talk about our plans. Tochan comes into the kitchen where Mama and I finish the dishes and pack six lunches for school. Tochan looks weary, a look that I haven't seen before. For the first time since the public notices appeared, a tinge of hopelessness threatens to break my *gaman*—perseverance. Hold on a little bit longer, Mama often reminds us.

"Bill came this morning and offered to look after our place while we are gone," Tochan tells Mama.

Bill must be about twenty-three or so. At Edward Kelley School, I remember being in awe over the tall, Caucasian boy in the eighth grade who was allowed to do grown up tasks. I don't know exactly what his family does. Grow grain, maybe.

Bill would harvest the crop, irrigate, pay the electricity bill and oversee the place. All the profits would be his. Tochan agreed to let him take over, having no other alternative, but I can sense his doubts. How can a young boy only a few years older than I am, and who knows nothing about strawberry farming, take over such a big responsibility?

"He seemed very eager," Tochan continues, "and maybe we won't be gone too long." Everything seems to hinge on the hope that our "trip" won't be long.

There is a cluster of four *Issei*-owned farms on Routier Road. What will happen to them?

The authorities are worried that food production will suffer with the abandonment of the productive Japanese farms in the state.

"Let's build one huge concentration camp in the middle of California and put them all to work," a politician suggests.

Other than at mealtimes, there is no rest for Mama, Tochan and me. We barely take time to sleep. But the children, Mama says, need to grow up happy and secure. They go to Edward Kelley School, where they are safe with Miss Cox. In her small, one-room schoolhouse, peace reigns. Fifty to sixty children come from surrounding farm families—Dagostinos, Durans, Sakumas, Cabrals, Hashimotos, Newtons, Sunaharas and others—children from diverse backgrounds, unaware of the hateful world around them.

I finally had to quit junior college in Sacramento just before the public notices were posted, and I was about the last hold out. Japanese-American students left to help their families.

No one goes anywhere any longer. It is as if we are already exiled. The only time we leave our farm is when it is absolutely necessary—like to get suitcases and follow government orders to get shots and turn in contrabands. No one drives down the lane except Herb or another driver to pick up our berries.

A half a mile away a cloud of dust appears as I am taking the clothes off the line. Who would be brave enough to be driving here, I wonder? Maybe Tony Yamamoto from the other side of Folsom Boulevard. As the car comes closer, I notice that the passenger is not black-haired and that the driver is wearing a hat. I prepare for the worst. Agents wear hats. Tochan is in the barn loading boxes on the Model T truck. It is too late to warn him to go out the back and hide in the orange grove. Besides, I can't see Tochan running. I can see him facing his enemy calmly.

The car appears around the pump house, and to my happy surprise, I see that it is my high school classmate Alberta and her father.

"We just dropped in to say hello," Alberta tells me. They have been by before to buy a crate of strawberries.

Tochan appears from the barn. Seeing Mr. Walker, he extends his hand, obviously happy to see him.

"I'm glad to see you," he tells him.

"We were driving by," Mr. Walker says, "so we thought we'd just drop in."

They walk to the barn and Tochan shows Mr. Walker what is being done now on the farm. They don't talk about the impending evacuation. Mr. Walker, a deeply thoughtful man and a Seventh Day Adventist, listens with apparent concern. Alberta and I stand under the scraggly Gravenstein apple tree and talk about nothing in particular. Knowing our limited time, they don't stay long.

Even though they didn't say so, I know they made a special effort to visit us. I worry that somebody may have seen them drive in here. When they turn onto Routier Road and no other car comes by, I go back to my clothesline, relieved.

It is our last supper at home. Curry stew and rice with everything in it—big chunks of potatoes, carrots, green bell peppers, celery and onions, with pounds of stew meat. Mama is seeing to it that our bodies are well fed for "the trip." To finish off, I have my *ochazuke* and *koko*. I never feel quite done unless I swish hot green tea over a small portion of rice and crunch on *takuwan*, pickled radish or cabbage or *nappa*. Then my mouth feels refreshed.

Even before everyone finishes, Mama gets up from the kitchen table, her hands and feet in constant motion as always, as if she hasn't got a minute to waste. Little hands shove their plates to the end of the table where I gather them and place them on the sink behind me. Masashi and Tomoko scramble for Tochan's lap and outstretched legs. He quotes to himself several lines from Longfellow, as if his thoughts are elsewhere, and pauses.

> Lives of great men all remind us
> We can make our lives sublime,
> And, departing, leave behind us
> Footprints on the sands of time

Ten days have gone by so quickly and there is a non-ending list of things yet to be done before we have to leave tomorrow. I fully expect Tochan to say "No story tonight," followed by unhappy groans.

"When I was a boy . . . ," Tochan begins. Around the crowded kitchen table, there is instant silence, with outstretched necks. Another *kitsune* story. The clever fox appears in different disguises each time, tricking unwary travelers. Tochan knows. He has seen them.

Walking home on a lonely mountain road at dusk, a pretty lady is lost. She asks Shinji, a young boy, to help her. He leads her around the next mountain and points the way for her. He must go around two mountain roads to his home and it is getting dark, but the lady tearfully insists that he accompany her down her path. His mother will be worried, he tells the pretty lady but she weeps helplessly.

Tochan spins a skillful tale of the lady and the unsuspecting boy— unsuspecting, until he gets a glimpse of her ugly, clawed feet under her long, bright kimono.

Frightened out of his wits, Shinji pivots and runs with all his might around the two mountains, his zori *flipping off his feet behind him. He reaches his house, puffing, bangs the shoji screen behind him and sinks to the* tatami *mat floor.*

"Yay!" the children all clap.

There is a pause.

"Another one."

"A Kuzu story!"

"Jean Valjean!"

"Yeah! Jean Valjean!" There is a chorus of voices.

"All right. Let's see . . . Where did we stop last night?"

Lately, he has not had time to read a chapter each night from Victor Hugo's *Les Miserables*. He retells the story of the kind priest and the stolen candelabras. Once the storyteller begins, the children are hooked. It does not matter that it has been told many times before.

"Time to take a bath," Tochan announces.

"Some more!" the children insist.

"All right. One more and we go take a bath," Tochan concedes.

They settle back for another episode from their favorite *Kuzu* stories. The children empathize with *Kuzu*, who is not so smart but always has solutions to problems. They clap with glee at his bright ideas. If you drop a grape into a hole and your hands are too big, use your chopsticks. They clap for *Kuzu*.

"Time to take a bath," Tochan announces again. They reluctantly leave the kitchen to fetch their pajamas.

Tochan swings Masashi onto his back and carries him to the bathhouse. Others follow, shouldering their well-worn pajamas. Sanji, Aizo, Kozo, Kazu, Naoshi and Tomoko. The boys run ahead on the moonlit dirt road.

The raspberry patch along the road is producing now. Straddling the ditch, Tochan checks the berries. He notices that they need to be harvested. He plucks a large, juicy berry and hands it to Masashi on his back. I remember it wasn't long ago that we were commissioned by the Berry Growers' Association for several crates of our large raspberries for the banquet table of the King and Queen of England! How we scrambled to pick the biggest and the best! How proud we were when they wanted more!

In America, dreams do come true—with hard work.

Warm steam rises from the square, redwood tub. Embers still burn below from the late afternoon when Sanji started his assigned chore of heating the bath water. Every Japanese family builds their *ofuro* with redwood and a sheet metal bottom, which, surprisingly, rarely leaks. Tochan uses putty but many people use strips of newspaper with homemade flour paste to seal the edges. Even before a house is built, the *ofuro* bathhouse is necessary. It is an unspoken rule that one always washes off the day's sweat and dirt before going to bed.

One bare light bulb hangs from the rafter. The children shed their clothes and pile them by the old wringer washing machine. Naked bodies step onto the wooden latticed platform. Tochan washes the little bodies while the older boys help scrub each other's back.

"Wash your hair," Tochan reminds them.

When Tochan pours a bucketful of water over each head and rinses it clean, it signals permission to jump into the *ofuro* to play.

First to be washed and rinsed, Naoshi quietly makes air bubbles with his washcloth in the corner of the redwood tub.

Outside the tub, two sisters chatter happily as they wash.

"Wash your hair," Tochan reminds them.

"Hey! Don't do that!" Aizo punches Sanji's washcloth balloon. The fun is in making squishy noises drowning each other's bubbles.

Tochan washes and rinses Masashi. He showers Kazu and Tomoko each with a bucketful of warm water.

"Time to get out, boys."

"Not yet."

"A little bit longer," they beg.

"Time." Their father's word is law. Reluctantly they hop out and the rest get in.

Tochan steps into the tub and lifts three-year-old Masashi onto his lap. The warm water reaches above their chests. Naoshi squeezes in beside his father and his sisters take the two opposite corners. Tochan leans his head against the edge of the redwood tub and closes his eyes, enjoying the soak while the children play quietly.

Scrubbed and clean, they walk back, wearing their pajamas and *zoris* on their feet. With the youngest on his back, Tochan stops to look up at the sky.

"Now, who can find the *mitsu-boshi?*"

"I see it! I see it!" Naoshi, the quiet observant one, points to the Three Sisters. *Mitsu* means three and *boshi* means stars, Tochan explains.

While everyone looks up to the sky to see who can see the first shooting star, Tochan gazes at the old rosebush, just beginning to bloom, at the edge of the garden, the first rose he planted ten years ago. The moonlight sheds an iridescent glow on the delicate, pink petals. The leaves appear to be brushed with a pale silvery film.

The screen door squeaks and Mama calls out "*Anata!*" When around the children, she calls her husband "Tochan," but when addressing him directly, she says "*Anata,*" a respectful pronoun meaning "You."

She is worried. "The children will get chilled," she says. With the warm bath and the brisk evening air, she is concerned that they might catch colds, and it surely is no time for that with "the trip" tomorrow.

"Brush your teeth," Mama reminds the children. In a jar by the sink, Mama keeps baking soda and salt, mixed half and half, for toothpowder.

The children scatter to their beds, their new clothes beside them lying on their own suitcase. Tomorrow is the big day. We don't tell them that tomorrow is the dreaded evacuation day and that we are soon to become prisoners of our own country. Mama does everything to protect her children. It's as if she is a silent and uncompromising barrier between the hateful world and the children.

Tochan returns to his unfinished task. He gathers into the corner of the living room tools he has carefully chosen to take—a hammer, nails, a roll of wire, a folding pruning saw, a carpenter's square and plane. Where is he going to put all that stuff? How does he plan to pack that bucket, and a gallon jug, I wonder, and why the bucket?

In the remaining hours, he cannot worry about the rotting strawberry crop, the raspberries, the farm equipment and house. Right now he must concentrate on how best to take care of his wife and children. He must trust that Bill will harvest the crop and pay the electricity bill for the irrigation. The remaining income, which will be Bill's, would have clothed and fed the family for the entire year.

If Tochan is troubled that there has not been any sign of picking the already overripe berries, he does not show it. To miss even a single day of picking during harvest time is disastrous, resulting in overripe berries, which cannot be shipped and must be discarded in the ditches. Tochan sees that Bill has made no visible plans to continue the picking, but there is nothing more he can do. Tochan has nailed two hundred boxes "ahead." He has stocked up enough shooks and baskets for the crop ahead. He has worked way into the night.

In the kitchen, Mama makes small rice balls with sprinkles of black sesame seeds and salt while I fix sandwiches, slathering plenty of peanut butter and jelly.

"Look at all this peanut butter left," I tell Mama. The five-gallon gold-colored can is still two-thirds full. On the shelves are cans of salmon, corned beef, pork and beans, abalone, sardines and so much more. And there are still the hundred-pound sacks of rice stacked in the bedroom.

Mama says, "Somebody will eat them." As long as some human being is fed, she is satisfied.

She scrubs and washes the rice pot and puts it away in its usual place in the corner of the counter. She cleans up as if we will be back for our next meal. I put away the partial loaf of bread.

We don't know where we will be taken, north or south or across the ocean. Rumors abound. Pinedale, somebody said. Where's that?

Mama takes no chances that her children will not be fed. We wrap the sandwiches in waxed paper and place them in a cardboard box over a layer of rice balls. Then Mama wraps the whole thing with a square *furoshiki* made from the hundred-pound rice sacking. The four opposite corners tied together make the package easy to carry over one's arm, freeing both hands for the suitcases.

"Kiyo-chan, you go and get some sleep," Mama tells me. I am numb from weariness and I don't want to take a bath, but my good sense tells me that this is the last chance to wash at home. Only God knows when my next bath will be. I reluctantly leave my mother to finish alone. I pick up my pajamas and walk down to the bathhouse.

A radiating warmth from the bottom of the *ofuro* awakens me. I don't know how long I have been asleep with my head leaning against the ledge of the redwood tub. My shoulders and upper body feel cold. My neck is stiff. The water is cool. I hear Mama stoking the fire below.

She removes her clothes and throws them into the washing machine, along with the pile left by the family, and fills it with buckets of hot water from the tub. While the washing machine runs, she washes herself from her long, flowing black hair to her toes. We both soak quietly, grateful for this last and brief time of rest and warmth.

Together we finish rinsing the clothes in the tub and wringing them through the rollers of the washer while it washes a second load. Mama removes the wooden pallet from the bottom of the tub, scrubs it and the tub and rinses everything clean, all ready for the next bath.

In the moonlight, neither of us talks, as we shake out the little overalls, shirts and underwear and clip them with wooden clothespins onto the long wire lines, which extend from the bathhouse to our vegetable garden. The lines sag in the middle with the heavy load. I place two eight-foot poles in the center of each line to keep the wash off the ground. By mid-morning it will be dry and ready to be packed.

It has been non-stop for ten days preparing for the departure; now it is zero hour. There is a strange kind of peace in knowing that there is no more tomorrow to finish our work. I no longer write in my diary, nor does Tochan, since the FBI agents ransacked our house and read my diary.

"*Oyasumi*." Sleep well, Mama says, as I go to my room. She walks back to the kitchen.

What will happen to our house? Will we come back home? Where are we going?

I hope no one will climb to the attic and find our boxes of picture albums and Tochan's books and his records. All our clothes are washed and packed away in boxes. It doesn't seem possible that we will live with the few things we will carry with us. Mama and I washed and aired our blankets and sheets for the allotted bedrolls. Leave the kitchen as is, Mama says, for whoever might live here.

Where will we be sleeping tomorrow night? I lie in my bed in my clean pajamas, feeling stripped like a non-person, like a dandelion puff at the mercy of every waft of air. We go wherever we are sent. We do whatever we are told to do.

There is no choice if we want to survive.

· 7 ·

Evacuation Day—
Executive Order 9066

Ashi wa doro

Medama wa ten wo

Mite kawazu

  – JOHN SHINJI SATO

Feet stuck in mud

Eyeballs looking skyward

A frog

  – TRUDY SATO, TRANSLATION

MAY 29, 1942.

THE RAPID, RHYTHMIC sound of slicing vegetables on the cutting board
awakens me. In my half-conscious state, I count as fast as I can and find
that Mama has left me far behind. The window shade barely lightens, or is
it moonlight? Has Mama gone to bed at all?

Softly, she sings a Baptist hymn, almost as if to coax the children to
awaken happily. There is something about Mama, like a continuous unbroken thread that knits the family together. She gets everything necessary
done, like feeding and washing and loving.

Light shines from the living room. I hear Tochan walking back and
forth. As soon as I get out of my bed, he takes my blankets and spreads
them out on the living room floor. He places a hammer, a large bagful of
nails of all sizes, and a roll of wire in the middle. Then he rolls my blankets, covers them with rice sacking and ties the bedroll securely with the
heavy rope we use to tie down loaded crates of strawberries. He makes
sure that nothing will spill out with rough handling.

With each waking child, he takes the well-worn blankets and sheets
and carefully hides inside the folds, the tools and supplies he has selected
with care the past week and has set in the corner of the room. Is he going
to hide all that stuff, I wonder, seeing the large pile? I worry that we might
get caught. We hear that searches are stringent and unkind and even cruel,
that young girls are patted down and touched.

Tochan wraps a gallon jug with a sheet and stuffs it inside a metal
bucket, then wraps a comforter around it. Why a jug, I wonder? He hides
a small pruning saw that folds in two, instead of his favorite big saw. A
carpenter's plane and a level go inside another bedroll. To my dismay,

he carefully packs my violin inside a thick comforter. Having struggled as second violin in our high school orchestra, I would not have minded at all leaving it with our old piano.

Inside the folds, he scatters little brown bags of seeds of all kinds—squash, *nappa*, *daikon*, cucumber, and flower seeds for Mama.

I know that my father is aware that this is a risk he must take for the welfare of his wife and children. It's scary to think how easily he could have disappeared, like so many *Issei* fathers. What's happening to Sam, I wonder? Where is his father? No one is told what the FBI did with all the *Issei* men taken into custody. Sam must be packing up his family right now. What did he decide to do with the farm and all that equipment?

Watching Tochan, I shudder to think what I would do as head of the family right now. I feel for Sam and for Mickey and for Frank and for Kaoru, all my friends and schoolmates, having to protect their *Issei* mothers and brothers and sisters from harm in an angry and hostile world. One step out of line would chalk up another "saboteur" for the FBI, where just looking like the enemy gets one put in jail.

We don't ask questions any more. It's no use. There are no answers. We keep working like our lives depend on it.

Children play on the bedrolls piled up on the porch, waiting to be loaded onto Mr. Iwasa's big old farm truck, which Masami gave Tochan, knowing that it would be left on the farm anyway.

One item is not a bedroll. It is a large, tightly rolled up canvas, in case we need shelter. A slim thread of security gives me comfort, knowing that my father will take care of us no matter what the circumstances. I've just turned nineteen; my baby brother is only three-years-old. In between are seven children, with Seiji in the United States Army. Sometimes I want to just crumble and give up, but seeing Mama and Tochan keep right on working without a complaint gives me no choice but to hold my head up and do what I can.

At the kitchen table, Mama serves hot *misoshiru* soup with thinly sliced *daikon* radish. She drops an egg into the bowl. Tochan sits down and bows his head. Mama appears surprised, as this is not the usual routine. She quickly wipes her hands on her rice sack apron and sits down beside him and bows her head. No words are said.

How long will it be before we eat at this table again? Will we be able to come back home?

———

"Dress after you eat," I tell my little brothers and sisters, "so you won't mess up your new clothes."

One by one they come to the kitchen table in their pajamas. Seeing the shaggy edges of their pant legs, I wish that I could have ordered new pajamas for them. The last check from the Strawberry Growers' Association barely covered the cost of underwear for everybody and shirts and pants for the boys. Aizo and Kozo wear the new boots Tochan picked up for them. For days the two of them followed Tochan in the field, all three wearing their green work boots with the tan-colored soles.

Kozo leaves the table, barely touching his food, quickly downing his cup of chocolate milk.

"I'm gonna wash my boots," he announces.

He carefully scrubs his boots at the back yard faucet and takes them up the attic steps.

"What are you doing, Kozo? You need to pack them in your suitcase," I tell him.

"I'm going to put them on the roof so they will dry fast," he answers and disappears.

"Are Molly and Dicky coming with us?" Tomoko asks.

They are her friends and constant companions. To Molly, the faithful collie, the two youngest children are her charges. Wherever Masashi toddles, Molly trots along and stations herself close by, nudging gently with her wet nose when danger lurks, like a car coming into the yard. Dicky follows his mother.

"Dogs aren't allowed where we are going," I explain.

"Why?"

Nervously, Molly and Dicky run back and forth through the front yard as if they know that we are leaving.

"Out of my way!" Sanji yells, almost tripping over Molly as he drags his suitcase to the truck.

I had contacted the Humane Society to pick up our dogs but they still are not here. Maybe they don't want "Jap" dogs. I wouldn't be surprised. What will our dogs do, left with nobody to feed them? Everybody I know owns dogs, mostly strays that found homes on the farms. I know that Molly and Dicky will follow us when we drive off.

"Put them inside the back shed," Tochan tells us. In back of our farmhouse is a small storage shed.

"Help me catch them!" I shout to my brothers.

It is difficult to catch Molly and Dicky, who seem to be trying to corral us to keep us from leaving. Sanji and Aizo finally catch them and drag them across the yard. Once inside, they paw frantically at the door, totally ignoring the food and water.

"We can't lock them up," Kozo says. "Suppose nobody comes for them."

I shudder at the thought of finding them dead inside the shed.

"Time to go!" Tochan calls.

We depart quickly, leaving the door open a crack.

No sooner do we reach the truck than we find the two dogs behind us, wagging their tails.

"Oh, no!" I groan.

Back again, we go, the five of us, dragging the reluctant dogs.

"Find me a big rock!" I order.

"What for?" Kozo asks, looking stunned.

"Just do what I tell you!" My patience begins to wear thin, and my voice demands immediate action, which is not like me. Time is running out. I hold the door closed while my brothers scatter. They return with three big rocks. I instruct Sanji to hold the door open just enough so that I can reach behind it and place the largest rock against the door leaving it open about five inches.

"Okay! Let's go! Hurry before they get out!"

There is no time to grieve. How can I explain this terrible, cruel thing we are doing to them? No one on this earth will miss us so much, certainly not in California. We are abandoning two members of our family. I turn and run, swallowing hard to stop my welling tears as Molly and Dicky whine and scratch frantically on the shed door.

The big truck starts forward with difficulty as Bill, who has volunteered to drive us to the train, steps on the accelerator. Piled high and securely tied with heavy farm rope, the bedrolls and suitcases sway precariously. This one truckload holds our survival. Sanji and Aizo, looking like they are on their way to Sunday School, ride in front with Bill.

The rest of us squeeze into our 1932 Studebaker, hoping that the axle will not break again or that we won't have a flat tire due to the extra heavy load.

As soon as we drive into the dirt yard of the old Washington School, six miles away, young *Nisei* men, most of them still in their teens, direct us and offer help. Mothers alight with babies, arms loaded with sweaters and coats, purses overflowing with baby bottles, food and water, and most of them with *furoshiki* of food slung over their wrists.

Guards with rifles and fixed bayonets stand at attention everywhere. They make no attempt to move out of the way of baggage being carried to the railroad cars. A chill runs through me, knowing what they can do to us if we get out of line. I worry for the children who are running around, unaware that we are now prisoners.

"You need to sign in over there, Mr. Sato," one of them tells Tochan. "We'll unload for you. You'd better go and get your number."

Like looking at a flat painting, devoid of feelings, I see long tables at the edge of the dirt yard, manned by unsmiling Caucasian workers busily processing papers. Immediately behind them stand at attention a long row of drab green, uniformed soldiers, armed and ready to protect them from the "Japs."

Masashi, three-years-old, awed by the soldier's big gun and boots, stares in fascination at the guard's rifle and bayonet and his feet. The soldier looks straight ahead. He avoids my brother's gaze. None of them acknowledge our presence or lend a hand.

Each family is issued a number. Each person must wear a baggage tag with the family's number. Even infants must wear a tag. Tochan gets ten tags and hands them to me to put them on my brothers and sisters.

I take Masashi's hand. "Come on, Sweetheart! Let's go!" He carries his own small suitcase, which I found in a second-hand store. He wears his brand new mail-order pants, rolled up at the bottom giving him room to grow.

Tochan has two suitcases under his arms and two more in each hand.

He tells the boys to carry what they can and follow him. Mama and I keep a watchful eye on the little ones, Masashi and Tomoko. Kazu, not to be outdone by her three older brothers, struggles with both hands, holding her suitcase in front, bumping her knees.

Totally ignoring the armed guards, the young men tie our tags onto our bedrolls and suitcases and carry them like busy ants to the train's baggage car, weaving around the guards who do not step out of the way. Much to my relief, our bedrolls get past the guards. I look around to see when they are starting the dreaded body searches.

Upon orders, the guards leave their posts and close in from all directions and corral us toward the train like a herd of cattle. The crowd moves peacefully, each helping the other with little children, older people and carryables. No one panics; no one yells. I keep an eye on Mama and Tochan up ahead, while I hold on tightly to Masashi's hand.

I worry about everything. Did we forget anything? What will happen to our dogs? Where are they taking us? Did I pack enough warm clothes? Did we bring enough food?

Little children, excited by their first train ride, run up and down the aisle. I pick an empty seat. The wooden slab seats are covered with a layer of sooty dirt. Everybody scrambles for anything to clean their seats— handkerchief, napkin, or even a scrap of paper off the floor. We pass on whatever works to the next person. Young men dust off their seats with their shirttails.

Through the dirty window, I see blurred images of clusters of Caucasian people talking. What are they saying, I wonder? Are they relieved to see us taken away? Do they really think that we are dangerous spies? Is there anyone out there who cares what happens to us?

No one waves.

Automobiles drive off. I don't see our Studebaker where Tochan had parked it.

"That's our car," I hear a fellow behind me tell his companion. "Somebody's driving it away," he says wearily.

An air of resignation consumes us. Armed guards stand at attention at both ends of our coach, rifles held upright with bayonets pointing to the ceiling, legs spread, prepared for any emergency.

I hope against hope that our President will realize his mistake and a messenger will come running to the train, waving a telegram telling us that we can all go home.

When the old train creaks, it is only the wind, I tell myself, but when it lurches forward, my whole world collapses and uncontrollable sobs well up from deep inside. I had dared not weaken. "*Gaman*," Mama would often say; persevere, don't give up.

Reality finally hits me. "We are putting you there for your own protection," the authorities had said. All I know is that my non-*Nisei* friends hate me. Like an arrow through my heart, I notice that not one of our school friends have come to see us off. The churches, the Caucasian farmers, the veterans groups, all of them, even the politicians who are supposed to be protecting the citizens, are now banding together to get rid of us. The Japanese Americans cannot be trusted. It is the political rallying cry, an open season on "Japs."

When our President signed Executive Order 9066, he put a stamp of national approval on ridding our country of everyone with more than one-sixteenth Japanese blood living in the west coast states. To the general public, it doesn't matter how it's done. It is a devastating loneliness to realize that there is no one in my own country to whom we can turn for help.

Last year, my winning essay. "What America Means to Me," placed in our school's finals. This year I am branded a "non-alien," no longer a citizen, and banished. To where?

Children curiously look at me from around the corner of the high seat where I sit alone sobbing. Embarrassed, I press my face against the dirty, opaque window. Taking a last look through my tears at the familiar scene about to disappear, I see two arms waving.

I frantically wave back. Miss Cox, our grammar school teacher and Mrs. Fairbairn, our piano teacher, stand beside the tracks, surrounded by a handful of little children from Edward Kelley School. Midst tears and sobs, I wave back until I can no longer see them.

We cross Fruitridge Road . . . then Elder Creek Road . . . Florin Road . . . Gerber Road . . . all familiar places. How I wish I could be driving my Studebaker, stopping for this train to pass.

"*Shikataga nai ne,*" women greet each other quietly. There is nothing we can do, they say. But with the welfare of the children foremost in their minds, they endure the insults. They have a word for it—*gaman*. Mama says it often when we are about to give up.

It reminds me of the time one of my brothers came home complaining about a bully. "I'm glad none of my children are like him," Mama said.

"*Ahh, soh desu ne. Kodomo no tame ni.*" Yes, that is so. For the sake of the children, I hear *Issei* parents say often. They board with arms loaded with food and warm clothing. Property is lost, home is gone, unloaded cars and trucks are left at the schoolyard and driven away by strangers, but the children are protected. The children wear their new clothes and happily explore their new surroundings, feeling safe with caring adults.

After several hours of going through the coach from one end to the other, the children are tired and hungry. Mama unties her *furoshiki,* and offers its contents to the children around her. Other *Issei* mothers do the same. Someone brings me a *sushi,* the kind we call *inarizushi,* with seasoned rice inside a fried bean curd pocket.

I feel better. We used to have them for our picnics. We had to get up early to cook the rice and season it. Then we had to stuff the *abura-age* pockets, which were cooked and seasoned the night before. Someone didn't sleep much to have made the *inarizushi.*

The guards begin to relax, leaning their weapons against the wall. They look weary. They must have finally realized that we are not dangerous. Seiji in the United States Army could be one of them. Mama extends her box of peanut butter sandwiches; they refuse.

For so long, we had tried so hard to avoid any incident which would give anybody an excuse to report us or take us in. Fathers are missing but they are at least alive someplace.

I think about the warm sweaters I should have packed for my brothers and sisters. I watch our *Issei* parents talking quietly. All that they have worked for is gone, their houses and farms abandoned, their possessions reduced to what each can carry. The children, fed and happy, play in the aisle with new friends, ignoring the armed guards at both ends of the coach.

We find comfort and safety in each other.

· 8 ·

LOCKED UP
GUARD TOWERS

Tai kai wo

Nogarete i ni iru

Kawazu kana

    – JOHN SHINJI SATO

A frog escaping

From the gigantic world

Lives in a well

    – TRUDY SATO, TRANSLATION

ARMED SOLDIERS CORRAL an exhausted and bedraggled band of men, women and children from the train and herd them onto waiting buses, the freshness and the vitality of the morning drained after a day on the dirty coal-burning train.

"Where are we?" I ask.

"Fresno, I think," a young *Nisei* answers. Responsible for his mother and five siblings, he sits glumly, flanked on both sides by his brothers and sisters, who cling to their big brother. Having been picked up by the FBI as "spies," many fathers are missing. I shudder to think how close we were to losing Tochan when the three agents ransacked our house. Now that I think back, it could have been my diary that saved him and the notations I made about teaching a Sunday School class at the Mayhew Japanese Baptist Church. Christians are supposed to be good; Buddhists are supposed to be evil, according to them. Tochan grew up a Buddhist. He can chant just like the Buddhist priests he used to hear as a little boy in Japan.

"Good Christian family," the agent had said, patting Mama's head. Right now it's dangerous to belong to the Buddhist Church. The FBI picks up the *Isseis* for just being Japanese to let the public know what a good job the FBI is doing. Why did they drag Mr. Saiki off his farm for no reason? Every day the headlines announce the number of "Japanese spies" the FBI agents have brought in—none of them spies or saboteurs.

The caravan of buses takes us miles out of town into the country. The blacktop ends and we travel along a barely visible road on flat dry terrain. Dusk lends an eerie look to the brown dust clouds churned by the buses ahead.

In the distance, in the middle of the vast dry, flat land, hundreds of black barracks enclosed by barbed wire come into view. Silhouettes of guard towers surround the compound. We stop by the gate, above which is one of the towers, where two guards armed with rifles stand. A machine gun at their feet, pointed at us, sends a chilling message. How come, I ask myself? Didn't they tell us that we were being sent here in "protective custody?" What are the guards thinking? Will they shoot anybody? Do they really think that we are dangerous?

I sneak a side-glance, hoping they do not see me looking. The young white faces look serious, as if we'd better not get out of line. Below, the sign says keep 10 feet away from fence, in English and in Japanese. I worry that we might be too close. I hold tightly to Masashi's hand and keep up with the crowd.

Tochan walks ahead and I bring up the rear, with the rest of the family between us. Hundreds of weary people, arms loaded with bundles, coats, and babies, trudge through the open gates. Jostled by the crowd, I am afraid that one of our children might be dragged away. I keep a close eye on my brothers and sisters in front of me while dragging my little brother. It is getting dark.

The barracks along the way are all occupied by the earlier arrivals. What will we do, I worry, if all of them are filled?

"Mr. Sato!" someone calls. A young man, probably my age, weaves through the crowd.

"There are empty barracks at the end of the camp. Follow me," he says.

It is a long, dusty walk down the middle of camp. We pass row upon row of black tarpapered barracks, already occupied. The dry, powdery dirt, left by the bulldozers during construction, stands a foot deep in spots. To my dismay, my feet sink into the ground, filling my shoes with dry dirt. There is not one blade of green grass, not one weed, and no trees. Masashi tugs at my hand to pick up a small piece of wood. The scraps of lumber left from construction are scattered everywhere, floating like dead tan-colored fish on the soft, brown undulating earth.

"Come on!" I urge Masashi, pulling him back. If he gets lost, there's no telling how we will ever find him in this camp of thousands of people.

The young man rushes ahead, goes from barrack to barrack, opening and closing one door after another. He finally finds one unoccupied and stands by the door.

"Here's one, Mr. Sato!" he yells from ahead. He holds the door open as we all march in. "Give me your number. I'll go and get your things."

Metal cots with thin gray and white mattresses are lined up on the black, asphalt floor. One light bulb hangs from the rafters.

"This is mine!" Aizo says flopping onto a cot, raising a small cloud of dust.

"This is mine!" says Kozo, following suit.

"You need two more cots," the young man tells Tochan. "You come with me," he tells Sanji. They bring in two more from the next empty barrack.

I go to the far end of the room and unload my bag and *furoshiki* on the bed in the corner. Even in the dim light, I see thick layers of dust on the two-by-four ledges holding the tarpaper. I catch Mama standing at the other side of the room, looking from corner to corner, lips pursed with determination, or is it to keep them from quivering?

CLANG! CLANG! CLANG! The sound is like that of a baseball bat hitting the bottom of a washtub.

The boys run to the door. Everybody hurries in one direction, back the way we came.

"Where are you going?" Sanji asks.

"Time for chow! Mess hall."

It is closer to bedtime than suppertime so this, I figure, is a special mess to feed the latecomers. People come from all directions forming a long line at the mess hall barrack. A pickup truck loaded with bawling children moves slowly along the line.

"Please pick up your children," a young man with a bullhorn announces, standing in the back of the truck with the children.

"See, Masashi? That's what happens when you get lost." I feel his little hands tighten in mine as he watches the children with sadness.

"Remember, all the houses are the same so you have to stay close by unless one of us goes with you," I explain.

He looks glum. "I don't want to stay here. I want to go home," he whines.

So do I, I want to tell him, but I say: "Let's go exploring after supper and get more wood."

"Okay," he says, brightening up. "Where are we going?"

"How about down that road?" I point down the firebreak.

The mess hall is like all the other barracks except that it is not partitioned into separate rooms. An overwhelming and unappetizing smell fills the hot, suffocating hall. Warmed over mutton stew, someone tells us.

After a whole day of munching on things, it is good to at least sit down and eat together. I scoop the white rice untouched by the stew into my teacup. It tastes good.

"All I need is some *koko*, Mama," I kid. Wouldn't that be good? Hot tea and rice and pickled *nappa* cabbage!

Mama doesn't think it's funny, I can tell.

My empty stomach repels my first spoonful of the mutton stew even before I swallow it. I try the leftover bread mushed with milk and raisins. It doesn't taste too bad. My brothers don't think much of the bread pudding. I see that Mama, who hates to see food go to waste, hardly touches her portion.

Everybody hurries back to the barracks to unpack and get ready for the night. We went in and out of ours so quickly that I can't remember which it is. I remember it was close to the west fence and along the south side of the road which runs through the center of camp.

Masashi and I walk past our barrack and northward from the firebreak. Masashi picks up pieces of scrap wood and stuffs them into his pockets. Usually his pockets are full of "treasures" found on the farm—nails, bottle caps, screws, rocks, silver gum wrapper and even tiny bones.

"Here, hold this," he says, handing me a foot-long piece of plywood.

"What are you going to do with all this?" I ask him.

"I'm going to make something," he says.

Pockets bulging, we return to our barrack. Tochan is already hammering away, putting up shelves with the nails he had smuggled inside the bedroll. He, too, has picked up boards.

"That's a nice piece, Masashi," Tochan says. "Let's put that by your bed for your toothbrush and cup." With two nails a new shelf forms on the two-by-four ledge. Below it he hammers three large nails for Masashi's towel and clothes.

"Mama, I need my towel!" Masashi yells, happy to have his own corner.

Curious neighbors knock on the door, wanting to know where Sato-san got the hammer and nails. They see the saw, the bucket, jug, carpenter's plane, drill and other tools piled in the corner.

"*Ma-ah!* You look like a *furu doh-gu ya*, a dealer of used equipment," one of them comments with a tinge of envy.

"After I am through here, you can use my hammer and nails," Tochan tells the grateful neighbors.

With two big nails, he hangs a rope diagonally from one corner of the room to the other to hang our clothes and towels. When he is finished, he takes his hammer and his bag of nails to his new neighbor. Other neighbors come. He does the same.

"*Arigatoh. Sumanai na,*" they apologize as if they are an imposition.

"*Yoku kangae ta monda.*" You planned well, an *Issei* father says, impressed with Tochan's good thinking.

A handful of nails triggers a ray of excitement when there seemed to be no more hope. The journey ends for the five thousand brown-skinned men, women and children now concentrated inside the heavily-guarded compound.

Mama brings back a wet bath towel from the shower barrack, wipes the children's faces and hands and feet and tucks the children in their beds. One by one they fall asleep, exhausted from our long day's trip.

I sneak out to wash up and brush my teeth. The grime from the sooty train permeates my whole body and I feel filthy. I brush my teeth in the wooden trough and leave feeling better.

Mama hurries by, carrying a large #10 can she found in the mess hall garbage.

"The toilet is so far away for the children," Mama says, and heads for the laundry room to rinse the can.

Curfew is ten o'clock. Lights have to be out. I hang my wet towel on our clothesline overhead. My mattress is so dusty but I am too tired to carry it out the door and shake it out. I spread out my bedroll on it and lie down, glad for my body to be horizontal. Tochan returns from the men's shower building.

"Mama, you better hurry. It's almost ten."

As long as Mama is upright, her hands and feet keep going, organizing the children's clothes for tomorrow, putting away clean clothes and gathering dirty ones. She stops, picks up her towel, soap and toothbrush, and a few soiled clothes, and leaves. As long as the water is running, she will do some washing. Tomorrow will be a big laundry day, to be done by hand.

We finally make it under our covers a few minutes before ten o'clock. Mama pulls the light bulb cord in the middle of the room and carefully makes her way to her bed along the west wall. Except for Seiji, we are all together. Seiji must be worried. He knows only that we had to evacuate this morning. As he is in the army, maybe he will he be allowed to go home and check on Molly and Dicky. Tomorrow I will write to him. Where are we, anyway? What is our address?

BAM! BAM! BAM! It is not a knock, but more the sound of a fist pushing on our tarpaper-covered door. The door opens forcibly and a light flashes on each of our cots.

Two heads pop up. "What happened?" a sleepy voice asks.

"Go back to sleep," Mama whispers softly. "Everything's all right."

"Ten," a guard says.

"Ten," the other with a clipboard, repeats.

I lie perfectly still, all my joints frozen stiff and straight. How do they know which ten we are? Do they think some of us escaped? Do they search the latrine, too?

If Seiji's army unit were assigned to guard this camp, I wonder if he would be allowed to visit us. Would I have to pretend that I don't know him?

It's not so easy for Seiji, according to his last letter. He writes that his rifle was replaced with a mop and bucket, and he included a snapshot to prove it, with a cigarette in his mouth, looking almost defiant.

It must be embarrassing for a soldier to receive letters from home from a prison camp. It must not be easy to be treated like less than a soldier, like his buddies' servant.

A deathly silence falls upon the camp. There are no dogs barking; there are no songs of summer insects or sleepy birds. No automobiles drive by. The night is warm and still. Huge searchlights scan the compound, causing weird shadows through the small windows. Each time the light hits my bed I feel cornered, and cringe inside my blanket. If I have to go to the latrine, will the searchlights follow me? I fall asleep thinking I would rather use Mama's chamber pot can.

In the middle of the night, I turn from side to side, hoping that my urge to go to the bathroom will subside and I will go back to sleep. I finally give up. It would be a simple matter to use the chamber pot, but somehow it doesn't seem proper for me, a nineteen-year-old girl, to go pee in the can by the door.

I slip on my shoes. When I step outside, it is not nighttime, but a weird day, with black barracks pasted against a beige background of powdery, brown dirt. I hear my footsteps in the deathly quiet. It all seems unreal, like a dream, as I try to dodge the paths of the searchlights.

The light sweeps over me from the opposite side. I feel cornered and make a dash across the open space towards the latrine.

At the first hole, just inside the door, a mother struggles with her child, holding her backwards over the large hole while a toddler whines beside her. The dozen holes down the center and back are all the same size, too big for children. To minimize the overpowering smell, I take shallow breaths, holding my tongue up against the roof of my mouth. To insure myself some privacy, just in case someone comes in, I walk to the very end of the elevated trough and sit down at the last hole, relieved that there is no one sitting beside me or behind me. My toes barely touch the dirt floor.

Latrine is a new word for us. When we moved to our farm in 1930, Tochan built a barn and an *obenjo*, an outhouse. The pump house and the outhouse were the two important buildings on the twenty-acre farm, other than the barn.

The *obenjo* was a place where dreams were born with the Sears Roebuck catalog beside you. Pages were torn out and crumpled to soften them, but the toy section remained until not even the back cover was left.

It was a place of escape from weeding the ditches in the strawberry fields in the hot sun. One could hear the occasional breeze rustling through the trees nearby. Sometimes birds would hop-hop-hop on the roof and a loud rap would scare them away.

Mama would scrub the tiny room with buckets of soapy water and a *tawashi* brush, which looked like a porcupine. Then she would splash bucketfuls of Clorox water all over the inside surfaces, including the door. Mama's strength and fury against dirt and germs wore out every *tawashi* to its wire core. Wherever there was a faucet, there was a *tawashi*. Every few days Tochan shoveled a layer of dirt over the excrement to control the smell and pests.

In our big family, the *obenjo* was the only place where one could be alone.

Oh, to be there now!

The door flaps open, interrupting my reverie. A young mother enters, carrying a sleepy child. The child's head flops to one side as she is being held over the large hole. The mother sees me at the far end and apologetically acknowledges my presence with a nod and leaves.

I walk back, feeling braver, into the well-lit night, ignoring the searchlights crossing my path and dissecting my body. Just before disappearing into my barrack, I look up at the tower, not without a tinge of defiance.

In the morning, the quiet explodes with the clang-clang-clang from the mess hall. Outside our door, hundreds of bodies hurry eastward.

At the mess hall we go through the line for pancakes and Spam and stewed prunes. I plan to hurry through breakfast to be the first occupant in the latrine.

To my utter dismay, the place is filled with children and parents, and the smell blasts my nostrils. I quickly close the door and retreat.

With the hundreds of men, women and children who filled the empty barracks last night, the shower, laundry and latrine are bustling with activity. Mothers line up with containers of clothes to wash. Mama, too, in line, has a huge bundle of laundry wrapped up in a sheet, with Masashi and Tomoko at her side.

I stand by the corner of our barrack trying to appear nonchalant, but in truth, I am miserable. How can I sit in the latrine between all those people, or have my back against a stranger? What am I going to do? I watch the latrine door and count the numbers of people coming out and going in. Even at this distance I have to hold my tongue against the roof of my mouth to avoid a gag reflex from the smell.

The waste products of two hundred and fifty people, deposited overnight in the middle of the block, overpowers the block. When the wind blows in one's direction one is forced to move away.

When three more people emerge from the latrine and no one goes in, I make a dash for it.

To keep our dusty feet clean, someone starts the fashion of wearing *geta*, the Japanese clodhoppers. The pieces of scrap wood we pick up and bring home to our barracks room become *geta* or shelves. Tochan cuts pieces little bigger than the soles of our feet and bores three holes in each for the sandal straps. Two vertical slabs keep the feet off the ground, like short stilts. Hot and dirty feet can now be rinsed or cooled under the faucet without removing the *geta*. We wear our *geta* in and out of the shower.

In the shower barrack, I choose the farthest corner of the huge barrack room. Showerheads protrude from the three walls, without dividers or stalls or curtains. The cement floor extends from one end to the other with several drainage holes down the center.

Several *Issei* women squat around their cans of water, chatting. With wet washcloths they wash and soothe their hot bodies, seemingly comfortable in their nakedness.

Embarrassed, I face the wall and awkwardly take off my clothes. No matter in what order I disrobe, I know that if I want to shower I have to be naked. The women sense my embarrassment and talk to each other in Japanese about how difficult this experience must be for the young people. Kindly, they avoid looking my way, for which I am grateful.

"*Shikataga nai ne.*" It can't be helped, one says sympathetically.

"*Soh-ne,*" another agrees kindly.

I feel as if they are talking about me. From the tone of their voices, I gather they feel sorry for me.

I wet my body and quickly wash the sweaty parts of me, feeling guilty about using so much water while the *Issei* women so carefully wash from their cans.

I am nineteen. My birthday was two and a half weeks ago. That was May 8th, twenty days before we had to leave our farm. Only Mama had remembered. At the supper table she said, "Today is your birthday, isn't it?" I was grateful just to be remembered.

My little brother is three. He will be four in August. Mama was forty-two when he was born. Masashi follows me everywhere. He never stops asking me questions.

"How come he has a gun?" he asks, as we pass under the guard tower.

How do I explain to him that we are in a concentration camp? How do I tell him that we are locked up in here? Only bad people are locked up. So are we bad?

He constantly asks, "Why can't we go home?" When he is tired he whines, "I wanna go home. I wanna go home to our house by the gravel pit."

To divert his thoughts, I suggest, "Let's go exploring."

"I want to go, too," says Tomoko.

It is midmorning. The three of us walk down the camp's main path, heading west, keeping a respectful distance from the guard towers.

We pass a group of boys playing.

"Where are you going?" one asks.

"We are going exploring," I tell them.

"Can I go, too?"

"You'd better ask your mother first."

"Okay," says one of them and runs into the barrack and quickly emerges with permission. I try to make a mental note of which barrack he belongs to.

Along the way, other children join us. I feel like Momotaro of one of Tochan's stories, on his way to conquer the monster that is creating havoc amongst the villagers.

Momotaro was the miracle baby who came inside a peach floating down the river to the old woodman and his wife. He grew up strong and wise and kind, much to the delight of his father and mother.

"Do you know the story of Momotaro?" I ask the children.

"I do! The Peach Boy!" one of them answers.

"I am Momotaro and we are on our way to slay the monster." The boys look at me strangely.

"Where?"

"That way," I point.

That terrible monster that put us here, I want to say, and is creating so much trouble is going to be brought to his knees and I would force him to say, "I was wrong. Please forgive me. You may all go home."

All I need is a *furoshiki* of *onigiri* rice balls tied to a stick and I would really look like Momotaro. Wouldn't the children love that, eating rice balls as we go along!

We come to the west fence. The same dry, brown soil stretches for half a mile outside the fence. Rows of clods formed by the heavy machinery still remain, baked hard by the hot sun. Inside the compound, the soil is ground up into fine dirt from the bulldozing. From below the mid-calf, our pants and shoes become brown from the dust. We don't even try anymore to avoid the dirt.

KEEP 10 FEET AWAY FROM FENCE, the signs constantly remind us. The children happily follow me, glad to have something to do in this cramped and desolate place. I no longer ask where they belong. There are too many of them.

We stop along the north fence, midway between two guard towers. On the other side of the fence, a distance away, a lone fig tree grows. It appears as if the bulldozer had missed it. One branch dangles downwards and lies almost flat along the ground, forming a perfect place for climbing and sitting. As if they, too, understand, the children quietly gaze through the fence. As I step closer to the fence, they take a step forward.

I don't like fig trees. They are prickly and itchy, and the figs are messy and sticky. In fact, on our farm, none of us paid much attention to them, leaving the figs to the birds or letting them fall to the ground to dry up. But right now I wish I could lead all the children right through the barbed wire fence to that fig tree, and let the children play to their hearts' content. I would sit on that low branch and feel its green friendliness.

Inside this fence, there is nothing green, no trees to climb, not one single weed. The brown and black and dusty scene is broken only by the colors of the clothes we wear.

I feel like Pied Piper, gathering more and more children as we walk along. Just before the next guard tower, we take a right between rows of barracks. As we come upon the firebreak, I see in the distance a crowd of adults gathering. They appear agitated. Someone may have gotten sick, I guess, or maybe died, and the children don't need to be exposed to that. A horrible thought crosses my mind. What do we do if someone dies in a place like this?

I lead the children quickly across the firebreak, hoping that they will not notice the commotion. I glance again towards the crowd and notice that they do not seem agitated. Several smiling *Issei* walk away.

Curiosity gets the better of me and I walk eastward, with the children following me.

All eyes are focused on the ground. I ease myself towards the front, fully expecting to find someone in trouble, maybe an older person who has fallen off the step. The center of attention is the ground in front of the barrack. I see nothing, but all around me the *Issei* exclaim enthusiastically "ooh" and "aah" and "*maah!*"

Stretching my neck further and upon closer scrutiny, I see inside a tiny, carefully roped enclosure of ground, two green leaves, a dicotyledon, which have just appeared above ground.

"What is it?" I ask.

"*Asagao*," the woman next to me tells me. I remember the morning glory. It climbs everywhere and has beautiful purplish-blue trumpet-shaped flowers. According to my father, during the night the *asagao* wound around the haiku poet Chiyo's water bucket rope. She could not bear to tear the vine; instead, she sat down and composed a haiku. The morning glory flowers greet you in the mornings and by nightfall the blossoms die to be replaced by new ones the next day.

At their front door, an elderly *Issei* couple holds court, answering questions. She places a pinch of tiny black seeds in the palms of a few standing in front. I wish I could have a few seeds for Mama.

From that day on, a continuous pilgrimage visits the tiny plant. It is on our daily route. It does not take long before the plant becomes a vine. It divides and climbs the vertical rows of string meticulously strung from the barrack roof and staked to the ground. When the first morning glory blooms midway up the side of the black tarpapered building, it is big news in camp.

Many plants begin to appear all over camp. Soon radishes and lettuce grow between the barracks. Colorful zinnias and cosmos appear here and there offsetting the drabness of the camp. Everybody shares seeds. We try hard to create our own livable world.

Just when life settles down to a bearable routine, we get an order to move again.

Mama wants all our sheets washed before we leave. Twenty sheets!

She plans to get up at the crack of dawn before the line forms at the laundry room. We'll get two tubs. It seems as if every day in camp has been washday. The clotheslines are full and tubs of wet laundry wait in line to be dried. You'd think that we are the cleanest people on this earth!

Our *Issei* neighbor digs up her plants and puts them in small cans from the mess hall garbage. She says she will carry them in her purse. Rumor has it that some of us are going south and others will be sent north. I'd rather not think about it.

Tochan reminds us that it'll be over, but how soon? He is like a rock in a raging river. Or maybe one must bend like the bamboo in the wind and when the storm is over, we will be able to stand upright again.

The bamboo never breaks.

· 9 ·

JOURNEY TO POSTON

Mikotoba no

Shōno oshie no

Tōtoku mo

Waga yaku mune wo

Kyō mo shizume shi

—JOHN SHINJI SATO

Sacred words

His teachings

Noble, inspiring

My burning chest

Today, again, finds peace

—TRUDY SATO, TRANSLATION

JULY 21, 1942.

In May I had to leave Sacramento City College, only weeks before I would have finished my freshman year. Stay in school as long as you can, Tochan had advised. I was the last of the *Nisei* students to stick it out. When the 18" by 24" posters, INSTRUCTIONS TO ALL PERSONS OF JAPANESE ANCESTRY, appeared on fence posts and power poles, announcing our removal, all hope faded.

Most of the sixty children from Edward Kelley School are on this train. Miss Cox now has only thirteen Caucasian children. The town of Sacramento and the whole state of California are completely cleansed of "Jap blood."

The orders came again: Pack up. Your permanent camp is now ready. It is not to be called "concentration camp." It is a "relocation center," the authorities say.

"Hold that down," the guard orders, bayonet pointing at my shoulder. The train had been mothballed for so long, its shade keeps rolling right back up, and only if I hold it against the windowsill does it stay down.

"What difference does it make?" I grumble to myself. "It's dark in here and it's dark outside."

When finally the shade stays down, I rub my stiffened elbow and carefully lower my exhausted body onto the wooden bench. I rest my head on the armrest of the two-passenger seat and fall asleep from sheer exhaustion. The long train, loaded with prisoners from the Pinedale Assembly Center, slowly winds down the California valley with all its shades drawn.

Suddenly a jolt awakens me. The train stops.

The guards at each end of our coach leave quickly. Very carefully, I pull open the side of the shade just enough to peek. Through the slit, I see only the boots and rifle butts of the guards standing at attention at the two entrances of the coach. I spread the slit wider. Hundreds of guards stand along the whole length of the train, while curious people stare from the yard of the old sand-colored stucco station.

What are they thinking, I wonder? They must be scared seeing a train so heavily guarded. No doubt they think that the train is loaded with dangerous prisoners. Does anyone see my eye through this slit? What would happen if we opened our shades and waved to them and they saw all the children?

Upon orders, the guards board their coaches and take their positions. I quickly close the slit. The train continues on.

Mama dozes fitfully, holding three-year-old Masashi, who has finally quit whining, "I wanna go home. I wanna go home." Tochan and my six younger brothers and sisters sleep soundly in their seats. Seiji is not here. Seiji's last letter came from Fort Leonard Wood in Missouri. I wish I, too, could be out there, free.

I curl up on the hard wooden seat, turning from side to side. Lying awake in the dark, listening to the clickety-clack of the wheels, I wonder where this train is taking us.

The soldiers at each end of the coach no longer stand at attention. The guard assigned to the back sprawls against the wall, his legs spread out into the aisle, his rifle leaning carelessly in the corner. Guiltily, I carefully lift the side of the shade again and peek. Where are we, anyway?

The scene passing by takes my breath away. It is a scene I have never seen before, not in the collection of our tattered, double-image travel postcards we look at with the stereopticon. Giant saguaros pass before my eyes. Bathed in moonlight, they stand like silent sentinels as far as I can see. Not until my elbows ache from bending do I realize that I have been peeking for a long while, mesmerized. I lean back against the seat and dream, "Some day, I'm coming back here to see the whole place as a free person."

The crisp, clean blouse, which I put on yesterday morning is smudged and wrinkled. None of us care how we look any more. The coal burning smoke permeates the coach and even into my empty stomach. I swallow saliva to quell the threatening nausea.

Several fellows walk past the guard without confrontation, stepping over his extended leg. I watch in the semi-darkness to see if they are sent back by the guard in the next car. They don't return.

Desperately needing to move around, I straighten up, survey the quiet coach, and with a breath of bravado, walk nonchalantly down the aisle and by the guard. He does not pull his leg out of the way. I step over it.

I hold my breath and walk on, past the next guard. Except for the sound of the wheels, it is dark and quiet. Carefully I avoid the sleeping children's little feet and legs sticking out into the aisle. To my surprise, the guard at the other end moves aside to let me pass. Suddenly emboldened, I walk bravely through the next coaches, not knowing what I will find, just glad to be walking. They must have finally realized that there is nowhere for us to escape to, that we are all imprisoned on this moving train.

My long walk finally ends in a huge baggage car, where I see a group of fellows sitting around. I let myself fall with relief against a bunch of soft bedrolls. Where are the guards, I wonder? Don't they worry that a bunch of us might be planning an uprising or something?

"Where are we?" I ask.

"I don't know," someone answers.

"Maybe Arizona."

"Where are we going?"

No one knows. An air of weary resignation hangs over the group. We accept each other, hair uncombed, shirttails hanging out and clothes wrinkled and dirty.

I snuggle into the soft crevices of the bedrolls and gratefully doze off. Conversation fades away. The rhythmic sound of the train wheels lulls me to sleep.

I don't know how long I had been asleep. I hear the murmur of voices and have the suffocating feeling of not being able to breathe. My damp hair leaves an indentation of perspiration on the bedroll where my head has rested. Apologetically, I lift up the area and shake it to dry. This is someone's precious belonging. Daylight peeks through the cracks in the weatherbeaten boards of the old train. The heat is oppressive in the windowless car.

The train cuts its speed. Occupants crane their necks like turkeys to listen. Clickety-clack . . . clickety-clack . . . slower . . . and . . . slower. It crawls on forever. Each second, we hope, will bring the last clack, and that the train will stop and the door will open.

We gather by the heavy sliding door and wait. Breathing becomes progressively difficult. I wish now that I had stayed in the coach with my family. Another five minutes and they might find the prisoners suffocated inside in this car.

Finally the train comes to a creaking halt. The door opens, grinding heavily on its rusted grooves.

Framed by the sides of the open door, a huge surreal view appears. Rows of neatly-lined drab-green army trucks cut the horizon in half, with the dry desert-brown soil in the foreground and the hot orange dawn sky above.

Taken by surprise, the soldiers lift their bayonets when they see their prisoners ready to jump out of the baggage car. I hesitate. Beneath me is a four-foot drop. There are no steps and no one offers to help. I remember the railroad cars by our farm that my brothers and I used to play in. I jump like the rest.

Desperately I decide, "I've got to get back to my family!"

As soon as my feet hit the ground, I dash towards my family's coach. Just as quickly, guards appear across my path, rifles held horizontally at their beltlines.

"Stay where you are!" the guards order.

They herd us towards an open army truck.

The first prisoners to load up sit on the side benches. Others stand. The tailgate closes when no more bodies can be squeezed in. I scan the crowd; there are no familiar faces.

An air of almost a happy anticipation hovers over the open army truck, knowing that this is the end of the line, and that the long and exhausting journey will soon be over. Bodies jostle against each other, as we ride over the dirt road in the treeless, sagebrush-covered terrain. The endless caravan of trucks swirl the hot, dry dust off the desert land, leaving it suspended in the still air. Occasionally, the back of the truck ahead of us comes into view and then disappears again into the huge brown dust cloud. The relentless, penetrating, midmorning sun plays hide-and-seek with the dust.

Dust seeps everywhere, attacking mouths and throats, causing dry coughs. I pull the collar of my blouse over my nose. Others use their handkerchiefs or lift the bottoms of their shirts to cover their noses. Brown dust settles on heads and shoulders. Our usually invisible eyelashes droop, weighted down with tips of brown. We look at each other and smile halfheartedly

Somewhere in the middle of the truck, squeezed in by adult legs and bodies, a child whines, apparently suffocating.

"Let her get to the side," someone suggests.

With difficulty, the little body weaves through legs to the edge of the truck and happily sits on a lap.

We ride further and further into the desert. I figure it's been at least thirteen miles, the distance from our farm to the town of Sacramento. My legs are tired and I want desperately to just squat on the floor but there is no room. We must stand pinned against each other. I worry about how my family is faring. Riding in one of the forward trucks, at least they won't be breathing all this dust.

"As soon as we stop," I plan, "I will make a dash for it and find them. The guards probably won't care, now that they've finally gotten us herded towards a concentration camp and there's no escaping."

A huge black and white sign appears, looking strange in the great expanse of desert: "Poston Indian Reservation."

Spirits soar.

"We are going to an Indian reservation!"

Weariness dissipates. Rivers to fish in, grounds to hunt on. We had studied about the Indians in our United States history class. How good of the Indians to invite us to their reservation!

The ride continues for miles and miles through the same sagebrush. Suddenly the realization hits us that we have been traveling on the reservation. The occasional cabin with a windmill we pass is the home of a family living on the reservation.

"Are they going to dump us here?" I ask.

Henry McClemore is getting his way. "Throw them out in the desert," he wrote in the *Sacramento Union*, "and let them become like the skulls of cattle."

Is this what our government gave to the Indians? Quiet anger rises as the realization of our plight hits me and the plight of the Indians before us who were chased off their land onto this arid, unfriendly desert.

The gravity of our situation sinks in. How can Mama and Tochan and all the other *Issei* parents sit quietly knowing that everything they worked for is now gone?

"*Shikataga nai ne*," I hear them say so often, a phrase of acceptance. They accept what is and do not use their energy to fight the impossible.

Instead they remind themselves, "*Kodomo no tame ni*," for the sake of the children.

Surrounded by human indignities, they never once succumb to the tactics of the perpetrators. I watch my father with awe and complete trust as he protects and leads his family, when the future looks totally hopeless to me, a nineteen-year-old.

My mouth is dry and grainy. I have no more spit left to swallow. My knees want to crumble. If only I could sit down right now, I know I'd be all right.

I can hear Mama's gentle urging: "*Gaman*. Just a little bit longer." Persevere.

As the truck slows down and hundreds of black tarpapered barracks come into view, my knees begin to weaken. Mama and Tochan flash through my mind. I want to tell someone that my name is Kiyo and that my parents are Shinji and Tomomi Sato. I try desperately to hold on to my fading consciousness.

"Don't do this. You will never find your family," I tell myself, but no amount of scolding holds me upright.

I feel someone's hand at my elbow as I crumple downward.

· 10 ·

POSTON CONCENTRATION CAMP II, BLOCK 229, BARRACK 11A & B

Kino omo asu omo

Ikinu hito no yo ni

Kyoh no ichi nichi

Ika ni kura san

– JOHN SHINJI SATO

Yesterday . . . tomorrow . . .

Like all those living

This one day . . . today

How will I live it?

– TRUDY SATO, TRANSLATOR

MY EYES OPEN. My blouse sticks to the canvas cot. A huge gray slab of cement hangs inches above my head. I have trouble breathing. Am I supposed to be dead? Is this where they bring the dead bodies?

Do I dare move? I shift only my eyeballs to the right and see a cement box attached to the wall. I look to my left, this time moving my head for a better view. Above my head and lined up to the end of the long room, I see eight or nine more gray cement boxes.

I don't know how long I have lain in the same position. My stiff arms lock at the elbows. My legs feel heavy and detached.

Still bodies lie on long rows of cots along both walls of the long barrack room. The bodies are deadly still. Immobilized, I wonder what I should do next?

I want some water. Inside my mouth, my tongue sticks to the roof of my mouth. With each breath, the suffocating heat dries my windpipe. I take slow shallow breaths. I can't tell if the bodies alongside of me are breathing. I wait for something to happen, for a body to move.

Slowly, curiosity overcomes my fear. I crane my neck and look for familiar faces. Should I lie here until help comes, or should I try to get out of here? Which way do I go to find my family?

Then with summoned courage, I sit up on the edge of my cot and peer more closely at the faces turned towards me. From the far end of the barrack, I see a live person walking down the aisle with clipboard in hand, looking very efficient. Underneath his safari hat, I am relieved to see that he is one of us.

"Your name?"

"Kiyo Sato."

"Number?"

Panic-stricken, I try to remember the five-digit family number we were all issued, knowing that finding my family depends on it. It's not by my name but by my number that I'm known.

"27 . . . 21 . . . I think there's a 6," I fumble desperately.

"That's okay," he says kindly. "Come with me."

He walks so quickly between the two long rows of cots that I have difficulty looking both ways, checking the bodies for my brothers and sisters.

He motions towards the wall. A small body hops off her cot. It is Kazu. With a wide, happy grin on her face, she is relieved to see me.

The hot scorching sun blinds me as we emerge from the barrack. My knees feel weak. Instinctively, the *Nisei* extends his arms behind me without touching, ready to catch me if I fall.

"You okay?" he asks.

He motions to an army jeep parked just outside the door.

"Get in," he tells me, as he goes to the driver's side. He motions to Kazu to get in the back.

It seems strange that a *Nisei* would be driving an army jeep that our guards were driving not too long ago. I want to know how long I was unconscious but I am afraid to ask him. He appears to be all business and not at all communicative.

"How hot is it?" I ask.

"Near 130," he replies. He says no more, as if he is duty bound to keep quiet. We ride in silence. Clouds of dust stay suspended behind us. There are no trees, no plants, no grass, only dry dirt, sand and sagebrush in all directions as far as the eye can see. A few people walk with their heads protected by a towel or some sort of cloth. Now and then, I see small groups of children playing along the shady side of a barrack. I check every face, desperate to connect myself with someone I know—a neighbor, a schoolmate, just anyone in this huge camp of thousands of prisoners.

On the driver's side, an endless expanse of scrubby sagebrush and sand disappears into the horizon through which we had come. I notice that there are no barbed wire fences separating the barracks from the desert. Did the authorities know that we would never attempt to go back the way we came?

At the last row of barracks, we turn right and drive a short distance along the south edge of camp. In the desert, I see people bent over around a large pile of straw, filling long white sacks. To my happy relief, I spot Mama dragging a sack three times her size.

"Stop!" I yell at the driver.

I jump out of the jeep and rush towards Mama to help her.

"*Yokatta ne,*" she says, dropping her sack. She looks me over from top to bottom. Relieved to see that I am all right, she picks up her bag and walks toward the barracks. I pick up the other end.

She leads me into one of the small rooms of a barrack in which are five canvas cots lined up, all of which are already topped with the fat straw mattresses. Mama explains that each family with six members or less gets one room. We have two rooms.

I plop onto a cot, relieved to be horizontal again. With effort, I keep my breathing shallow. I want to take a deep breath but as soon as I try, my windpipe shuts. A tremendous urge to sleep overtakes me.

Mama returns.

"*Ohiya?*" Water, she asks me.

Oh, how I want some water to loosen my parched tongue from the roof of my mouth.

Tired, thirsty and irritable, I wonder why it is taking Mama so long.

She appears, finally, with a tin cup. "Here you are. Drink it slowly," she advises, but I am so thirsty that I gulp a mouthful. My throat closes automatically and I choke and cough out the contents onto the floor. The water is not only hot, but it is foul as if it has come through a sewer pipe.

"*Sukoshi zutsu,*" A little bit at a time, Mama advises.

Desperate for liquid, I take tiny sips to wet the inside of my mouth. It becomes more tolerable when I close off my nostrils to avoid the smell.

Mama brings me a clean, wet diaper cloth for my head. The sun pounds mercilessly on the black tarpapered barrack, radiating its heat inside like an oven. The straw mattress sticks to my back. Relieved to be with my family again, I fall asleep.

The sound of hammering from the next room rudely awakens me. I resent being awakened to my breathing, the feel of hot air going through my nostrils and windpipe. Oh, to be able to sleep until the cool of nightfall!

Bright sun shines through the small, dusty window. I sit on the edge of my cot, head cradled in the palms of my hands, feeling miserable. I am miserable sitting up; I am miserable lying down. With a groan I fall back on my sweaty straw mattress. One could cook in this room if not for the gaping floorboards and the open partitions separating the "apartments." Through the floorboards, I can see the dry, sandy ground below. A huge hairy spider crawls between the floorboards and disappears underneath. I let out a scream! It is not like any spider I have seen on the farm.

Mama appears.

"It's probably a scorpion," she tells me. "From what I hear they are all over camp and are poisonous. They say to be careful of scorpions and rattlesnakes."

They found a rattler underneath one of the barracks, she tells me. With legs crossed on my bed, I am even less inclined to move.

"I don't know what to do," I mumble. Mama looks at me sympathetically. It is not like me, the eldest, to be so helpless.

"Why don't you go and help at the mess hall?" she suggests gently.

I carefully shake the sand and dirt out of my shoes, put them on and follow Mama's suggestion. My legs don't seem to want to hold me upright. I haven't had anything to eat for I don't know how long, but I am not hungry.

As I step outside, the sun blinds me. In a half-daze, I walk down the firebreak, past five or six rows of barracks and eastward to the mess hall. I know now to breathe very slowly, giving each breath time to cool off along the way.

In the drab, dark interior of the mess hall, I see silhouettes of a few helpers busily moving back and forth. I set out the aluminum teapots. The strong smell of stew cooking makes me nauseous. Warmed up mutton stew, somebody says.

At five o'clock, the cook bangs on the back of a large aluminum pan with a smaller skillet, the first mess call for supper. Servers behind the counter dish out stew and rice. A few children smell their food and crinkle their noses. I forget my misery for a short while, filling teapots and water pitchers.

My family sits all together at the far table against the wall. When the crowd thins, I join them. Everybody is talking. They've found friends their ages and can hardly wait to go out and play with them again. Tochan finds his brother and our cousins in Block 208, which is at the other end of the camp. Our block is 229.

There are supposed to be five thousand people in this camp. Camp I is already filled to capacity with ten thousand people. Three miles south of us, another camp is supposed to hold five thousand more people. Tochan tells us somebody named Camp I, Camp II and Camp III "Post 'em," "Toast 'em," and "Roast 'em."

For a while it seems like old times, just sitting around the table talking. No stories. Tochan reports on what is happening in this place. He talks about Mr. Crawford, the director of Camp II, like he was already an old friend.

"Mr. Crawford is a good man. I think we will get along fine," he assures us. "The first thing we have to do is to appoint a manager for our block."

Most of the *Nisei* are young and the *Issei* are still in charge, but to be a block manager one has to be a citizen, according to Administration rules. As Tochan speaks both English and Japanese fluently, both generations depend on him as an interpreter, but being an *Issei*, he has no voting power. As it stands now, no *Issei* can become an American citizen, but he says the law will change one day.

They throw us in here as enemy aliens, strip us of all rights as citizens, call us "non-aliens" and now one has to be a citizen to be a block manager. Makes no sense.

I sip hot tea, the only way I can tolerate the strong, metallic tasting alkaline water.

"You must drink more water," Mama encourages the children. They take dutiful sips.

"Yuk!" Naoshi crunches his face and puts his cup down.

"Yuk," Tomoko mimics.

I reach over for a heaping spoonful of white rice from Kazu's plate of stew and drop it into my teacup. The *ochazuke* of tea and rice hits the spot, my first mouthful of food. My brothers watch me and follow suit, scooping out ungravied rice into their cups and filling them up with hot tea. They slurp up the *ochazuke* without the usual tasty *takuwan*, the sweet and salty *daikon* pickle.

Tochan leaves the table. He seems preoccupied. In the short time we've been here, he has been to so many meetings.

"Can I take my cot outside?" Sanji asks.

"No," Tochan says.

"It's hot in here," he complains. "Everybody's sleeping outside."

"We will all sleep in our rooms," Tochan says.

I don't know how I am going to stand it. I wish I could make myself unconscious again and sleep for another three or four hours.

My canvas cot lies parallel to the far wall of the room. Scattered in the center of the room, my four brothers, Sanji, Aizo, Kozo and Naoshi, have their cots. Our suitcases are under our cots. My one small suitcase holds my two blouses, two skirts, my anklets, underwear, a light jacket, note-pad and pencil, and in the corner are tucked away the clean diaper squares and safety pins for that time of the month.

"I want to sleep in that room," I hear Masashi complain through the wall. He wants to be with his big brothers. He doesn't want to be with Mama and Tochan.

Overcome by the long and exhausting day and night, my brothers are dead to the world. I can hear our neighbors in the next section talking. The Sueokas, a big family like ours, have the next two sections. I hear a baby crying somewhere. A little girl whines; a mother shushes her. I can hear every little sound in this barrack as if we were in one big room. Thin partitions, open at the top, divide the long barrack into four or six "apartments."

I kick off my army blanket and sheet. My flannel pajamas, the only ones I have, stick to my body. I envy my brothers, who strip down to their pajama bottoms. Rolling up my pant legs as high as they will go, pulling up my sleeves and lifting up my midriff, makes me feel the stiff straw through the mattress, but I feel less hot. My wet diaper cloth gives me some relief as I stroke it lightly over the bare parts of my body.

Having been unconscious for three hours this morning, I am now awake and totally miserable.

I want to take my cot outside; but I know that Mama and Tochan won't let me, as I am nineteen and a girl. If I have to go to the bathroom, I will have to walk by all those sleeping bodies. And I'm not going to sit on Mama's pee-can.

I get up and push the bulky straw mattress off my cot, lean it against the wall and flop back into bed. What a relief it is to lie on the smooth, firm canvas! But it is not long before every point of contact of my body and canvas is wet. I get up again and throw my sheet over my cot and lie on it. Nothing relieves my misery.

The night does not cool the vast hot desert. It continues to "cook" like an oven that is never turned off.

Far in the distance the eerie howls of the coyotes float over the sleeping camp.

A guttural groan breaks the silence, scaring me upright. Next to me, the dark silhouette of Sanji's body bends upwards as if on a hinge and then falls back.

Sanji is awake; now I have someone to talk to.

"Sanji?" I whisper. There is no answer.

Terrible thoughts go through my mind. Will we dry up in here in the middle of the desert?

The shower went dry on me already, and they are telling us to be careful with the use of water. If we dug deep enough would we get water, I wonder?

Our block borders the south edge of Camp II. From our "front" room, looking south, there are no fences and no guard towers, only sand and sagebrush as far as the eye can see. One could shrivel up with dehydration if one tried to escape in any direction. Is that how they planned it?

A band of coyotes comes closer. They seem to be coming in our direction. Do they attack people? They eat sheep. There are no fences to protect us, and our barrack is in the last row at the edge of Camp II.

The coyotes come closer and closer. I hear scurrying footsteps along the back of our barrack and then the sound of overturned containers. I freeze.

They rustle further into camp.

I fall asleep from sheer fatigue.

CLANG! CLANG! CLANG!

For a second I think I am back home, turning over in my bed, only to feel my body against the stiff, bare canvas. The first mess call, the sound of one giant pan hitting another, reverberates throughout our block of fourteen barracks with two hundred and fifty people.

Sanji sits on the edge of his cot, looking as if he's been zombied. Kozo, slowly and methodically, puts on his pants and shirt. Aizo and Naoshi don't move.

I reach for my bloomers, which I had washed and hung on a nail beside my cot. They are dry and stiff and out-of-shape like my washcloth, and both look like long, fat clubs. Nothing stays wet for long here. I sit on my cot, face the wall and discreetly remove my pajama bottoms and quickly put on my underpants. My brothers strip down naked and walk around as if they'd rather stay that way. The thought flashes through my mind: What do I do at that time of the month? There is no place to go. The open latrine? The open room?

Mama reminds us with a knock on the wall: "Wash your face and brush your teeth."

We gather in the "front" room.

"Let's go," Masashi impatiently implores. Having awakened and gone to the washroom early, he is hungry.

"We have to wait for Naoshi," Kozo reminds us.

Tochan busily nails the canvas he smuggled in as a bedroll across the rafter, standing on a large suitcase upended.

"Get a bucket of water, Aizo," Tochan requests.

Dutifully, Aizo leaves with the bucket and fills it at the far end of the building.

Aizo sloshes in. Tochan throws the bucket of water against the canvas, much to the delight of the boys. They rush to lean against the wet canvas, clothes and all.

"Another bucket," says Tochan.

"I'll get it!" Kozo grabs the bucket and disappears. He returns followed by curious friends.

After several more trips to the faucet, the miserable hot night is forgotten with backs pressed gratefully against the coolness. Word spreads quickly and children appear from nearby barracks to sit for a few minutes against the canvas.

Happy children in their wet, cool clothes scamper along with us towards the mess hall, joined by newly found friends along the way.

After the first night, none of us sleep on our straw mattresses. I drag mine into the open desert and shake out the contents, fold the bag and place it under my cot. Who in their right mind, I wonder, would have thought up this crazy idea? The heat, the sweat, the straw! Didn't they understand at all? I can hear them around the conference table sounding important.

"The army has a surplus of body bags. Why can't we use them?"

"For what?"

"Mattresses."

"What do we fill them with?"

"Straw."

"I'll go to the feed store in Parker and find out how much it will cost."

"We could have them dump a truckload of straw at each block. It'll be cheap and the farmers will be glad to get paid for what they throw out."

"How about issuing the bags to the Japs when they come in and let them fill their own mattresses?"

"Good idea."

No one objects. They requisition ten thousand body bags for Camp I, five thousand for Camp II, and five thousand for Camp III.

They adjourn, feeling smug about their solution to a major problem, solved at minimum cost. As they sit in their air-cooled meeting room, no one addresses the more serious problem of men, women and children having to survive in the desert heat. After all, they are only Japs.

At 120 degrees to 130 degrees, our bodies cook inside our black tar-papered barracks, while "they" send out directives from their air-cooled white buildings on how to run these three camps with 20,000 prisoners.

Internees return from their jobs with envious reports of serving dinners, complete with crystal goblets and wine glasses, inside a cool dining room.

⁓

Tochan finally relents.

"Tonight we will sleep outside," he tells us.

"Yaay!" my brothers yell.

The children can hardly wait until nighttime.

"I'm going to take my cot by George." Kozo plans. The Toguchis live one barrack over.

Tochan hears him.

"We will all sleep along the west side of our apartment," he announces.

When the sky darkens, wearing my flannel pajamas, I carry my cot outside. I carry my sheet just to be discreet.

We line our ten cots against the outside wall of our two "apartments." Would you believe it, they are to be called "apartments" like we were living in town somewhere? Ours is apartment 11-A and B.

⁓

Our camp, they tell us, is now to be called a "relocation center" and not a "concentration camp." We are internees, not prisoners. So now we are "relocated" into a relocation center!

I live in an apartment in a relocation center. I am fed three meals a day. If I don't want to I don't have to work. I am an internee.

Here's the truth: I am now called a non-alien, stripped of my constitutional rights. I am a prisoner in a concentration camp in my own country. I sleep on a canvas cot under which is a suitcase with my life's belongings: a change of clothes, underwear, a notebook and pencil.

Why?

⁓

Tochan stations his cot at the far south with Mama's next to him. Between my cot at the other end and theirs, the seven cots for my brothers and sisters line up.

On my right I see that the Sueoka boys are still out and about. My brothers are restless. They would rather be with their friends.

"Who can find the *mitsu-boshi?*" Tochan asks looking up at the sky.

There is instant quiet as all eyes look upwards. The sky is filled with brilliant stars. Some appear close, some farther and millions of others seem to disappear into the limitless beyond. Back home, there were not so many stars but they seemed so friendly and secure. Now I wonder where it all ends. It's like a darkness that goes on forever and forever and there is no escape.

A small band of people, banished into this vastness, is left to survive. Will we really become dried-up bones? And when our remains are found, what will they say about us, that a bunch of hapless immigrants wandered in the wrong direction? Is there anyone out there who is trying to get us out of here before it is too late? Is there anybody who cares?

Seiji. He's out there. He cares. Makoto cares. Susumu cares, and so do all our *Nisei* sons and brothers in the army. And Molly and Dicky. I hope someone is feeding them. I hope they will wait for us.

"I see it!" exclaims Naoshi. He points to the Three Sisters in the sky exactly as we see them from our path from the *ofuro* bath back home.

A falling star streaks across the sky, much to the delight of the children.

"There's one!"

"There's another one!"

There are so many of them. Where do they go, I wonder? Attention focuses on who will spot the next one. One by one, quiet gently and kindly falls upon the tired bodies and the children fall asleep. The eerie howl of the coyotes floats into camp.

The oppressive heat continues. Men, young and old, stripped down to their shorts, line up at the outside faucet, carrying their cots. Like the rest, I place my cot under the running water and slosh it back and forth to cover the canvas surface. My whole body relaxes with relief as it hits the cool cot. I fall asleep.

It is not until several hours later that I awaken, bone dry and hot. The nightly howl of the coyotes sounds closer. Reluctantly, I wait in line again to wet my cot.

Just before dawn, the coyotes rush through our block. I hold my body still. The band hurries on to the next block. No one moves. I don't know if they are asleep or scared stiff, as I am. There is silence.

Kozo, barely awake, appears around the corner, carrying his cot. He woke up and found himself sleeping next to George Toguchi. George and his brother had carried Kozo, sound asleep on his cot, to their family group on the other side of the next barrack building.

Mama is already sitting on the edge of her cot, mending something, when I report in to our "front apartment." We know that if Mama is not sitting and mending, we can find her standing in line at the laundry room or washing at the tub. I wonder sometimes what will happen if our clothes finally become unmendable. Maybe my blouse will become a whole new crazy weave.

With his small folding pruning saw, Tochan busily saws through our common wall.

"What's that, Tochan?" I ask.

"This will be our doorway."

"Don't you have to have a permit to do that?" I ask. He grunts, just to let me know that he heard me. Sometimes I worry about my father. He doesn't seem to care about things like rules and regulations, like the time he allowed me to drive into town over the five-mile limit without a permit. He keeps on doing what he thinks is right.

He smoothly cuts across three sections of the one-by-twelve boards at a height for the tallest of us to get through, which is my father at five feet six and a half inches. With his hammer he rips the boards loose and slices the tarpaper with his sharp pocketknife.

"Yaaay!" Three-year-old Masashi runs through the opening, happy to see his brothers on the other side.

Naoshi is still asleep.

"Wake up!" Kozo shakes him. Naoshi mumbles and turns over. "We gotta go for breakfast. Hurry up!"

Tochan pounds out the nails from the boards and carefully straightens each nail, and then adds them to the bag of nails that he brought from home. He continues to share his nails with curious neighbors who pop in to see what is going on.

"I still have that roll of wire, which will make plenty of nails," he says. "After breakfast, I will make a door."

⁓

"Where do you want your shelf, Mama?" he asks. Mama's mending supplies sit on the floor beside her cot.

It has taken him four days to finish the doorway, working with the few tools he smuggled in. Sawing an opening in the partition had been simple. Creating a frame on which to hang a door has taken much thought, given his limited resources. His time, too, has been taken up in meetings and with requests for a translator.

With no metal hinges available, he uses double strips of canvas cut from the edge of our big canvas, which now hangs from the rafters as an air cooler.

Using lumber left from the swinging half door, Tochan puts up a shelf just above Mama's cot for her sewing supplies.

"*Maah! Yoku kangae ta mono desu ne.*" How did you think of all this Mrs. Kuwabara from the next barrack comments, impressed with Tochan's skill.

He plans next to construct two chairs and a small cabinet, which will store his papers. Children bring back to Tochan any piece of scrap wood they find. Even the smallest piece of wood becomes useful.

⁓

"*Ohayo gozaimasu.*" Good morning. The *Issei* greet each other with a nod as we all head in the same direction. We know everybody—the Yamasakis, the Hironakas, the Kobatas—and strangers are no longer strangers.

"*Atsui desu ne.*" It is hot, isn't it, they say as they greet each other.

"*Taihen desu ne.*" It is difficult, isn't it, they say, empathizing with mothers carrying little babies who had to be shushed during the night so neighbors would not be disturbed.

"That's a good idea," a mother tells Mama, who shares her idea about the can from the Pinedale mess hall garbage that she used for an *omaru* chamber pot to avoid the long walk to the latrine. The young mother, trailed by four little children, looks tired and haggard, as if she has not slept at all. "I will do that tonight," she says with gratitude.

In the mess hall, a group of teenage boys sit at one table.

"Can I sit with my friends?" Aizo asks.

"No," Tochan says firmly.

Families are already fractured. Older children sit with friends. Mothers and fathers have only their little children with them.

Not having eaten much since we got to Poston, I am hungry. The pancakes, flattened under huge stacks, stay warm at room temperature. Nothing gets cold here. I'm not used to drinking coffee but it is more drinkable than the water, which still refuses to go down my throat. Even the tea and coffee do not camouflage the foul-tasting water.

Mama encourages us to take little sips. The children are not drinking enough water and Mama is concerned that they will become dehydrated.

"I'll get some good water, today," I hear Tochan tell Mama.

"Where would you do that?" she asks, surprised.

At the far end of the camp, detached from our black tar-papered barracks, stand legitimate white buildings, which house the Caucasian personnel. He had been there on many occasions to talk with Mr. Crawford.

After breakfast, he takes his gallon jug, which he had hidden inside a bedroll, puts on his old straw hat and leaves. Remembering my passing out while riding through the desert, I worry as he trudges out into the unforgiving heat. It is a long way to the Administration buildings.

The sun hits directly overhead when he returns. Only a sliver of shade on one side of the barrack offers any reprieve. There is no shady side to walk along. His hat droops from the frequent stops at the outside faucets along the way to wet his hat.

"*Atsui-na!*" It is hot, he exclaims, as he deposits the gallon jug on the crudely constructed table, which he made from the doorway he sawed off.

"Would you like some water, Masashi?" Mama asks.

"Unh, unh," he refuses.

"Drink a little bit," Mama coaxes.

"Okay." He takes a swallow, looks at the tin cup suspiciously and then drinks half the cup with great gulps.

"Slowly . . . slowly," Mama advises.

She methodically sees to it that each of her children drinks a cup of water, and gives equally to an accompanying friend. After the initial grumble, the children drink gratefully.

I have the last cupful, which I insist on sharing with my mother.

"You finish it, Kiyo-chan," she says.

It is almost like drinking the clear, cold water from our irrigation pump. My throat does not constrict. I want Mama to enjoy it. She takes a sip just to please me.

Pata-pata-pata, pata-pata-pata. Back and forth, back and forth, I hear the sound of footsteps. Who in the world would be walking when the sky is barely light and most of us are still asleep, I grumble to myself? I turn over and cover my head with my pillow.

An *Issei* man waters the long furrows he has created at the far end of our barrack. Back and forth he carries water, one can at a time. The desert soil soaks up the water as if it had never had a drink. He pours can after can of water as if he will conquer the relentless August heat.

A curious neighbor asks, "What did you plant there?"

"Radishes."

"In this desert? They say nothing will grow here. See that white ring by the faucet? That's how alkaline this soil is."

From the beginning of time there has been nothing but sagebrush and mesquite trees in this desert.

"I don't have anything else to do. I might as well do this," the *Issei* man responds, shrugging his shoulders.

The farmer does not let up irrigating his little plot, even in the hot midday sun. He knows that the seeds need to be kept moist constantly in order to germinate. If he allows them to dry out even for five minutes in this heat, it is the end of his project.

"*Ojisan*, you'd better take it easy," a young man advises. "It's 125 degrees right now." Curious people stop to chat and sometimes to help water.

Every morning for weeks, I hear the pata-pata-pata before sunrise. The little garden becomes "our" project and I no longer feel put-upon. It is the first thing I check on my way to the latrine.

Early one morning I see through a tiny crack in the sand, a green tip pushing up.

"*Ojisan*! There's one coming up!" He turns in mid track, drops his empty can and hurries toward where I stand.

"Ahhh! *Dete kita, dete kita!*" He repeats over and over: It's come up! It's come up!

By midmorning the first leaf appears above the soil. It is a celebration. Word spreads and from blocks around people come to see the first radish plant growing in the desert. There is a constant pilgrimage. No one walks by without checking on the progress of "the farm."

The leaves grow rapidly and soon small red roots appear. As they swell one by one, the *Issei* plucks the largest and offers it to a friend, who thanks him profusely while looking at the small red radish in his hand from all angles. Radish isn't my favorite vegetable but I am caught up in the excitement of this new birth.

The *Issei* man gives them away one by one, enjoying the pleasure of other *Issei*.

"This is very good," Tochan says, crunching into a fat radish. "What are you going to plant next?" he asks, as he hands me the half-eaten radish.

The fever spreads. Yes, plants will grow in this uninhabitable desert! More vegetables appear between the barracks. Soon colorful zinnias and cosmos add color to the drab surroundings. Purple morning glories climb the sides of the black tar-papered walls with vigor.

The rush is on!

Seeds of all kinds are shared. It is not just Tochan who had hidden little paper bags of seeds inside our blankets. Every *Issei*, it seems, had packed some kind of seeds—*daikon* radish, *nappa* cabbage, lettuce, carrots and even *gobo*, the Japanese burdock.

Rumors abound. News gets passed from person to person. We depend on rumors.

"There's going to be a canteen in Block 119."

"The canteen is open."

"They have ice cream!"

"It's not open yet."

"They're going to sell sewing stuff."

By the time rumors make the rounds, it seems that one can buy anything the outside world has.

Rumors are a way of life around camp. Who's seeing whom, which mess hall serves the best meals, who's had a baby, etc.

Somebody says there's going to be a nursery school.

"Where?" I ask, thinking that working there would be better than working in the mess hall.

"Somewhere in Block 228."

That's in the next block. I decide to investigate.

The "apartments" are all occupied, as far as I know. Would it be in the Block Manager's office or maybe the mess hall? After breakfast, I walk towards Block 228, asking anyone along the way if they had heard about a nursery school.

At the edge of the block, I stop to watch an old man scrubbing a gnarled piece of wood under the faucet. My first reaction is that of resentment, that he would use water so wastefully when I didn't have enough to rinse the soap off my body in the shower room.

He rubs the wood with total concentration, occasionally dipping his dirty cloth in the sand. I stand a respectful distance away, wondering what it is that he sees in his crooked piece of desert wood. Sensing my quiet presence, he turns around and smiles, so I ask.

"*Ojisan, nani o shite imasu?*" What are you doing?

"*Kore wa,*" he explains in Japanese. It is a piece of ironwood he found in the desert. It is a beautiful piece, he tells me. "I am trying to smooth out the rough exterior."

He turns the piece over and shows me where the weeks of rubbing with dirt and sand have brought out the deep, dark purple sheen of the petrified wood. How did he know that beneath that scraggly, rough branch would be such a beautiful sculpture? His rough, brown hands tell me that he has probably worked hard on a farm. If I had come across this piece of wood, I would have stepped over it. If I had tried to kick it out of my way, I would have realized that it was stone, not wood, and maybe paid attention.

He seems the least likely person to know, but I ask him anyway where the nursery school might be.

"*Soko, soko!*" There! There! he says, pointing his dirty rag to the barrack across the firebreak.

I thank him and walk over.

The barrack appears deserted. There are no sounds inside. Slowly I open the door a crack and peek.

The room, the size of our apartment A, is empty. Sunlight shines through the small, dirty windows and through the pine floorboards, which had dried and shrunk in the heat. A foot below, the dust and dirt lie ready to be churned up through the slits at any moment by the devastating, frequent dust storms. When a storm comes without notice, there is no escape. Indoors and outdoors, the sand permeates our nostrils and hair and even sticks to the tarpapered walls.

An older *Nisei* woman, arms loaded with books and files, enters.

"Is this the nursery school?" I ask.

"It's going to be," she says. "Would you like to help?"

I am delighted. But what can I possibly do in this barren room, I wonder.

"Which block are you from?" she asks me.

"229."

She dumps her materials on the floor. There is no desk or bench. Only a bare light bulb hangs from the rafter. Sunlight leaks through along the roofline.

"You can check your block and tell the parents of three- to five-year-olds that they can bring their children on Monday. I'll sign you up for Nursery School Attendant. We will start at nine o'clock and go until noon every day. We will have afternoon sessions if more children enroll. Your salary will be twelve dollars a month."

—◌

I am elated, not only to have a job but to have some spending money. Now I can order burlap from Sears & Roebuck for our windows. I'd like to have something bright. Green? Blue? The problem with colored burlap is that it fades in no time where the sun hits. Maybe with my second paycheck I will have enough to replace my army blanket partition with burlap.

First things first: we need some toothbrushes. Mama cleans her teeth with a washcloth wrapped around her finger. And I've got to get some monthly needs. Mama showed me how to fold a piece of a diaper and pin one inside my underwear. I don't like having to change behind my blanket partition, which Tochan hung from the rafters for my privacy. I never know who's going to come looking for me, like my little brother, for instance.

I miss my room where I can read and write and watch the moonlight through my window and hear the symphony of frogs down by the creek. Right now I hear the Sueokas on the other side of the thin wall, and more garbled sounds from three and four walls down. The only privacy I have is inside my small suitcase under my cot.

Here, I shower with a half a dozen people, eat with two hundred and fifty people, and sit in the community latrine with people I don't even know.

To wash out my monthly personals without being noticed, I wrap the soiled diaper squares with my clothes and take them to the laundry room and wait in line with mothers shuffling huge bags of dirty clothes wrapped *furoshiki*-style with sheets. I carefully unwrap my blouse in the bottom of the deep tub and do my washing. Everything dries up in no time, even inside our rooms, so two sets is all I need. Within an hour I fold the diaper squares and put them inside my suitcase under my cot.

Everybody knows everything about everybody—when you go to the latrine, when you go to the shower room, and on and on. But hardly anyone pays any attention to what one wears. We all came with what we could carry and that's what we wash and wear and mend. The laundry room is never empty. We look so fresh and clean in the mornings, but by mid-afternoon the desert dirt permeates our clothes and body.

Mama mends constantly. No matter when I come in, she is sitting on her cot with her needle and thread. No doubt she wishes she had her old Singer sewing machine. With only a change or two of clothing for each of her eight children, the washing and the mending pursue Mama.

Occasionally I see her take out the few yards of bright green corduroy she brought with her.

"What are you doing with that, Mama?" I ask.

"I think this might fit Tomoko. Maybe a skirt and a vest."

⸻

I live in Block 229, Apartment 11-B in the Poston Relocation Center in Poston, Arizona. With such an address, who can tell that my order from Montgomery Ward is being delivered to prisoner #21716-C? My father is #21716-A and Mama is #21716-B. I am C and down the line to Masashi, who is #21716-K. The government reclassified my brothers and sisters and me from "citizen" to "non-alien," whatever that means.

Soon, with my first month's paycheck of twelve dollars, I plan to decorate our "apartment" windows.

⸻

The Administration sets aside a plot of land at the edge of camp "for farming." It is decided that the prisoners will do the manual labor at camp wages of twelve dollars per month for eight hours of work daily. The machinery is to be operated only by the white personnel, the Administration decrees.

"Why?" a *Nisei* asks. Work to prepare the land is slow and inept. The young internees are pulling at the bit to get moving, excited by the new challenge, that of being able to grow something in this desert.

"Why can't we drive the tractor?" they complain.

Work progresses slowly.

A Caucasian supervisor convinces the Administration. "They are the experts," he tells his board. "They made California productive. Why not give them a chance on this desert? We have nothing to lose."

The *Nisei* boys take over, with the enthusiasm of young bulls released from their pen. They maneuver the machinery with expertise that no administrator has. They level the land. They ditch hundreds of rows, each one so straight that a string could be pulled through the center of each ditch for a mile and not touch its sides. Water flows evenly.

A *Nisei* project supervisor earns $19.00 per month, while his Caucasian counterpart earns more than the prevailing wages outside. The camp farm exceeds production of fresh vegetables, which includes Japanese favorites such as *nappa*, *daikon* and *gobo*. They are from seeds that the *Issei* brought with them. Not only does the crop feed the Poston inmates, but eventually inmates of other camps as well.

Another crew digs a canal to bring in water from the Colorado River. When they reach Camp II, three miles from Camp I, someone suggests, "Hey! Let's dig a swimming hole here."

"We might get into trouble."

"What's the difference? We couldn't be in any worse trouble."

"I heard somebody talking about a swimming pool."

"What the heck," the driver says, and takes bold, wide sweeps with his front loader. "Just widening the canal," he says, grinning from his high seat.

Rattlesnakes crawl out from everywhere, trying to escape from the unearthing. The ground crew whacks those nearby with their shovels. Hundreds of baby rattlers slither away.

"I sure wouldn't want to swim with those guys," one says.

With renewed vigor the young men continue in the 125-degree heat, with visions of making the unbearable heat bearable for everyone.

At least twice a day I walk over to the Block Manager's office to read the bulletins tacked onto the outside wall. That's the only way rumors become substantiated. Plastered with information, flyers overlap—War Relocation Authority edicts, announcements, baseball practices, judo lessons, church services, etc. They help keep hope alive. We devour every bit of news. Some fellows practically live on the Block Manager's doorstep and can tell you what's been posted lately. Anybody interested in singing? A chorus is being organized.

School will start in September as usual. Where? Where there are empty barracks? Teachers, college graduates and college students may apply. Salary: sixteen dollars a month.

The hospital needs personnel—also the mess hall, the hospital and clinic and the farm.

I can't believe what I am reading. Flower Arrangement Show! Block 219, Saturday. This I've got to see, I tell myself. A flower show in this desert?

On Saturday I ask my little brother, who is occupied with his favorite pastime, making canals and hills in the sand.

"Want to go with me, Masashi?"

"Where?" He asks, dusting himself off.

"See a flower show."

"Okay," he says, always happy to go with me. Just four, he is forever asking questions and "experimenting" with his buddies. Since Mama caught him under our barrack playing with matches with his friends, she does not let him out of her sight. If I didn't take him this morning, he would probably have to stand in the laundry line with Mama.

It is another hot day, probably in the 120's. Back home in Sacramento, even on the hottest of days, one can look forward to a cool evening. But here the great expanse of the hot, sandy desert holds the heat all night. The only thought of the prisoners, day and night, is to find a cool spot. Some sit on the doorsteps of their barracks. Some go to the shower with their cans and washcloths to soothe their hot bodies with the minimum use of water. No one hogs the water. We try to be considerate of each other's needs.

With a wet diaper over my head and my brother in hand, we walk towards the center of camp. Masashi, already the color of the desert, seems to have become a part of it. While I am conscious of every hot breath going down into my lungs, he hops along beside me like a happy little desert rabbit.

The double doors at the north end of the barrack are wide open. Displays of hundreds of arrangements line up on long wooden, mess hall tables. My heart thrills to see the colors—a rose, a peony, a pink carnation, one or two with buds, each one elegantly arranged. Some kind person must have sent us a truckload of flowers, I assume. A large, white peony dramatically arranged with the stark desert branches catches my eye. I gently touch the petal. To my surprise, I find that it is paper. There is not a single real flower in the show!

The vases appear to be made of wood, some of them in the shape of tall Japanese buckets. A few black and brown glazed ceramic vases probably are treasures, carefully carried from home.

I can hardly wait to tell Mama. I want her to see this flower show.

Back at the barrack, Mama doesn't seem all that excited. She finds a small piece of wrinkled tissue paper. We don't throw away anything. She pulls down her sewing kit from the shelf. She carefully smoothes out the wrinkles in the paper and cuts out oval shaped pieces. Then with white thread, ties them all together at the base, forming a rose just beginning to open its petals. It is beautiful. I can hardly believe that my mother, who spent all her life in the fields, even knew how to create such flowers!

"If we had some green crêpe paper, we could cover the base and cut out some leaves," she explains. For lack of a piece of wire, Mama sticks the rose on the end of a chopstick.

She cuts a two-inch wide, long piece of tissue paper and serrates one side. She rolls the piece around the small end of a chopstick and secures it at the base. She fluffs it open and a carnation blooms on a stem!

In a small box, I learn to keep all sorts of colored paper scraps, thin wires, dried up stems, a pair of small scissors, thread, paste and anything else that might become a flower. On my ledge by my cot, my cup begins to fill up with straight, stiff-stemmed flowers, adding a bit of cheer to our drab room. I find a small scrap of an odd shaped piece of colored paper on my cot, probably an offering from one of my brothers. Funny how things we would usually throw into a waste paper basket become precious.

A lady in another block saves every piece of string and makes string baskets. Mrs. Machida in our block makes Indian baskets from every kind of tissue paper. She even helps herself to gobs of toilet paper. I wonder where she learned to make baskets. The Machidas own twenty acres and as long as I've known Mrs. Machida, she has worked hard in a strawberry field. Like Mama, she has had no time for anything else.

—

"The laundry tubs didn't have any plugs."

Mama says it like she is just stating a fact. She never gets upset.

"I had to find a little pebble and wrap it inside a washcloth to hold the water in the tub," she tells me. "I wonder where they all went."

The word gets around.

And now I vaguely remember seeing a young boy wearing a chain going into his pocket hanging from his belt. At the time, I thought it was odd.

"They're getting those chains from the laundry tubs," Aizo tells us. I give him the once over to see if he is wearing one.

The next time Mama and I go to the laundry room, the chains with the plugs are there.

⸻

Tochan, who keeps constantly busy with camp government, sits at our small table today talking seriously with Mama. I quietly sit down on the edge of the cot.

"I guess we will have to let those ten acres by the railroad tracks go," he tells Mama.

The east half of our property runs along the tracks, which end at Mather Airfield. Young almond trees grow on five acres. The rest are in oranges, and walnuts grafted not too long ago.

A realtor wants the property. Tochan explains that if he doesn't sell, they are threatening to seize the property for wartime use. He sees no choice but to accept their offer of one hundred and seventy-five dollars per acre.

Disturbing news comes from home. I receive a letter from Bill, asking me to ask the internees for any tires they want to sell, of all things! And when Tochan receives a bill from the power company, he begins to suspect that all is not well back on the farm.

Having no choice, he writes to Mr. Coyle, the attorney in Sacramento, of his decision to let go of the ten acres.

⸻

Suspended in the center of a long pole, shouldered by two young boys at each end, hangs a large gunnysack filled with squirming rattlesnakes. A parade of noisy and excited boys follows them.

"What are you going to do with them?" one of them asks.

"It's for the mess hall."

"Yuk!"

"Really?"

"We pickle them for medicine."

"Naw . . ."

I find out later that they skin the snakes to make wallets and belts. They save the largest snake and build a cage for it.

"Would you like to see the biggest snake in Poston?" I ask Masashi.

"Sure. Where?"

"Somewhere in the middle of camp."

We walk in the hot mid-August heat to the center of Poston Camp II, inquiring along the way.

"I'll show you," a young boy says. "It's really big!"

I am scared of any kind of snake, but my curiosity gets the better of me. I can't believe that I am looking straight at the camp's biggest rattler, curled up inside a homemade cage made of scrap wood and chicken wire. Masashi is fascinated. He checks it out from head to toe, asking me questions I can't answer, like how do snakes walk.

The rattlesnake is twice the size of my forearm and not as long as I had imagined. The tail does not rattle. It looks almost dead.

If we ate snake meat, we wouldn't starve in this desert. I probably would starve first. Some *Issei* like the small rattlesnakes, they say. They preserve them in alcohol, which supposedly will cure all kinds of sicknesses.

Kuse, pronounced "koosay," has an interesting meaning. The way Tochan talks about it, *kuse* is a habit one tolerates or even forgives. Living in a place like this, with five thousand people, one can't help but notice people's *kuse*.

"That is his *kuse*," Tochan says, meaning that the poor man can't help it, that it came with birth, that perhaps there was a tiny kink in one of the millions of nerve threads in his body.

I wonder if Henry is one of them. No matter what I say he has a negative retort.

I say, "Great day" and he says, "What's so great about it?"

"That's dumb," he says, when I mention that some fellows might get released to work in the beet fields in Colorado.

"Why work? They put us in here; let them feed us."

He doesn't think much of my brother either.

"I sure as hell wouldn't volunteer," he tells me. "Fight for a country that treats us like this? And get killed? Dumb."

I don't tell him I wrote to the War Relocation Authority, asking for a release to go to college.

Tochan says some people create their own ulcers.

"There is a violin teacher in camp," Tochan announces at supper.

I cringe, thinking he is going to suggest that I continue my lessons. He had insisted on packing my violin. If I had a choice I'd much rather continue with piano.

"I think she lives in Block 219. She said she would be happy to teach me."

For a moment it's like the earth stood still. I can't believe what I am hearing—my father play the violin?

He talks about doing so many things, but this?

I can see him teaching English to the *Issei*, which he says he will be doing soon. Learning to repair shoes at the camp shoe repair shop, I can see. His cobbler skills leave much to be desired.

He talks about having a *tofu* factory in camp. He says a professional shipbuilder in camp is willing to make *tofu* boats, the trays which separate the whey. Soybeans should be easy to get from the feed store in Parker, Tochan says. That, too, makes sense.

"Besides, it will be good food for the children."

But it is the violin lessons that he starts first.

Lois Kanagawa does not have lesson books. She sends him home with copies of her own few, a precious collection which she brought with her to camp. At night, Tochan laboriously copies the notes on whatever paper or cardboard he finds. He brings home a paper carton. He cuts the sides, and on them he copies whole pages of the music.

"I can do that for you," Kazu offers.

She carefully draws five equally spaced lines across the page, and then a half-inch space down, another row of five lines are drawn. Soon the whole page is a music sheet, ready for the notes to be drawn in. He copies a Japanese folk song.

People turn their heads when they walk by our barrack and hear strange notes coming from Apartment 11-A. Some poke their heads inside the door. When the bow grates heavily across the violin strings, I grit my teeth. The notes seem to have no specific sounds.

I am impressed with Tochan's perseverance. It reminds me of his typing at his old Remington typewriter, tapping late into the night, repeating over and over r-t-y-u, r-t-y-u.

"Mah, soh desu ne. Kodomo no tame ni." That is so right; for the sake of the children, they say, as if they have to keep reminding themselves what is important. In the outside world, such was taken for granted. Parents toiled to send their children to school.

In September school starts. Wherever there is an empty barrack space, classes are held. Children bring their own stools made from scrap wood and their own paper and pencils.

Interned teachers are few, as the average age of the *Nisei* is between seventeen and nineteen years. College students teach in the elementary grades until teachers are hired from outside the camp. Caucasian teachers earn more than the prevailing wages, whereas credentialed *Nisei* teachers get paid nineteen dollars a month for the same hours of work.

A semblance of normalcy resumes, as the children, neatly dressed, traipse off to school every morning after breakfast at the mess hall. Gone are the happy noises of summer play. Mama continues mending. Tomoko trots off, wearing her new green suit. Tochan goes off on camp business as usual. I resign myself to working as a nursery school attendant for the duration.

With Masashi in hand, clean, bright and combed, we walk to the nursery school. Along the way we pick up his little friends, all eager and happy. Parents stand at the doorway to see them off.

"*Arigatoh*," Thank you, they nod. Although they don't know me, they know that their children will be safe wherever they go inside this camp.

The double doors of the barrack are wide open. In the middle of the empty room, a large army blanket, spread out on the floor, beckons the children to gather. In the corner by the door a small table made of scrap wood holds the teacher's supplies. Cans, large and small, from the mess hall trash, serve as containers for used pencils, crayons, scissors, paste, etc. A small stack of odd pieces of paper and cardboard and several old picture books lie scattered on the floor.

"Kiyo-chan!" somebody calls in a loud whisper.

I turn around and am delighted to see Mrs. Tamano, my friend and neighbor, standing against the far wall of the room. She is pretty, petite and her pearly white skin betrays the long hours of hard work on their vegetable truck farm in Sacramento. She is only a few years older than I am. Everybody loves Mrs. Tamano and affectionately calls her "Mommy."

Months before our evacuation, the FBI dragged her father off their farm without even giving him a chance to say goodbye or to change his dirty work clothes. He became another one of the numbers of "Jap spies," to make headlines and "prove" to the public that the FBI was making our country safe. From people like Mr. Saiki? What is scary is that everybody believes the lies.

The morning goes by quickly, mostly with latrine duty. No sooner does one of us start on a project, then a child wants to go "*Shi-shi*." And if one goes, others want to.

"Okay, anybody else?" I ask.

With three preschoolers in tow, it is a slow, long walk between the barracks to the latrine building in the center of the block. The community toilet is always busy with mothers and children going in and out. There are no stalls, but unlike the Pinedale Assembly Center's communal outhouse, the smell is controllable with flush toilets. The place is always picked up and clean. Still, I find it difficult to sit on a toilet in one big room with everybody else, without any partitions.

I lead the children to the outside faucet, where a sliver of soap sits on a small rock. Thoughtfully, someone has dug a shallow ditch, coaxing the pool of muddy water away from the base of the frequently-used faucet. A wide ring of white alkaline deposits circumscribes the dried edge, slashed here and there by the slats of the *geta* clodhoppers.

On our way back, I meet Mommy Tamano with several more happy children. Nursery school seems like field trips to the latrine!

For now I resign myself to camp living, feeling good that I have a small and useful part in it.

With the scrap lumber we bring home, Tochan starts sawing pieces to make a small end table with a drawer where he can keep his important papers. The project sits in the middle of the room. It seems that he goes to more and more meetings lately and has little time to work at home. Mama sweeps the sawdust and picks up his tools each time he leaves.

Frustrations begin to creep in. At the mess hall, young teenagers sit with their friends. Parents bring their little children. My brothers reluctantly join the family because they know they have to. In a mess hall feeding 250 people, one can no longer see family groups, only fractured families.

Young men respond to the notices posted at the Block Manager's office for laborers to work on the sugar beet farms in Idaho. Release and legitimate earnings encourage many to apply.

Restless boys too young to work explore their surroundings. As there are no barbed wire fences, they walk into the desert. Kozo and three Toguchi brothers head five miles northwest and discover the Colorado River.

One morning before the heat of the midday sun, I decide to head south. To my great surprise, in a grove of gnarled mesquite trees, I come upon a beautiful and austere Japanese garden. I walk up a curved bridge skillfully crafted from scrap lumber. A dry bed of rocks marks the river below. A small swing for a toddler hangs from a branch. Several benches and a picnic table beckon parents to rest. I sit down and ponder: who is this person who carried all this wood into this hot desert to create a place of beauty and fun for children?

Beneath the stoic attempts of parents to make life livable for the children, problems simmer. As a Councilman Advisor, Tochan meets frequently with other *Issei*, *Nisei* and camp authorities to prevent uprisings before they happen.

· 11 ·

FREE! FIRST CHILD RELEASED FREE! SECOND CHILD RELEASED

Ookaze ni

Ima wo sakari no shiro-momo wa

Ookiku yurete

Hana chigire tobu

— JOHN SHINJI SATO

Amidst the storm

Flowering white peaches

Blooming at their peak

Swaying wildly

Tossing petals in the wind.

— TRUDY SATO, TRANSLATION

SEPTEMBER, 1942.

August passes by and September is almost gone. I give up all hope of going to school, as the fall semester has already started.

The October sun brings no relief. It's still hot. After lunch I decide to write to Seiji. Protected from the mid-afternoon sun by a sliver of shade on the back of the building, I write on my tablet, leaning against the barrack wall.

"Hey, you got a letter." Our young postman comes around the corner, hands me a large envelope and hurries off. It's not often that one gets a letter here. It's usually our soldier brothers and sons who write. My last letter came from Sacramento, from Mr. John Beskeen, the nice man from the Mills Station Grocery Store. And then there was that letter from Bill, asking me to send him names and addresses of anybody who wants to sell him automobile tires. I wonder what he is up to.

The letter looks official. I read, "You have been released to attend . . ."

I scream!

"I can get out of here!" I announce to the whole world.

Children come running around from both sides of the building.

"What happened?"

"Did you get bitten?" Scorpions are everywhere and sometimes rattlers crawl under the barracks.

I run around to the front to tell Mama that I can now continue with college.

"Yokatta ne." That's good, she says, dropping her needle and thread in her lap. Her eyes look at me with deep concern—fear, perhaps. To go back into the outside world that sent us into this dreadful place seems worse than staying here, but I can't rot in here. I'll be fine, I try to convince myself. After all, that's where I belong, outside.

"Where are you going?" Sanji asks me. When I am gone, he will be the oldest one home. He is almost sixteen.

"Michigan," I answer.

"Where's that?"

"I don't know. Back east someplace. Hillsdale College, it says here." I show him my letter.

I am to let them know immediately of my "decision." Decision? What decision? To stay a prisoner, or to be free?

Tochan returns. "Good," he says as if everything is going just fine. I know, then, that I'm going to be alright. No one questions where I will be going. It only matters that I am getting out.

Mama says, "You don't have any shoes."

My shoes have long deteriorated in this sandy desert and I have been wearing a pair of *geta*. I don't know how I will adjust to wearing shoes again. It is great to just rinse my feet under the faucet with my *geta* on. No dirty ankle socks to wash.

"I'll see if I can get permission to get to Parker to buy a pair of shoes for you," Tochan says. I am surprised that my father would even think of the possibility of getting seventeen miles away from this camp. He tells us that army trucks go out every day for supplies. Even then! Those are the trucks that transported us here, for heaven's sake!

By nightfall the whole block knows that I am being released.

"How can your parents let you go?" an *Issei* parent asks.

"You might get killed out there," somebody tells me.

At night, lying on my cot, looking up at the sky, my excitement wanes. Do I really want to leave? Do I want to leave my family, my brothers and sisters, my friends, this safe place?

No one is hateful in here. We are considerate of each other. Nobody steps over a piece of trash. We pick up every piece of paper and every little piece of scrap wood. No one locks anything; no one steals anything. We wash and wear the same few clothes. Children can wander off anywhere and know that somebody will help them find their barrack home.

This is my only chance to get to college, I remind myself. If I wait, heaven only knows how long that will be. As the night deepens, my resolve weakens and I want to stay where I am safe and where I know that the people like me. If I run into trouble out there, to whom do I go? To a church? I might get reported as a possible escapee from a Japanese camp. I surely can't depend on the police. And I have no friends out there. All my friends are in here. Will I be able to come back here if things don't work out? I quickly push aside images of finding myself in a strange town surrounded by angry people.

The howl of the coyotes in the distance only deepens my fears. How do they survive in this unfriendly, waterless desert? Will I be able to survive as well?

Flat on my cot outside, I look up at the limitless sky, filled with the most brilliant stars, the same stars that people outside are seeing, the same stars that I would see from our farm in Sacramento. Is there anyone, I wonder, who is trying to get us out of here? Or did they plan for us to shrivel up in this desert and just quietly disappear?

There is a knock on the door. Usually people call our names or poke their heads in the open doorway. Helen Kazato from Block 211 appears with a package.

"I heard you don't have shoes for school," she says. "You can have these. I hope they fit."

She has another pair, she tells me.

The shoes don't fit me.

Helen's family has property in Fresno. Helen has received permission and a scholarship to attend Smith College in Massachusetts to study music. We find out that we leave on the same train. Two other students from the other camps are to join us.

Mrs. Crawford drives through the gate without stopping. Sitting beside her in the front seat of her sedan, I feel like a fugitive being whisked through to freedom. I notice that this time we travel on a well-defined road, unlike three months ago when it was only a dusty path. It seems like a bad dream that we had ridden through this hot desert for seventeen miles, standing up in open army trucks. So many of us passed out. No one died, fortunately.

From the railroad tracks I had not seen the stores along the short main street. As soon as I get out of the car, a man stops in his tracks and stares. We find a small variety store.

"We're looking for a pair of shoes for school," Mrs. Crawford tells the salesman. He measures my foot. I am embarrassed by my old shoes, which I have cleaned as best as I could. My anklets are stained but clean. Across the floor a mother and her two children, waiting their turn, look at me curiously.

The salesman brings out a pair of saddle shoes in two shades of brown. I'd rather have a white pair with brown through the middle but I don't say anything.

"How does it feel?" Mrs. Crawford asks.

"Fine," I tell her. I want to get out quickly.

I need a suitcase. Mine has a broken lock. In the far corner of the store, several suitcases sit on the floor. I pick out a small one for four dollars. Though it is smaller, I figure it should hold what I have. It has a shiny, dark brown nubby cardboard surface.

As soon as I return to my room, I pack my new suitcase. From the few clothes that Miss Findley, the camp social worker, collected, I choose a cotton dress, two blouses, two skirts, a cardigan sweater, my underwear and bobby socks. My notebook, writing pad and envelopes fit easily. My pajamas hang on the clothesline, drying. I plan to wear my new shoes, carry my suitcase, my small, brown purse and a red jacket.

Even though the October sun shows no signs of cooling, the purple flowers of the morning glory climb the tarpapered barracks as if to herald the coming of autumn. Only three months ago we had arrived on this barren, arid desert. We have managed to create a safe haven for our children. Now I leave its security and the people I love and trust for the unknown. As I wait for the army jeep to pick me up, people mill around. I am the first student to be released from our block.

Issei mothers, with tears in their eyes, place in my hands white envelopes with a few dollars of their precious savings, the only money they have left to face an unknown future. Tochan takes me aside and advises me not to accept the money. He gives me two envelopes, which he had decided to accept in my behalf, from Mr. Yamamoto and from Mrs. Kuwabara

"*Ki wo tsukete, ne.*" Be careful, they tell me, grasping my hands.

I feel Mama's concern. She looks worried. For my father it is almost as if he himself is about to face this challenge with me.

One by one my *Nisei* companions who left Poston with me leave the train to head for their assigned schools, one in Philadelphia, another in Nebraska, another a Baptist seminary somewhere. The Quakers, we are told, had something to do with our release. From Arizona to Illinois, Helen Kazato, several years older, watches over me like a mother hen. It is not until my seatmate leaves that I feel alone.

"Always keep your purse around your wrist," she tells me as she leaves the train to catch another going to Massachusetts.

For hours we ride through green, rolling countryside. Abruptly the terrain changes into old gray buildings and smokestacks. Trash flies along the sides of the train as we go by. In the Poston camps with 18,000 people crammed in, why is it that there was not one piece of trash and here it is everywhere?

As we travel deeper and deeper into the big city, the train slows down. The tracks converge and for almost an hour the train threatens to stop but never does. It keeps going on and on.

"How am I ever going to find the Embrees in this huge place?" I worry. Their daughter Catherine, a teacher at Poston, has asked them to pick me up for the night.

The train stops, flanked on both sides by rows and rows of tracks and trains. I follow the crowd and enter the cavernous, high-domed station. I stand there, not knowing which way to go. To my great relief, I hear my name. Dr. and Mrs. Embree drive me home. In their presence, I feel safe again.

As we sit at the dinner table, thoughts of home well up, threatening homesickness. I wonder when it will be before we can all sit around our farm table again.

Mrs. Embree shows me Catherine's room. She opens the closet. Never have I seen so many clothes!

"Let's find something you can wear," she says. "You pick what you want."

Everything appears large. I figure Catherine must be six feet tall, but she must be thin like me. I find a two-piece, dusty blue, nylon print dress, which I can wear by shortening the skirt about three inches. I also pick a tailored, dark brown velvet suit to shorten. They both fit nicely in my small suitcase.

The next morning, after a tour of Dr. Embree's office at the University of Chicago, the Embrees put me on the train going east to Hillsdale, Michigan. Only three other passengers sit by the door of the coach. They disembark and others get on. The train travels slowly through the pretty countryside and stops at every town. As the late afternoon shadows lengthen along the rolling hills, I worry, wishing that this old train would hurry up. I had hoped to reach my destination before dark.

"Elkhart!"

This must be a big town, I surmise, as the conductor hurries through the car.

As I step outside, I ask the trainman how long we will be here.

"Twenty minutes," he says. I decide to look around, making sure that I keep within safe distance of my coach.

A young, blond redcap about my age approaches me.

"Hi. Where are you from?" he asks me.

Not needing his services, I politely nod and walk on.

"Would you like a cup of coffee?" he asks, following me. He should be working, I think, but he seems sincere, so I accept his invitation and sit at the long counter inside the station. Straddling his stool sideways, hardly drinking his coffee, he questions me.

"Where are you from?" he asks again.

"Poston internment camp."

"Where's that?"

His honest curiosity prods me on. I have never told anyone about our experience of being evacuated and imprisoned. With his neck craned forward, he listens to me with incredulity as I tell him of our eviction from our home in California.

All too soon, the conductor yells "All aboard!"

He walks with me to the coach. I thank him for the cup of coffee.

"Good luck in Hillsdale," he says, waving as the train leaves.

The town passes by without my seeing. I think about the redcap who listened to me. All the inner turmoil and the fear that I had kept under control eases. I feel better about what's ahead.

When the train stops in Hillsdale, I hear someone run up and down the tracks with a flashlight.

"Are you Kiyo?" a young woman asks as I alight.

She directs me to a waiting group, an older person and several young students.

"Let's get your baggage," Mrs. Morgan, the housemother, suggests, walking towards the small station.

"I have it here," I tell her, lifting the small suitcase in my hand. The four of them look at me aghast, making me feel as if I had committed some awful crime.

The ride up the hill to the campus is filled with chatter. I look out the window, trying to acquaint myself with my new place. Along the dimly lit streets stand many tall trees and cozy houses.

One of the students shows me to my room on the second floor of Mauck Hall. A single bed with a thick mattress, a homemade quilt, chenille bedspread and a large, fluffy pillow welcome my tired body. All I want to do is to lie down and sleep. There is a washbasin with hot and cold water right in my room! The closet looks big enough to hold the contents of ten suitcases like mine. By the window I have my own student desk, lamp and a chair. This is more than I had in my room back home. But right now all I want to do is to wash my face, brush my teeth and go to bed. I'm too tired to shower.

Tomorrow morning I will look out of my window.

School started four weeks ago, and to my dismay, I have to pick from what courses are left at the bottom of the barrel. What will I do with a course called The Geography of South America? I find out that two professors voted against my coming to Hillsdale College and one of them teaches The Geography of South America. I enroll in the class to prove to the professor that I am a loyal American citizen, to prove him wrong. Like facing a dare, I take the class. What kind of an instructor would not like me sight unseen? Would he fail me because he "hates Japs?"

At the end of the semester he says, "I hope you sign up for my next class."

With trepidation, I walk up the stairs of an imposing mansion. I have walked by it many times, looking over the high white fence and seeing the huge double doors, wondering who is this person who is supposed to be my sponsor. What is a sponsor? Is she someone I can talk to? The three-story house does not seem like a place one can go with one's troubles.

My sponsor invites me to "tea" to meet the ladies of the community. I wear my brown saddle shoes and the brown velvet suit, which I have shortened. I picture Catherine Embree, a tall white version of me, small busted, thin, and from the hem that I trimmed off, probably three and a half inches taller.

When I knock, the huge double doors open and my view is filled with a magnificent chandelier sparkling from the ceiling. The room is filled with well-dressed ladies chatting in small groups. The maid, in her black dress and white ruffled apron, leads me through the crowd to the back.

My sponsor, a tall, matronly figure bends over and takes my hand. "Let me introduce you," she says and hurriedly leads me by the hand to a cluster of women in the next room.

"This is Kiyo Sato, who came from the Japanese internment camp." The women politely nod, and just as quickly return to their conversation.

She interrupts several other groups and introduces me. Miss Beeney asks how I am finding Hillsdale College. My hostess quickly takes the opportunity to leave and goes back to the kitchen, leaving me in Miss Beeney's care.

Feeling my five-foot-two smallness, I stand awkwardly beside the tall, well-dressed, Caucasian women, pretending to be interested in the conversation being bantered above my head. After a while I slip away with no one noticing and sit in one of the straight-backed chairs lined up against the wall. The maid serves me a cup of tea. Sensing my discomfort, Miss Beeney sits beside me. She seems genuinely interested in my experiences. I feel that my presence is only a symbol of a "Christian duty" performed, that of having helped in the release of a "Japanese student from an internment camp."

Animated conversation fills the rooms. I wonder how long this is going to last. The bite of cookie is dry in my mouth. I sip my tea to wash it down. I wish desperately that I could slip away and end this agony. No one really seems to care whether I am here or not. I know that if I were to walk out the door, no one would notice, but that would be rude. Good manners tell me that at least I should thank the hostess.

I find my hostess and tell her, "I need to get back to my studies. Thank you for your invitation." She seems busy and preoccupied and I am relieved that she allows me a quick getaway. There is no offer of a small plate of cookies to take to the dormitory, something my mother would have done.

When the doors close behind me, I sigh with relief.

I stand on the steps, not knowing what to do, feeling inside like a stirred up pot of hot stew. Going back to Mauck Hall to study seems out of the question. By some miracle I want to plop myself into barrack 11-A in Poston Camp II. I want to be with my family. I want to go home.

I walk eastward towards a park-like estate, one of my favorite places in town. Leaning against the railing of a small, curved bridge, I fight the welling tears of loneliness.

Watching the elegant white swans glide along the water smoothes the ragged edges of my terrible homesickness. Suddenly, I shudder from the chilly air, which tells me that I have been here for a long while. The shadows of the trees extend into the lake.

With renewed resolve I walk up the hill towards the campus.

Excitement fills the air. Students are eager to go home for the holidays. Going home to Arizona is out of the question for me. I plan to find a job and stay in the dormitory.

"Mauck Hall will be closed," Mrs. Morgan tells me.

"I will take care of the building," I suggest.

She advises me that the whole campus will be totally closed.

As I ponder my next move, a letter arrives from Mr. and Mrs. Nicholson of Gary, Indiana, inviting me for the holidays. I am not sure that I want to go to a strange place to spend several weeks with people I don't know. Besides I need to earn some money.

I learn later that their daughter, Goldie Nicholson, a missionary to our church before the war, had written them of my situation.

With no short-term job and with no place to stay, I accept the invitation and take the train from Hillsdale, Michigan to Gary, Indiana, where the elderly, kind couple picks me up. It is a cold, blustery day. We have a near miss when the automobile slides and spins, but Mr. Nicholson appears calm as I sit in the back seat, stiff and straight.

Her knees swollen from arthritis, Mrs. Nicholson has a difficult time climbing the stone steps to their neat, grey two-story house on the outskirts of the city. She shows me to my room on the second floor, a small, bright, cheery room with sparkly, white lace curtains. She leaves me to unpack.

I spread the curtain to see outside. Snow falls gently past my window. From above, I see a beautiful white world, with the tops of roofs and trees covered with snow. I sit down in the straight-back chair by the small, doily-covered table and look outside, mesmerized. Tochan would compose a *haiku*. The thought bursts a dam I've held together so bravely all these weeks, and my sobs and tears flow uncontrollably. I try to muffle them so my hosts won't hear me downstairs. I cry until there are no more tears left.

I go down the staircase and make a quick turn into the bathroom before anyone sees me. I wash my face and then go to the living room to talk with my kind hosts.

The weeks pass by quietly, with much time spent writing home in my pleasant room. On sunny days I walk, exploring the neighborhood, when there is nothing more I can do to be helpful.

When the Nicholsons drive me back to the station, I am ready again to face whatever lies ahead, having had a kind of rest I've never known before. For a short time, my body was not on alert.

JANUARY, 1943.

As I busily man the dormitory switchboard, three students stand around waiting for my attention, with serious, mysterious smiles on their faces.

"Here. This is for you," they say thrusting a large brown box in front of me.

"For me?" I question, surprised.

"Open it," one of them urges.

They seem so eager for me to do so that I become very curious as to what may be inside the box.

Unfolding the white tissue paper, I find a soft, blue knit slipover sweater, which takes my breath away. It is what the students are wearing. I hold it up to my chest, not knowing what else to do or say. It is my first new piece of clothing since we left our home in Sacramento.

"Perfect! It fits you fine. Try the other one."

The other one? Another one? I unfold the bottom layer and pull out a beautiful blue and white pleated skirt with a large, diagonal plaid pattern. I am overwhelmed and choked up and don't know what to say except "thank you."

When they see that all is well, the trio disappears just as my board lights up.

They had passed the hat at Mauck Hall, I find out later, to buy me the sweater and skirt. Just the thought eases the terrible sting of not belonging that I had been feeling.

The formally set dining hall fills with happy chatter as students gather at their respective tables with their sorority and fraternity mates. I sit with the "independents," who could not, or did not, join a sorority. In the sea of white faces, I feel as conspicuous as a piece of coal in the snow. No matter how many times I join the group, it does not become comfortable and fun, like it seems to be for all the others. I try hard to belong, singing the college songs and listening to their conversation.

"I didn't get my check today," a student announces angrily.

"It'll come tomorrow," her friend consoles her.

"I needed it today!" she complains. "What's the matter with them, anyway?"

I am stunned. She condemns her parents because they are a day late in sending her allowance. I cannot believe what I am hearing.

A student sitting across the table says: "Did you hear that Nate was kicked out of his fraternity?"

"No! Why?"

"They say he's colored." A quiet chill shoots through my body.

Nate is a tall, handsome young man, so erect that his eyes focus much above my five-feet-two. I begin to understand why he does not acknowledge my presence whenever we cross paths going to classes. He looks straight ahead as if to tell me that to be associated with me would be incriminating. He looks white, except for the slight tinge of olive under his skin. I wonder what led him to enroll at Hillsdale College. They say he is leaving.

During the first weeks of school, students wait to be invited into a fraternity or sorority. Rejection leads to depression, bordering on suicide for some. Many follow a family tradition of attendance at this private Baptist College.

There is some comfort in knowing that I am different and that I don't have to fit certain social standards. I wash and iron and wear the same clothes over and over. I am excused as "the student from camp." I doubt if my schoolmates even know what that means.

Spare hours on my schedule fill up with working in the library and manning the dormitory switchboard while I eat lunch. They pay me thirty-five cents an hour, hardly enough to buy new clothes, but it helps with basic necessities like toothpaste and monthly needs and notepaper and stuff.

Unlike the students who take huge duffel bags of dirty clothes home on weekends, I spend considerable time in the dingy dormitory basement, washing and ironing my few changes of clothes.

"You sure can iron," a student at the other ironing board remarks, impressed with my quickness. "I hear you people are real good at it."

I look at her; I don't know what to say. Then it comes to me. She must see me as a descendant from a long line of Chinese laundrymen.

"I gotta get out of here," I tell myself.

I finish quickly, go upstairs, deposit my clothes and hurry outside. Emerging from the dark basement, the air is liberating.

A gentle drizzling rain falls like a soothing veil. I walk to the arboretum, my place to be alone and yet not alone. Over the small wooden bridge, east to the pond and along the woods, jumping muddy spots. Along the slope, daffodils begin to poke up their heads, with a few buds about to bloom. I am tempted to pick one for my room. Watching it unfold would continue to nourish my soul, but I know it is against the rules to pick them.

Darkness falls. I hug my thin jacket and hurry back to the dormitory, feeling better.

It is almost two o'clock in the morning when I finally finish my studies and go to bed.

"You don't seem to remember that you're not white," a classmate tells me.

I am so taken by surprise that I am lost for an answer.

What can I say? You mean to say that I should always remember that I am brown? Why? Does she always remember that she is white? I suppose so. She was born into the majority white class and I owe it to her to honor her status, and know my place. When I forget where I come from, does it threaten her? Is that it?

I know deep down that there is no answer, that whatever I say is a waste of time.

I walk away.

The day is overcast and gray. It is the annual Spring Sing on campus, even though there is no sign of spring. The students perform outdoors on the college steps. Students, faculty and friends of Hillsdale College gather in front of the old impressive building with its 1800's spire reaching up to the sky. The air is chilly.

From the fifth row of steps where I stand, I spot a figure weaving through the crowd. He wears a gray felt hat and an overcoat. He looks as if I had seen him before. I freeze.

"Not here! It can't be!" I tell myself. "Not in Michigan!"

He stops to talk to someone. They both look my way. I feel as if our whole group is seeing this man watching me. After stopping several times to ask, apparently, he approaches Dean Rowe, standing in front. They both look at me. She seems to be saying, "That's her," and looks at me with deep concern. I mouth the words of the song. No sounds come from my throat. Memories flash through my mind of the three FBI agents who searched our house and read my diary, of our neighbor Mr. Iwasa, who killed himself after the agents interrogated him, and Mr. Saiki and Mr. Okazaki, who were dragged off their farms with no time to say goodbye or pick up their toothbrushes.

The stranger stations himself directly below me, facing the first row of singers. He keeps a constant eye on me, as if I might escape. It does occur to me that I could rush up the stairs, go through the administration building and down the fire escape.

"No," I remind myself, "that will get you into more trouble."

Even before the last song ends, he rushes forward, ignoring the applause, rudely pushing aside those in the way. It is as if he is afraid that he will lose me.

Several steps up, he sees me coming down towards him. He decides to wait. Faculty and students go their way. No one comes my way. I desperately wish for a friendly body beside me. I submerge the scary, lonely feeling, hold my head up and walk down the steps.

"Where can we talk?" he asks.

I lead him into the administration building. We find a vacant conference room with a small table and two chairs. He sits down and pulls out a pad and pencil. I sit down and wait. Under the brim of his hat, his eyes do not meet mine, as if there is a glass panel between us. He hardly acknowledges my presence. I feel no kindness from him.

"Name?"

"Spell it."

"Age."

"Where were you born?"

The routine questions go on and on.

"Father's name."

"Spell it."

"Mother's name."

I answer each question clearly and patiently.

He meticulously records my whole family, all eight siblings and their birthdates. I wonder what thoughts go through his mind when I tell him that Seiji is a soldier with the United States Army and is stationed at Camp Shelby in Mississippi.

Where was your father born? When did he come to America? Where did he land? What did he do? What organizations did he belong to? The questions about my father are endless. He repeats them. I become weary. I want to tell him that he has asked me that already but I patiently repeat the answer. I realize that he is trying everything to trip me into incriminating my father, to say that he is a spy.

I worry that they might take him away, as they did our neighbors. I want to tell him that my father's heroes are Thomas Jefferson, Abraham Lincoln and Longfellow and Wordsworth and many others, that he deeply respects the United States Constitution and the Bill of Rights. But something tells me that I had better not irritate this man.

An hour goes by and another hour. It is getting dark outside. I feel weak and shaky from hunger and exhaustion. I know that if I give him the answer he wants, he will let me go.

"*Gaman*," I can hear Mama say. "*Moh sukoshi gaman o shite.*" Persevere a bit longer, she would encourage us, when faced with a difficult task.

My answers come automatically now. The questioning continues relentlessly. I begin to understand what brainwashing means and why soldiers break down to the enemy.

When we finally emerge from the room, the building is deserted. I look towards Mrs. Rowe's office, hoping to see her at her desk waiting for me.

Outside in the dark, I see no moving figure on the usually bustling campus grounds. To keep from crumbling, I try not to think about home. Taking a deep breath, I head for the dining hall on the hill. I sit at my usual table of "independents." A working student brings me food. Others are having dessert. The clamor hides my loneliness. No one asks where I have been.

The official letter addressed to me states: "You are the first internee to be released to the state of Michigan. Upon your deportment depends the future release of students to Michigan."

It's a heavy responsibility and I take it seriously. There is no choice. I am keenly aware that one misstep and I will jeopardize the future of many others.

Bill Onoda arrives on campus, followed by Alice Yoshioka. Although we don't talk about our past, there is a certain comfort in knowing that we share the same experiences. Bobby Takatsuka joins us. Like me, they were willing to go wherever the door opened. All of us study hard, as if our lives depend on it.

Betty Deguchi also leaves Poston Camp to live with the Reverend Whitaker's family while attending Hillsdale High School. My brother Sanji comes as a high school student. Sanji rooms at Mrs. Waller's, where Bobby and Bill stay. He tells me he wanted to go to Detroit but Mama would not allow it. He is sixteen.

"If you want to leave, you go to Hillsdale," she told him.

He wastes no time finding after-school jobs to pay for his expenses. Every day he walks to Dr. Martin's home from Hillsdale High School to wash dishes and clean the house. Jobs seem to come his way, such as cleaning the basement and furnace for Dr. Douglas and working at Ward's Nursery all summer. He puts up shelves at Loese's grocery store. I don't know how he manages to pay for his room and board and other expenses and still get his studies done.

He gets paid forty-five to fifty cents an hour. I get thirty-five cents an hour working in the campus library and at the dormitory switchboard during lunchtime.

"You want to go with me to the Junior Prom?" Sanji asks me.

I am surprised that he is even considering going to the Prom. "I have to speak," he says.

Later, I hear that parents are outraged that he has been voted to represent the class. They want him replaced by "one of their own," but the students stand firm on their vote.

I don't have a long dress and I can't afford to buy one. I now wish that I had packed the blue gown with the voile ruffles I wore at the recital of our Sacramento High School orchestra. It's up in the attic at home. How did my parents ever afford to buy that dress, let alone the violin and the piano?

"You can borrow mine," Jane Cornelius tells me back at Mauck Hall. Jane, a soft-spoken and kind person, comes from Berea, Kentucky. She is thin and about my height.

The beautiful white gown, with a ruffled collar slightly off the shoulders, fits me perfectly. I certainly don't look like a big sister. Proudly leading the class of juniors down the dance floor with Sanji, I don't feel like one.

As he speaks from the stage, I am bursting with pride and the words blur. I don't remember anything he says.

My grades slip from A's to B's. I write home that there have been too many requests to speak at churches all year long. This week I speak in Kalamazoo and Detroit. I have no time to study those nights. People are curious and ask all kinds of questions about the camps.

"What did you eat in camp?"

"What did you do in camp?"

"How did you happen to come to Hillsdale?"

"What happened to your family's property?"

"Why did the FBI search your house?"

Usually it is late when I am dropped off at Mauck Hall, wearing a corsage. Guiltily, I wish I had the money instead.

Tochan writes, "You must continue to talk. That is more important than your grades."

But am I doing it right, I wonder?

I ask Dr. Wells, our Public Speaking instructor, for advice.

"Why don't you come and talk to my class? In that way, we will be better able to give you advice."

The students listen as if they are dissecting my every word. I talk for almost an hour. I am prepared with my notebook for professional advice and am almost afraid to find out what I have been doing wrong, but no one speaks when I am finished.

Dr. Wells says, "You just keep on doing what you've been doing," and dismisses the class.

After the first week of June, my dormitory living ceases. If I am to continue in school, I have to find a place to live and a job to pay for tuition, which is $125.00 per semester. At thirty-five cents an hour for several hours a day, I see no way that I can manage.

I make an appointment with my dean, Mrs. Della Rowe, to let her know of my tentative plans, quitting school and working for a while.

She has been concerned, she tells me, and had been inquiring.

"There is a job opening in Litchfield, the next town north of here."

"What will I be doing?" I ask.

"Egg candling."

"But I don't know anything about egg candling," I answer.

"He says he will teach you how to do it."

Lloyd is the middleman for egg producers in the area. He needs someone to grade the eggs. What that means, I have no idea, other than to separate them by size: small, medium and large. Needless to say, I am grateful for any job.

"Do I take a bus to get there?" I ask.

"You will be staying with the Reverend and Mrs. Hoover in Litchfield."

I will be helping them with the care of their children and a new baby, she explains.

I thank Mrs. Rowe for her concern. It is good to know that for the next two and a half months I have a job and a place to stay.

SUMMER, 1943.

After a day's run, gathering eggs from the farmers in the area, Lloyd brings in a large truckload of eggs to be graded.

"You won't have any trouble," he tells me as he unloads the crates.

An egg is held in front of a hole in a 10" x 10" piece of cardboard. A forty-watt bulb shines from behind the hole. The inside of the egg appears translucent, with a dark, round blob in the center.

"This is for shipping," he says and places it on a flat, forty-eight-egg cardboard holder. "The best ones are shipped out of state," he tells me.

"This one is a little darker." The white of the egg is grayer; it is not top grade and will be trucked to area markets. "Anything else goes to the local restaurants."

"Anything else" means every egg that does not meet the first two standards, even eggs that appear to me to be on the verge of hatching.

That's it.

My boss drives off in his big truck, leaving me alone in the old dark room, surrounded by hundreds of dozens of eggs, which I am to check one at a time!

I look intently through my first egg. It is two shades of gray with a darker middle. Should I place it in grade one or grade two? There is no one to ask. I put it in the flat for local markets. I reason that eggs for shipping, like our grapes back home, have to be of top quality.

The decisions don't come easy. With each egg I wish Lloyd were around. The regular egg candler is supposed to come any time, he had said. I wish she would hurry up so I have someone to ask.

Eggs don't come in clear-cut, specific grades. Like embryos, one stage blurs into the next and I continue to have a difficult time deciding in which tray to place the eggs.

With a great sense of accomplishment, I carry my first crate of forty-eight dozen eggs, all candled, to the open elevator as Lloyd has instructed me to do. When he returns in the afternoon, I have three lugs on the elevator. He lowers the load down to the basement by untying the heavy rope by the door and slowly giving it slack on the pulley. When the platform hits the basement floor, he hooks the rope on the nail and limberly slides down the narrow, wooden ladder.

By the end of the day, my neck is stiff. All the eggs begin to look alike, from the fresh-looking eggs headed for New York to the pre-hatcher for a South Bend restaurant. I swear I will never again have eggs for breakfast at a restaurant, unless, of course, our own chickens have laid them.

At the end of the day, I turn off the candling light bulb at my workstation and open the door. The late afternoon sun blasts me. I feel like a mole emerging above ground. After eight hours of standing in the same position and bending my neck over the light, it is good to walk upright. Taking deep breaths and swaying my arms, I feel better.

Walking in the door of the Hoover household, I don't have to ask what to do. The sofa on which I sleep overflows with laundry to be folded. In the corner, the baby lies on the floor drinking from her bottle.

"Hi," I greet the little children sitting on the floor. They are surrounded with odds and ends of toys. "Where's your mother?"

"Sleeping," one of them says.

I see her on her bed in the bedroom and quietly close the door. Most of the time she appears overwhelmed and weary.

My days at work improve. I am getting to be as fast at candling eggs as I am at picking strawberries. The crates pile up on the elevator. But I never seem to catch up with the loads coming in. I wonder why the other worker does not come. Two other workstations remain unmanned.

I try each day to increase my speed, six crates, seven crates, eight crates, then thirteen crates! My boss says nothing but I am pleased with my own progress. I think of Mama and how she picked strawberries. No one could beat Mama but she paid no attention and did what was necessary.

By early afternoon, I finish my tenth crate. By mid afternoon, I lift my thirteenth crate onto the piles on the elevator. Just as I step off the platform, I hear a strange tearing sound and seconds later a huge hole opens at my feet, followed by a heavy crushing thud below.

Incredulously, I find myself looking down into the dark hole, my crates of eggs toppled over each other below, all my day's work ruined! Shall I climb down below and start cleaning up the mess? It would take a day to re-candle and separate the broken eggs. Where is the light switch? How do I get the crates back upstairs? As I ponder my next move, I hear Lloyd's truck drive up.

As soon as he walks in, I explain what had happened. He does not say a word and clambers down the ladder. He gathers up the scattered broken eggs in a bucket, gives a cursory check of the top layers of the crates, fills in where needed and he is done. He pulls up only one crate upstairs on the elevator to be refilled.

"I'll finish that," I tell Lloyd knowing that I would not be here tomorrow.

After he is finished unloading his truck, I ask him, "Am I fired?"

"No," he says matter of factly. It is frustrating not knowing what he is really thinking. A whole day's work was lost, but he is willing to keep me on.

On my way home, I ponder over the day's happenings. I had been an inch from falling down the one-story hole with the crates. It was luck that I did not lose my balance, landing head first onto the scattered crates of broken eggs below.

Suddenly, it occurs to me that I had overloaded the elevator. I realize now that the old elevator had never held thirteen crates of eggs before, four stacks of three crates each, which left no space for the thirteenth. I had hoisted the last crate up onto the center of the stacks. The elevator shuddered. The rope tore and I stepped off just in time.

I don't think Lloyd had suspected that I would exceed the elevator capacity in a single day. Although he is not pleased with the day's loss, he probably thinks that I can easily make it up.

The eggs pursue me all summer long. The other egg candlers never appear.

FALL, 1943.

It's fall, and I need work. If not for Dean Rowe's concern, I probably would have gone home.

"A family in Hillsdale would like someone to help with cleaning in exchange for room and board," she tells me. That means I can stay in school if I can pay for the tuition.

I move into a small room on the second floor of a mansion. It's the home of Dr. and Mrs. Moench. My job is to clean the house, help with the meals, do the dishes and see that the three children have breakfast before leaving for school.

"You will be treated as a member of the family," the lady of the house explains. I receive an allowance of one dollar a week, as do each of the three children.

I divide my day into half hour segments and fill in my nineteen hours of courses and my job hours on campus in the library and at the switchboard. Two half-hour segments are taken up walking to and from campus.

Each day, after I return from school, I schedule myself to clean a part of the house, so that the whole house is finished each week. I do two bedrooms one day, two bathrooms the next day and so forth. On Saturdays, I clean the large living room, the dining room and whatever else is unfinished. Going through the whole house requires twenty-seven to twenty-eight hours each week.

As soon as my daily after-school cleaning work is done, I start in the kitchen. From five to eight o'clock each day, I help with dinner and dishes. I wash and peel the potatoes, removing the eyes very carefully. At a quarter after five, they are ready to be boiled, so that they can be mashed and buttered and served warm on time, exactly at six. Mashed potatoes and gravy are served at every meal, like steamed rice at home. I stir the gravy and see that there are no lumps. There seems to be an understanding that a lump in anything can cause major consequences. I am not used to that. It seems such a waste of time to keep stirring so much. At home no one paid any attention to the blobs of tiny, unmixed flour "dumplings" in my big pot of stew, and everybody ate it like I was the best cook in the world.

I work as quickly as I can in order to get to my homework at a decent hour. I miss Mama as I work alone, carefully washing the "good" dishes and scrubbing the piles of pots and pans. Back home, in our small farm kitchen, I didn't have to walk back and forth to the dining room. I turned around and grabbed the dirty dishes from the supper table. Mama put away the food, wiped the dishes and after a while she would tell me, "Go and do your homework. I will finish the dishes." By eleven o'clock Mama would turn out the kitchen light and bring me a dish of canned peaches, telling me not to stay up too late.

It is after eight when I turn out the kitchen light and go up the back stairs to my room to study. The house is quiet, with each member of the family holed up in his or her private space.

I dread breakfast time. Each child wants something different and if it's not right, I try again. I wish they could be like my brothers and sisters, who will eat anything I fixed with never a complaint.

What a relief it is when I finally close the front door behind me. In the giant trees the birds are chirping; the air is crisp. Only a few people are out on the streets. My body stiffens only when another body comes towards me. I prepare myself to smile. I've learned that my survival depends on it. In my days since my release from camp, I've learned how to cope with stares. I am a curiosity. I look at each person full square in the face and smile. Little do they know that behind those tilted lips is a twenty-year-old trying to be brave. I squelch the tiny wave of homesickness in my chest. I long to be home where I am safe.

I can see Mama looking at me with deep concern, telling me, "*Moh sukoshi gaman o shina kereba.*" You must stick with it a bit longer. Her perseverance knows no end. When I recall Mama dozing at the supper table with her chopsticks halfway to her mouth, I know I can do more.

I remember asking her, "How can you work so hard, Mama?"

"When I think I can't take another step," she tells me, "I whisper *'Kamisama!'* God! And cling to His hem."

⁓

"I have a job working in the melon fields in Poston," writes Aizo. "I get paid twelve dollars a month. I work every day. Please split this check with Sanji."

I look at the government check for a long while, hardly able to hold back my tears. Aizo just turned sixteen in May. This check is the result of one month of hard work in the hot desert.

I can't take this check, I argue with myself. It would buy so many things that the family needs. By now their underwear is probably beyond Mama's mending. But he wanted us to have it. He would be hurt if I returned it to him.

I sit down and write him a thank-you note.

I remember my first check after working a month as a nursery school attendant in Poston Block 228. The twelve dollars went into the family pot. We had not seen any money since we left home and we were short of toothpaste, and our toothbrushes were flared and worn out. I had to wash and fold my own monthly sanitary pads. I decide to share Aizo's check with Sanji, as he has asked me to do.

I need to earn more money to pay for the second year tuition. Students are working at the bowling alley at nights. After the dishes are done, I plan to work two or three nights a week until midnight. Four dollars a month hardly pays for miscellaneous expenses.

I announce my plans and to my total surprise, I am met with angry refusals. I don't understand why. The job is within walking distance from the house. It will be on my own time. The bowling alley is a family place, but somehow I get the impression that it is not good for their family image for me to be working nights in a bowling alley. I go upstairs to my little room, confused and on the verge of tears at having my hopeful plans shattered.

In a small town, like in camp, news travel fast. The local beauty shop needs help. I have no experience but I walk to the other side of Main Street to find out about the job. The owner-beautician, very businesslike and unsmiling, leads me down to the small basement.

"I need these towels and sheets ironed," she says. "Do you know how to use the mangle?"

"No," I reply. I have never even seen one in my life, but I don't tell her that.

She sits down, places a folded sheet on the large ironing board, smoothes out the wrinkles carefully and then pulls down the handle of the top board. I am silently impressed that a sheet is so nicely ironed in a short time. I have never before ironed sheets. Ours come off the line stiff and smelling of sunshine.

"Can you start now?" she asks.

I had not planned on it but I tell her I can.

"You can do the towels on the mangle." She places a hand towel on the board. I can see that she is very meticulous by the way each towel is folded and ironed several times. "The uniforms have to be done with the iron," she tells me, and leaves hurriedly up the stairs.

The basement is well lit, with extra light coming from the sidewalk windows above, where I can see legs walking by.

Ironing while sitting down is a new experience and I find it easy. Steam puffs out with each contact. When it becomes too warm and steamy, I move to the ironing board to do the uniforms, which I soon dislike. One wrinkle ironed in error never smoothes out. It takes forever to do one white uniform and there is a pile of them ahead. I can see why she hired me on the spot. Another day and she probably would not have had one to put on.

I work steadily all afternoon. My employer appears once to pick up some pins. She says nothing.

It is after five. When my employer appears again, I stop her and tell her that I need to be back at the house to help with dinner preparations. She looks at me as if I have said something wrong, that she should have been the one to decide the quitting time.

"When can you come back?" she asks.

"I can come back next Sunday afternoon."

"All right. I will pay you then." She turns quickly and returns upstairs. I unplug the iron and mangle and leave, walking past the shop as unobtrusively as possible. Several ladies curiously look my way.

When the front door of the beauty shop closes behind me, I feel my body relax. I hurry across Main Street to avoid having to smile at curious stares. It is a comfort to walk along the side street, with elegant maple trees by my side.

⁓

Kozo writes that he was looking at a seed company catalog. The advertisement said that if he sold fifty packets of seeds, he would get a fishing pole, so he wrote to them. They sent him the packets of flower seeds to sell.

"I think I sold about half of them when Mama heard about it. I didn't think she would be upset. Everybody's planting things between the barracks and they liked looking at the different kinds of flower pictures I had."

He continues, "Mama said no one has money to spend. If we have seeds, we share them. We don't sell them. She made me return the ones I hadn't sold with the money I collected."

That was a long time ago and everybody had forgotten all about it until yesterday, he tells me. "The mailman brought me a long box and inside it was a fishing pole. Tomorrow I am going to the Colorado River with George Toguchi. It's about five miles. Nobody says anything anymore when we go out into the desert. We will save some food from the mess hall to take and use bread for bait."

Who is this wonderful, kind man from the seed company who would send a fishing pole to a boy in a concentration camp in Arizona, even though he failed to complete his contract? There are some good people in our country, I remind myself.

Disturbing news comes from camp. Saburo Kido of the Japanese American Citizens League reports on plans by the government to recruit volunteers for the army. A small group argues that internees should not serve until our families are released from camp. Tochan spends a great deal of his time as liaison between the Administration and the Law and Order Committee.

The government, in an attempt to separate the "loyals" from the "disloyals," demands that all internees over the age of 16 sign a loyalty questionnaire. *Isseis*, who are denied the right to become American citizens, are asked to forswear their allegiance to their country of birth. They become a people without a country, as they are forbidden by law to apply for United States citizenship.

Children are torn between their parents and their country. Many young men feel that the only way to get out of camp is to answer "Yes" to question 27 and "Yes" to question 28, a poorly worded statement which asks that *Niseis* "forswear" allegiance to a country to which they had never sworn allegiance. Government demands create havoc within the families.

Past midnight, I sneak quietly downstairs for something to eat.

Something smells. The good doctor sits at the dining table. Whatever he is having smells awful.

"Well!" he says. "How about limburger cheese and crackers?"

The odoriferous cheese is not what I want but I am famished and ready to try anything. He smears the cheese on a cracker and hands it to me. The first bite is difficult, but after the second I don't smell it anymore and I enjoy the creamy, soft cheese on the crisp cracker.

I keep smearing more and more cheese on the crackers while he tells me about his work, his public health nurses, what they do, and the problems they deal with.

I never see the doctor at breakfast time. He leaves before any of us come downstairs.

SPRING, 1944.

On campus I fill up every open period with a job, several periods in the library shelving books. If anyone needs a substitute in the kitchen, I fill in. Like a sculptor chipping away on a piece of marble, at thirty-five cents an hour, slowly my tuition whittles down. One hundred and twenty-five dollars a semester seem at times like an impossible boulder to move but I have no choice. This semester I have no scholarship. I try not to think about it and keep on working.

From the limited course choices, I change my major many times— art, journalism, psychology, sociology and biology. I find myself enrolling in classes just to earn credits toward my degree, and I find some surprises. "Thirteen Living Religions of the World" challenges my Baptist views, teaching that none of us are the chosen people. Courses in French and Spanish almost convince me to become a translator. Dr. and Mrs. Davidson are impressed with my ease with foreign languages. My having learned Japanese first may have something to do with it.

With the gentle encouragement from Dean Della Rowe, I finally find a direction in the mish-mash of courses I have taken. Nursing. As a nurse I can always find a job.

"You have a good academic record. Let's apply to schools which require a bachelor's degree," she advises. "There are three in the United States: Yale University School of Nursing, Johns Hopkins School of Nursing and Western Reserve University School of Nursing."

I send out application letters and wait with anticipation, excited that my goal is becoming a reality.

A letter arrives. I can hardly believe what I am reading. "We cannot have anyone of your ancestry around the patients."

Hurt, I shrug it off.

A second letter states that under the school's policy, they cannot admit anyone of my ancestry.

It doesn't look good. When universities of such high standing stoop to such practices, whom can we depend on? How did all this happen? And how did the highest court of our country, the Supreme Court, bless our internment? What is happening to America?

A letter arrives, postmarked Keenesburg, Colorado. It's in Tochan's handwriting. He writes that the family obtained a permit to work on a 50-acre sugar beet farm several miles away from the Jakel farm, where our cousins now live. Tochan received twenty-five dollars per person and a one-way train ticket. "This is much better for the family," he writes.

When a Navy recruiter comes on campus, I decide that if nothing is going to materialize, I can volunteer for the military. There is no one in the room waiting to sign up.

"I'd like to volunteer."

The young recruiter, looking efficient in his Navy uniform, becomes nervous. He must be new, I figure.

He fumbles for words. I wait. All I want to do is to serve my country like my brother. I don't understand why he is so agitated.

Finally he tells me, "Just a minute. I have to make a phone call," and leaves the room.

He returns shortly with a restored look of authority. "I can't sign you up," he tells me.

I could have asked him why, but why waste my breath, I tell myself. I know why and he knows why. Nothing I say is going to change things.

I look at him. His nervousness tells me that he may think that this is not right. Or, who knows, he may think that I am a spy trying to infiltrate the Navy! Isn't that why they threw us in camp?

School will be out for the summer soon. An air of excitement fills the campus, but for me it is a time of uncertainty. What will I do? Where will I go? I still have to earn about twelve more units. Summer session will do it but I need to work first to pay for tuition and room and board.

Sanji hands me an envelope. "Here's enough for a bus ticket. You go home."

"No," I tell him. "You earned the money. You go."

"You haven't seen the family for a long time. You go."

I am choked up that my brother, who is four years younger, would help me to go home. I try not to let Sanji see the tears welling in my eyes.

"You haven't, either, Sanji. I think you should go home."

"I plan to work at Ward's Greenhouse this summer," he tells me.

My heart overflows with happiness, knowing that I will see my parents and my brothers and sisters again. For two years I have not allowed myself to think about going home. Holidays have been especially difficult, when all the students happily left campus. Only those of us whose families were still in the concentration camps remained.

I pick up little gifts here and there and put them inside my suitcase. What had been such important priorities now are practically forgotten. My degree can wait. Nursing school can wait. My whole future can wait.

I am going home!

· 12 ·

SUGAR BEETS, *OFURO*, AND WINDMILL

Senso ya

Koko no sanka wa

Aki no tsuki

— JOHN SHINJI SATO

It is war

The autumn moon shines peacefully

On this land

— TRUDY SATO, TRANSLATOR

THE LONG EXHAUSTING ride from Michigan ends as the train slowly comes to a crawl in Denver, Colorado. The anticipation of soon seeing my family gives me renewed energy. I pick up my small suitcase and purse and with brisk steps follow the crowd into the old station.

Outside again, I look for a bus.

"Keenesburg? There is no bus going there," the driver answers.

"How do I get there?" I ask.

"I don't know."

"Where is its closest town?"

"Probably here, Denver," he says.

"Denver? How far is Brighton?" I ask having heard it mentioned in a letter.

"Don't know."

Now what? Take a taxi for how much? How far?

Darkness descends rapidly. I have not had anything to eat since noon and my stomach is complaining. Right now I want to get home before too late.

I don't want to take the wrong bus and be dumped somewhere in the dark. Maybe I should stay here in the station until morning and decide what to do in the daylight, I ponder. Sitting on the wooden bench, feeling *kokoro-bosoi*, as Mama would say, sad and lonely, I lean my head on my arm draped over my well-traveled suitcase. Not knowing where to go in the dark night, hungry and tired, I sit and wait for an answer.

The Toguchis, from the neighboring farm, moved to Denver, I remember. So did the Kitadas. They lived in Block 229, in Camp II. Maybe they will know where my family has moved. I look for a phone booth.

To my relief, I find the Toguchis listed in the phone book. Where is this place called Keenesburg that no one knows about? I hope that one of them will give me directions on how to get there.

"Hello. Takeo? This is Kiyo."

"Kiyo! Where are you?" he asks, sounding genuinely pleased to hear from me.

"I'm at the train depot. I need to know how to get to Keenesburg."

"It's not too far," he replies.

"You mean, you know where it is? Where is the closest town?"

"Brighton," he tells me. "But that's maybe about eight, nine miles from Keenesburg."

Quickly I decide I can't walk that tonight. Maybe tomorrow.

"I know where your family lives. I can take you there."

"You have a car?" I exclaim, surprised that in such a short time he has earned enough money to buy himself a car, and he is only a year or two older than me.

"I'll come and get you right now."

With a voice about to tremble, I tell him I will wait at the front entrance.

Swallowing tears of relief, I sink onto a bench. Finally I am connecting with my family!

⁓

"I came to Denver first, and looked for a job," Takeo tells me. "We got twenty-five dollars and a one way ticket to anywhere we wanted to go. I chose Denver because there were lots of jobs posted at the Block Manager's."

While staying at a hostel where internees could get room and board for a small fee, he was able to save enough money to rent an apartment and write his family of three sisters, three brothers and parents to come.

"All of them attend school. My mother does housecleaning. They are all well," he says with gratitude. "Your family relocated to a sugar beet farm. It's hard work. So did your uncle. They're in Keenesburg, about three, four miles from each other."

"You've been there?"

"Couple of times. You are lucky you have some land back home to return to. We lost our twenty acres," he tells me. "So when this is all over, we can't go home."

"I'm so sorry. Who has your farm?" I ask.

"I guess the bank or the realtor," he replies, shrugging his shoulders.

It is not just the Toguchi family. So many Japanese farmers have lost everything they owned, all that they had worked so hard for. They were reduced to a bedroll for each member of the family and what they could carry, evicted by government orders. Nobody helped; nobody listened. And here they are, forced to survive in a strange city— their land, their cars, their trucks, their dishes and pots and pans, their treasured family photographs all gone along with their farmhouse and land. Takeo has no choice but to take care of the family, which he does with such caring.

"The government told us to get out but did nothing to protect our properties," I tell him, anger mixed with sadness. "It's terrible. When all the families are released, where will they go?"

"When we left Sacramento, I suppose everybody helped themselves to the stuff we had to leave behind. I wonder what happened to my car. Do you think your Studebaker will still be there?" Takeo asks.

"I doubt it. I only hope somebody is watching out for our dogs."

Their productive strawberry farm, which had adequately supported the family for many years, is gone, and now Takeo, as head of the family of nine, is their sole support.

Time passes by quickly, talking about old times. The narrow asphalt road occasionally crosses creek-like ditches covered over with slabs of wood. Power poles disappear. We ride farther and farther into desolation.

"We're almost there," he assures me, as we drive down a long, narrow dirt road. What terrible place have they moved to?

Takeo takes a quick turn off the road and stops beside a tiny, dark house. It is almost midnight. In the moonlight, the silhouette of a tall windmill comes into view. Takeo hurries to the door and bangs loudly.

"Kiyo's home!" he shouts. "Kiyo's home!" Suppose it's the wrong house? How does he know this is it?

Then an overwhelming gratitude sweeps over me. He knew exactly where to bring me. Bodies in pajamas spill out of the door, everyone talking at once.

Mama thanks Takeo-san. "*Taihen deshita ne.*" It was a long and difficult drive, she says, and suggests that he stay the night.

After listening to everyone, I turn around to thank my friend, but find him gone. "It's not too far," he had said. It will be a long night of driving for him.

Masashi, an unhappy three-year-old at the Pinedale Assembly Center, is now a tall six-year-old. He pulls me by the hand, eagerly leading me into the house.

Mama fires up the big black stove, which appears to take over the tiny kitchen. She stuffs paper and twigs into the side door, lifts the round lid on top with a metal hook and drops large pieces of scrap wood on the starting fire. It seems like old times again as we squeeze in on the two benches along the wall and around the small table, the chill of the room lifting.

"Look at this!" Masashi says, pointing to the hurricane lamp, which sheds a comfortable glow in the kitchen. "You have to take the top off to light it," he explains. Everyone wants to report to big sister.

"I wanna show you my bed," Masashi announces.

"She doesn't want to see your bed!" big brother Aizo tells him with disdain.

I follow Masashi around the corner, followed by the rest, where in the next tiny space are bunk beds stacked up on both sides like in a Pullman car.

"Tochan made them," Masashi explains proudly. "He cut down the trees outside. That's my bed." He points to the lower bunk.

I flip aside a sheet hanging from the ceiling. Neatly piled high in the small corner space are boxes of family belongings ready for the next move.

Everybody dutifully follows Masashi, the tour guide, through the house and to the outside.

"That's where we take a bath every night," Masashi explains. "Tochan made a *furo-ba* just like the one at home."

Beneath the windmill, inside four walls and a roof sits a square red-wood tub, its lid leaning against it. The *ofuro* sits scrubbed and empty, ready for the next day. The embers below have been scraped out with a shovel and dumped out in the garden area in back.

I am overcome with a tremendous desire to lower my weary body into the warm, steaming water, lean my head against the redwood rim and close my eyes. I would feel my shoulder muscles taut from emotional assaults soften and melt away. Tomorrow I can do that.

"Kiyo-chan, you can sleep here." Mama shows me the "couch," constructed much like the bunk beds, with roughhewn, six-inch logs around the edges and boards across the top, neatly padded with layers of old comforters. Beneath it is storage space with doors. I slide in between Mama's fresh, sun-dried sheets and fall asleep with thoughts of moonlight shining through my window back home, the long difficult two-year journey now only a memory.

I am home.

Sleep gently lifts its warm wrap. My tired body has sunk onto the hard surface like Jell-O and remained unmoved the whole night. Happy chatter from the kitchen invites me to join them. I pull my old red jacket over my shoulders and leave the chilly room to join my brothers and sisters. They squeeze in closer on the bench to give me space on the end. The warmth from the old iron stove fills the tiny room.

"Hot Ovaltine?" Mama asks. A big pot warms on the stove, a gallon of milk from the Ewerts' cow already half consumed. Each day Kozo walks a half a mile down the road to buy a gallon from Mike Ewerts. The warm milk sits all night in a box outside the kitchen window, cooling.

Pancakes sizzle on the stove.

"What's all that racket?" I ask, looking out the window over the sink.

Hundreds of large, black birds circle wildly, cawing and vying for a spot on the roof of the outhouse a distance away.

"Aizo's in there," Kazu announces, and sure enough he is not at the table.

"Listen! Which one is Aizo cawing?" I ask.

Silence.

"That's him!"

"Naw."

"I hear him!"

No one can tell the difference between the crows and Aizo. The birds are frantic, pushing each other for perching space on the small outhouse roof. Other birds wait patiently, lined up on the peak of the shed roof nearby. Only Aizo, our family clown, would sit in that cold, teasing the birds.

"It must be freezing in there," I remark, noting the layer of white frost still on the ground.

With every move, Mama readies each of our beds and then puts out the *omaru*, the pee-can. The white, enameled pot with the lid is usually almost full by morning. Mama empties it, still steaming, and scrubs it and rinses it with Clorox, like she does everything else, and then leaves the pot and lid to dry in the sun all day.

I remember those cans from the mess hall garbage at the Pinedale Assembly Center, the disposable ones which you just threw away. In Poston Camp II, when someone knocked it over, Mama just washed the spill down the loose floorboards with a bucket of water, the bucket Tochan smuggled inside one of our bedrolls. No Clorox. The desert heat scorched the germs.

This time, a legitimate and squatty chamber pot with a lid, probably from the local hardware store, sits in the boys' bedroom, looking like a misplaced stew pot.

KEENESBURG, COLORADO.

At the crack of dawn, each member of the family big enough to handle a short hoe with some precision lines up at the beginning of the long, green rows of tiny sugar beet plants. I look down my row, wondering if I will reach the end, which disappears over the horizon. We scrape off eight- to ten-inch swaths of the plants, allowing one or two to become full-grown sugar beets. Usually it takes our fingers to pull out the unnecessary, small plants, which are too close to the one to keep. Sometimes the corner of the hoe hacks off the lone plant, leaving an empty spot, never to be filled except by weeds.

Mama and Tochan, Aizo, Kozo and I move along, with Mama always in the lead. Mama waits for no one, as if survival depended on her. She accomplishes twice the work of Tochan, who brings up the rear with his charges who try to keep up to hear his stories. Aizo, the quick hare, rushes ahead and sits and listens. Kozo prods along at a steady pace, helping the slower ones nearby. I hop from row to row, like a sheepdog, helping ten- and twelve-year-old Naoshi and Kazu to keep within listening distance of the story.

"Water boy, here!" Aizo calls.

Struggling over rough ditches, Masashi and Tomoko deliver water and snacks of Graham crackers or cookies wherever needed.

⸺

"Mama, I have an idea. What do you think about using long-handled hoes for thinning? It would be much easier on the back."

"*Soh, ne,*" she muses. But will it be less accurate, she questions? One would be stooping over anyway to pull out the missed plants.

"My back is troubling me again," Tochan says.

Maybe, he suggests, he could scrape out plants at eight to ten inch intervals walking upright with a long-handled hoe, and Mama could follow doing the fine work of leaving two plants. Mama smiles. She remembers the excruciating pain Tochan had suffered carrying a large crate of canta-loupes, and the resulting days of bed rest, or more accurately, floor rest, unable to climb onto his bed.

"That sounds like a good idea, Tochan," Aizo comments.

"I will try it tomorrow. If it works, we can buy enough long-handled hoes for each of us."

⸺

News travels fast.

Thinning beets standing up?

Who?

Where?

Can't be done. Can't be precise. You can try to leave one plant to mature into a beet but suppose you cut that by mistake. No plant, no beet. You have to use a short-handled hoe and pull out unnecessary plants by hand.

Old habits never die.

But the Sato crew, outfitted with new long-handled hoes, steadily thin down the plants just as quickly, stooping only when plants are too close to separate with the hoe. They finish thinning their fifty-acre contract in good time. To Mr. Craig, the boss, it doesn't matter how it's done, as long as it is done.

June passes. The sugar beet plants grow in neat rows, evenly spaced.

July. The sky turns a menacing gray. A welcome rain falls, only to be followed by pelting hail. Inside our small cabin, chattering stops when the noise on the roof drowns out the conversation. We step outside the door under the eaves and watch in fascination as little white balls dance on the ground, a few of them almost as large as baseballs.

My brothers dash towards the garden to grab the large ones gathered in the ditch.

"Ow! Ow!" they yell as they run back, pelted by the falling cold, white stones.

To the delight of the children, soon the whole yard turns white.

Tochan watches. What is this doing to the beet field?

"This is dangerous country," Mama says.

FALL, 1944.

Reluctantly we leave the warm and cozy kitchen and emerge into the early morning cold of fall. Every breath condenses into white vapor. It is harvesting time.

With headlights warning of large clods, Tochan drives the old Chevrolet to the far end of the sugar beet field. All bundled up, Masashi, Tomoko and Naoshi sit in the back seat. The water jug, Graham crackers, and Mama's ubiquitous folded old rags sit on the front seat inside a crate. Mama mostly uses the rags for blowing her nose.

The rest of us walk in the early dawn, carrying our beet topping knives, aware that tripping on a clod of dirt could slash us.

Aizo puckers his lips and blows hard. Kozo imitates him sending out a long white vapor trail.

"Mine went farther," he announces.

"Oh yeah?"

They line up at the ditch and blow together, each trying to outdo the other.

"Can you do a ring?" Kozo asks.

Aizo tries. "Mr. Miyasaki used to do that," he says.

I can see Mr. Miyasaki sitting in the sun, leaning against his cabin, rolling his Bull Durham, licking the edge of the thin, brown paper and lighting the cigarette. Then he'd lean back and slowly puff out round rings of smoke and watch them as they disappeared one by one. Mr. and Mrs. Miyasaki were like family. They stayed in our uncle's cabin and worked in the fields whenever necessary.

When we reach the field, Tochan already has the headlights shining at the starting point. Where there used to be tiny green plants are now round beet heads of all sizes, rolling in the furrows having been dug up by Mr. Craig's horse and plow. The beets are small, due to the devastating hailstorms, which flattened the growing plants twice. Tochan says, philosophically, they will be easier to harvest.

Just as the sun appears above the horizon, we claim our rows. The children rush to position themselves next to Tochan, within hearing distance of his stories.

During the week, Mama, Tochan and I work quietly while Tomoko and Masashi play in a ditch nearby, digging with their hoes. Today is Saturday. Aizo, Kozo, Naoshi and Kazu join the family work crew, adding four more rows.

"Tell about Kuzu, Tochan," Masashi requests, playing in the ditch nearby with Tomoko.

The small cluster of beet-toppers moves slowly northward in the vast, green 50-acre field.

Large beet heads can be as big and as heavy as a bowling ball. To spear each one, lift it on my knee, lop off the green tops and throw it into the sled path all day long is exhausting work. The rows seem endless, melting into the horizon, but the time goes by. Soon Tochan calls for someone to go home to prepare lunch.

"*Kiyo-chan, yatte cho dai, ne?*" Will you do it, please, Mama asks? Her right arm is bandaged with strips of rice sacking to control the pain from overuse. She moves her arm twice as fast as the rest of us. She knows that I welcome the change. What a relief it is to straighten up and walk upright!

When I hear the chatter of the family and the old hand pump creaking up and down by the windmill to wash hands and faces, I throw the sliced *nappa* cabbage sizzling into the hot oil in the large skillet, filling the small kitchen with aromatic vapors. Salt and *Ajinomoto*, monosodium glutamate, gives the *nappa* its final flavor. Mama never goes without *Ajinomoto*, which she buys by the pound. It is good for the brain, she says.

In the afternoons, fieldwork seems never-ending.

Mama's right arm, now wound tightly with a bandage, suddenly refuses to move.

"You'd better quit, Mama, and go home," Tochan advises. "Rest your arm."

Reluctantly she goes back to the house to do other chores, which can be done with her left arm. With rest, the arm slowly recovers.

The children follow Tochan. At times, only the quiet sound of beets being topped fills the silence. Birds sing in the distance.

"Tochan?"

"Uh?"

"Will you tell us another story?"

"What will it be?"

"About that mean man, Shylock."

"We know that already."

"I know! Remember that wagon? It broke down all at once? Tell that one, Tochan."

"All right. *The One-Hoss Shay*."

So the story begins, and everybody closes in on the slow lines. Tochan embellishes the words of Oliver Wendell Holmes, to make it interesting to a five-year-old. Step by step, the great storyteller describes the building of the wagon in such a way that the listener thinks that he, too, can one day build one. The children listen with bated breath, knowing already what is about to happen to the deacon and the deaconess.

Have you heard of the wonderful one-hoss shay,
That was built in such a logical way?
It ran a hundred years to the day,
It went to pieces all at once,
All at once, and nothing first,
Just as bubbles do when they burst

And the Deacon and the Deaconess find themselves on a big pile of wood in the middle of the road. Tochan describes in detail, in Japanese, the total look of astonishment of the Sunday-dressed Deacon and the Deaconess.

"Another one!"

"Let's see." Tochan pulls out his watch. "Almost four o'clock. It's time to start the *furo* bath. Kazu, why don't you and Naoshi do it today?"

"Okay."

"And you can throw some potatoes into the fire," Tochan suggests.

"Oh boy!" Naoshi exclaims, already savoring the half of a big hot potato with plenty of butter and salt.

Tochan composes a *haiku*.

Nagaki hi o
Tsukarete tsuma ko
Iru iye ji

A long day of toiling
An exhausting home-bound trail
For my wife and children

Old sweaters and jackets slung over their shoulders, carrying hoes and water jug and leftover snacks, a tired family, this time without Mama, trudges back to their cabin.

It is almost like home again. Everybody waits for grace. Tochan thanks *Kamisama* for the good day and then asks Him to watch over Seiji in Europe, fighting with the 442nd Regimental Combat Team, the segregated *Nisei* fighting unit. He also asks God to watch over Sanji, attending Hillsdale High School in Michigan. Amen.

Mama serves from the big skillet on the stove and I fill the rice bowls. There is *koko* of *nappa* cabbage and *daikon* on the table again.

Beet harvesting is done. Mama gets well. Tochan busies himself around the house while the children play.

"Naoshi!" Tochan calls, as he finishes scrubbing the inside of the *ofuro* bathtub the second time, and rinses it clean. It is midmorning.

"Yes?" Naoshi answers. "I want you to start the *ofuro* fire."

"Now? It's early. It's not four o'clock yet."

"We are going to make *miso*."

"*Miso?* In the bathtub?" Unbelieving, he stands with one foot on the battered can, with which he was playing kick-the-can with his sisters.

Mama says *misoshiru* keeps the children healthy. In California one can buy *miso*. Every Japanese family uses *miso*. Denver is the closest town where Japanese foodstuffs are available, but that's over fifty miles away.

"Around here cows get better food than people," Tochan says, as the children gather to help Naoshi start the fire under the *ofuro* tub. They listen expectantly, as Tochan always has something interesting to say.

"Soybeans are only used for cattle feed here in Colorado. In Japan, people have been eating soybeans for centuries. You see how it makes cows grow fat and healthy and give lots of milk? Soybean is the milk of Japan. It is more nutritious than milk because it is made from a vegetable.

Babies drink *misoshiru*. Children eat boiled green soybean pods for snacks. Everybody likes *tofu* made from soybeans. Lots of food is made from soybeans, even desserts."

"Desserts? Like what, Tochan?"

"Remember *manju*?"

It's been a long time since we've seen a *manju*. Masashi doesn't even know about the sweet round pastry eaten on special occasions, having been only three years old when we had to leave home.

"Does this mean we are going to eat what cows eat?" Kazu asks, perplexed. She often makes the *misoshiru*. It doesn't seem right to her to make it with cow food, but she has seen Tochan return from the feed store with a sack as large as a hundred-pound rice bag, filled with dried soybeans. She thinks it is what Mike Ewerts has in their barn where she has watched him milk the cows.

"Help fill the tub," Tochan tells the children. They move the wooden trough, which carries water to the kitchen, and redirect the water from the holding tank under the windmill to the *furo* tub.

Tochan slashes the top of the sack and dumps its contents into a large washtub. He rinses the soybeans, picking out the culls. Then with the help of Aizo, he lifts the washtub and places it inside the *ofuro*, now steaming with ten inches of hot water. From time to time, the children gather around the edges, lift the wooden cover and peer inside the tub with curiosity.

"Keep the fire going!" Tochan reminds them. They scamper down and poke branches and scrap wood into the fire below.

While the soybeans cook, Tochan scrubs his green rubber work boots with a *tawashi* brush and soap until there is not a sign of mud on the bottom treads.

"Kazu, will you wash Mama's boots?" Twelve-year-old Kazu wonders why. Tochan never cleans his or Mama's boots. Their boots have always stood outside the kitchen door, covered with mud. Once in a while Mama scrubs them and rinses them off under the hand pump.

Since moving to Keenesburg, Colorado, to live in this small worker's cabin, the children have helped cut trees and build their bunk beds. They have watched Tochan build a bathhouse. While in camp, other children knew that they could cool off in our room, leaning against the wet canvas

Tochan had hung from the rafters. He had cut a door for Masashi's very own use in the back side of the barrack room. All this he accomplished with the tools he had smuggled inside our bedrolls.

And now what is Tochan going to do?

After many hours of cooking, a cloud of steam pours out of the tub as Tochan lifts the lid. He picks out a bean and squashes it between his thumb and forefinger to test its doneness. Satisfied, he leaves the tub open to cool the beans.

With the handle of a hoe, he stirs the beans to aid in the cooling.

"Give me a hand here, Aizo." They lift the washtub out onto the cement floor to cool, stirring the beans occasionally.

He puts on his clean boots and steps into the washtub.

"Look what Tochan's doing!" Masashi exclaims. The children gather around fascinated as Tochan stomps on the cooked soybeans.

Aizo, tall and slim and almost as tall as his father at 16, puts on Tochan's boots. He stomps around the inside edge of the tub, enjoying the challenge of pulling his boots out of the gooey mass of the softening beans.

"Let me do it," Kozo asks after quietly observing everyone.

There is barely enough room for the four boots inside the tub. Clowning around, causing rapid, squishing sounds with each foot lift, Aizo loses his balance with both boots stuck to the bottom, much to the delight of the onlookers. Like dancing partners, the brothers hold on to each other by the shoulders, stomping the beans into a mush.

Tochan returns from the kitchen with a sack of salt and sugar and *koji*, fermented rice with which to seed the *miso*. *Koji*, not unlike yeast, is treasured and shared. It is survival food for Japanese immigrants.

Tochan finishes alone, carefully stepping on any uncrushed beans until it is a smooth paste. He adds the ingredients and vigorously stirs them with his arms. He covers the tub with a clean cloth and sets it aside to ripen.

<hr />

"Lunchtime! Wash your hands!"

From all corners of the yard, the children gather at the outside faucet, barely soaping their hands, as the water is ice cold.

In the crowded kitchen, the table only a foot away from the big, black stove, Mama serves bowls of hot *misoshiru* with thin half moon slices of turnips. Heated canned sardines in tomato sauce, rice, pickled cabbage, hot green tea and hot cocoa complete the meal.

Crunchy bits of uncrushed soybeans remain at the bottom of the bowls, unlike the store-bought *miso*, which is smooth.

Tochan holds his warm teacup against his cheek and closes his eyes. Masashi looks at his father intently and quizzically, holds his cocoa cup with both hands and presses it gently to his cheek.

When the old yellow school bus stops to pick up Mike Ewerts a half a mile down the road, the four Sato children, neat and pressed, lunch bags in hand, rush out from the back door of the little cabin and wait along the roadside. It is a long, slow and bumpy ride to Prospect Valley School.

At lunchtime, Naoshi joins his classmates for baseball.

Naoshi, at bat, takes his stance and swings several times to get the feel.

The pitch is too high. The pitcher has trouble changing from the tall batters.

"Ball one!"

Knees bent, his torso on a slant and bat extended, he swings with all the might in his body, sends a fast grounder to right field. He drops his bat and runs speedily to first base.

"Go! Go!" his teammates yell.

He flies around first base and without slowing, heads for second when he hears coming from left field, "Hey, you Jap!"

Like a snapped rubber band, he whirls around and runs full force into the player's body, knocking him down to the ground. The game stops, with everyone zeroing in on the two boys. With all the strength of every fiber in his little body, Naoshi pummels the boy with the fury of a tornado. He knows that Jap is a bad word.

The two tumble and hit each other until a teacher lifts Naoshi, kicking and flailing his arms.

"What goes on here?" the teacher demands.

"He called me a Jap!" Naoshi yells.

"I did not!" the boy counters.

"Both of you. Let's go tell that to the principal." He leads them to the office.

The two boys sit quietly on the bench in the office for a long time. Others come and go but the two are not called in to see the principal.

The bell rings.

The principal appears. "You may go back to your classrooms," he tells the boys.

Naoshi and Johnny exchange puzzled glances. They get up and return to their classrooms.

The bell rings for dismissal

Naoshi rushes to the waiting school bus and sits beside his brother.

His cousin, sitting in front, turns around and points a finger at him.

"You bad boy," she says, emphasizing each word with her finger. "You got sent to the principal!"

Having forgotten what had transpired earlier, Naoshi finds it difficult to understand what she is saying.

"You got sent to the principal's office?" Kozo asks.

"Yeah."

"What happened?"

"Johnny called me a Jap so I hit him."

Kozo tousles his little brother's hair and smiles.

A strange car parks by our cabin. From the distance I can see that the driver is wearing an overcoat and a hat. Under my breath I tell myself, "Not again!"

They seem to be everywhere, the agents. Back home in Sacramento, in Hillsdale, Michigan and now even in this isolated sugar beet farm in Keenesburg, Colorado.

He steps carefully over the rough terrain of dirt and beet tops. He approaches Tochan who, as always, extends his hand when he greets anyone. The stranger does the same. Unlike the cold and unsmiling stance of the FBI agents, this man appears relaxed and friendly. I strain to hear what they are saying.

"You are Mr. Sato?"

How did he know Tochan's name, I wonder?

They talk for a long while about churches, mainly. Dr. Foote has something to do with the area's Baptist churches. He invites the children to attend Sunday School in Brighton. I don't hear him say anything about the parents.

"Pastor Duncan will be happy to see them," he tells Tochan.

When Dr. Foote leaves, Tochan is way behind in his row. We hop into his row to get him closer to us to listen to what he has to say.

On Sunday morning, crisp and combed, Aizo and Kozo ride with Tochan in the dust-covered '36 Chevrolet. They pick up their two cousins, Osami and Satoru along the way to the Brighton Baptist Church.

In the churchyard, boys and girls in their Sunday clothes play and mingle. As soon as the boys alight from the car, all activity ceases and heads turn in one direction, like seagulls facing the sun. Pastor Duncan hurriedly approaches the boys and welcomes them warmly. Eyes follow them silently as the pastor directs them inside the church door.

Just before the hour, Tochan returns and waits. The children pour out of the front door of the church, tow-haired children now mixed with a sprinkling of black, jostling and talking.

"We would like to invite your boys to become members of our church," Pastor Duncan tells Tochan.

"Thank you. That will be fine," Tochan answers. Both Mama and Tochan are members of the Mayhew Baptist Church, which now houses evacuee belongings and they welcome the opportunity for the children to have a Sunday School to attend.

"I will let you know when the baptismal service will be," he says. They shake hands.

A month passes.

Reverend Duncan approaches Tochan as he waits for the children after Sunday School.

"Mr. Sato, can you bring the boys to church next Sunday afternoon?"

"I will be glad to. Is there to be a special program?"

"I will baptize the boys in a private session. It saddens me deeply to tell you that the congregation voted against Aizo and Kozo and their two cousins becoming members of our church."

Tochan is not surprised.

"I will be here next Sunday afternoon," he tells Pastor Duncan and thanks him. They shake hands.

He knows that this decision did not come easily for the pastor, that he had had to face the ire of his flock and still do what he thought was right in the eyes of God.

Months pass.

News reaches us that Pastor Duncan is no longer with the Brighton Baptist Church. He was fired.

"Military necessity? What do they mean 'military necessity?'" I exclaim, thumbing through Aizo's high school homework.

It states that it was a military necessity to evacuate the Japanese from the west coast after the attack on Pearl Harbor. I am incensed! How can they claim that we were a military threat? Seiji volunteered for the United States Army. So did his buddy Makoto. There's Kengo Abe, our neighbor, Susumu Satow, my cousin, and so many of our sons and brothers who volunteered to fight for our country, trying so hard to prove our loyalty.

What more can they do than to lay down their lives?

Holding the full *omaru* chamber pot with both hands, each morning Mama carefully walks out backwards, pushing the screen door. Its warm contents vaporize from the sides of the lid as she walks in the narrow, shoveled pathway to the outhouse. She empties the *omaru*, then walks to the hand pump under the windmill, rinses the chamber pot in the freezing water, leaves it to drain, and returns to the warm kitchen.

The school bus has not come for over a week. We are snowbound. Deep, sparkly white snow covers what is underneath, thousands of dead sugar beet tops, cut off one by one. Ridges of snow mark the furrows where the horse had pulled the sled of beets.

Inside the cabin, laundry hangs from clotheslines strung in every room. Nothing dries outside. We dodge overalls, underwear, sheets and socks.

No eggs, no green vegetables, no fresh fruits.

Mama misses the abundance of fruits and vegetables she had in her garden at home at all times of the year.

But Mama cooks big pots of nutritious stew. Then there's *misoshiru* every day, with dried *wakame* seaweed or Japanese *sato-imo* potatoes from the garden.

Outside the cabin, Tochan buries carrots, turnips and *daikon*, which we dig up when necessary. Mama keeps on hand canned corned beef, sardines, Spam and all sorts of protein for quick emergencies. She never runs out of food. And there's always peanut butter and jam.

Mama says. "Growing bodies need healthy food."

"Mama, can we have popped rice?" Tomoko asks.

"If there's enough dried rice," Mama says.

Tomoko steps up on the bench. She stretches her neck to check the cookie sheet on the top ledge of the stove where leftover rice is drying. Then she checks the coffee can.

"It's full, Mama," Tomoko reports. Dried rice collects faster now that Molly and Dicky aren't around to eat all the leftovers.

Mama pours Wesson oil into the large skillet in which she cooks *tempura*. Little bodies crowd around and watch with anticipation.

"Can I test it?" Kazu asks.

"Drop just one grain," Mama advises.

It stays at the bottom of the pan, not moving.

"Not yet."

"My turn."

"It's getting hot."

"Wait."

"Your turn, Masashi."

The rice hits the oil and in seconds puffs into triple its size, like a tiny, white popcorn.

"It's ready, Mama!" they shout.

The large mixing bowl fills up as Mama places a handful of dried rice into the hot oil and quickly scoops the grains up with a large, flat, mesh ladle. She sprinkles salt in the bowl. The children watch mesmerized as she deftly tosses the contents in the air with every kernel falling right back into the bowl. Only Mama can do that without spilling.

Little hands eagerly reach into the bowl.

"Something smells good!" says Aizo, as he and Kozo come in from playing in the snow in the back yard.

"Popped rice!" Aizo exclaims. "Did you leave some for us?"

Tochan returns, driving backwards down the road. He has dug only a half a mile, a shovelful at a time, towards Prospect Valley School, still many miles away.

"We'll just have to wait for the snow plow, Mama," Tochan says.

"Yaaay!" Masashi yells, glad to have his brothers and sisters at home.

Happily marooned in the small cabin, children eat popped rice, drink hot Ovaltine and listen to Tochan's stories.

There was a man named Job who lived in a faraway land called Uz. He was a good man who did everything right. He worked hard. Each morning, he looked up at the sky and said:

"Thank you, God, for the dawn

Thank you, God, for the birds

Thank you, God, for my children

Thank you, God, for the trees and flowers."

He thanked Him, also, for his 6,000 sheep, 3,000 camels, 1,000 cows and 500 donkeys.

"What are camels, Tochan?"

"They are animals that live in the hot, desert countries. They have a hump and sometimes two humps, four long legs and a long neck. They can go without water for many days.

"How come he had 3,000 camels?" Kozo asks.

"I suppose one or two would be enough," Tochan answers. "For having so many animals, he was known as the richest man in his country. Some people accused him of stealing from the poor.

One day the Devil said to God, "If Job did not have all his riches, he will not think you are a good God. I will prove it to you."

"What's a devil?" Kazu asks.

"He is a symbol of all the bad things on this earth."

With his evil hand, the Devil zapped all the sheep and killed them.

A servant came running to Job.

"Master! Master! A big lightning came down and killed all our 6,000 sheep! I am the only one alive to tell you!"

Job was terribly saddened, but he told his servant, you are alive and that is good.

No sooner had he said so than another servant came crying down another field.

"Our 3,000 camels are dead! And I am the only one alive to tell you!"

"O, no!" lamented Job wringing his hands. But you are alive, he said.

"We have yet our 1,000 cows and 500 donkeys," Job told his distraught servant. "That will be enough for us."

No sooner had he said so than his third servant came running down weeping.

"Master! Master! All our cows and donkeys are gone! And I am the only one left to tell you!"

Job sat down on a rock and grieved, holding his head in his hands.

"Why, God? Haven't I been a good man? I have lost everything. Why, God, are you doing this to me," he wailed.

A maidservant came running hardly able to talk.

"Your seven sons and three daughters are dead. A storm came in from the desert and swept them all away.

"God, what have I done to deserve this? Haven't I obeyed all your laws?"

To lose all his children was more than Job could bear. "Why? Why?" he cried.

When there was nothing more left in Job's life, painful sores appeared over his body. Every day more sores appeared. Nothing relieved his pain. He scraped the sores but more appeared. His skin hung loose on his body. His friends avoided him. Children ran away from him. Job has displeased God, they said.

"I used to be like a tree, with plenty of water for my roots and dew upon my leaves. Why this now?" he implored.

Alone, he had much time to think.

No one in this land of Uz had 6,000 sheep or even 500 donkeys. To have one donkey is sufficient. There are many people who have none. To have good health is enough and to be able to work.

Soon his sores disappeared.

"It is not enough to be just a rich, good man," he said.

He thanked God for the new dawn.

He thanked God for the birds and the trees.

He thanked God for those who worked with him.

Soon more children came to him and his wife.

Soon, one by one, through hard work, he acquired camels, sheep, cows and donkeys for his family and each of his children.

"I am now a wiser and a happier man," Job said.

And God blessed him.

"Tochan, what happened to the Devil?"

"The Devil likes to be where there are bad things happening, where people fight, where there are wars, where they are not kind to each other. Then the Devil likes to come in and create more trouble."

Listening to Tochan tell stories, I marvel at his ability to hold our attention, from Masashi, six-years-old, to me, fifteen years older.

⸺

Lying in bed, I strain to hear the serious discussion coming from the kitchen.

"We don't have enough money to move," Tochan says.

"Seiji will be discharged soon. I want him to be able to come home to home," Mama implores. After three years of fighting with the 442nd Regimental Combat Team in Europe, and with the war's end, she wants more than anything else that Seiji will be able to return to the family farm and that we will all be together again.

"If our crop hadn't been hit with hailstorms, we might have been able to move."

"If we can just get to Sacramento," Mama says, "we can find jobs on the farms, and we can grow our own vegetables."

"One more year and we will have enough to start again," Tochan says. "We don't know what's still left on the farm."

Mama does not budge. She wants to go home. For three and a half years, she has protected her eight children with her whole being. Buffeted from place to place, she saw that the children were properly clothed, forever mending in camp, when all we had was what we could carry. When it seemed impossible, she saw that her children were nourished. Wherever we went, she carried a *furoshiki* of food.

I lie in bed in the next room, feeling sad, listening to Mama and Tochan argue for the first time in their lives.

They argue way into the night.

Wiping my tears on my sheet, I fall asleep,

"Yaay! We can go home! Yay!!" Masashi yells, emerging from the bedroom to the kitchen for breakfast.

"Who said?" I ask warming up by the stove.

"I heard Mama and Tochan talking about it last night."

· 13 ·

Home Again:
the Bittersweet Journey

Kubi tare te

Tada mokushi ori

Fuji no hana

        –JOHN SHINJI SATO

Head drooping,

Uttering not a word,

The wisteria blossom

        – TRUDY SATO, TRANSLATION

JANUARY 14, 1945.

ALONE IN THE coach, heading westward, my white permission papers in my purse, I look out the window, wondering what is in store at the other end. Why do I need this permit, I ask myself, when the west coast ban has been lifted? Don't they trust us, even after all these years? My permission paper isn't yellow, for which I'm glad. That would mean I am on the suspect list and require further investigation. If my name had been on the gray or black lists, I wouldn't be allowed to return home.

Even after almost four years, memories are raw. Like an apparition, I can see the soldiers with bayonets standing guard at both ends of my coach. As clear as yesterday, I remember thinking, what will I do if I have to go to the toilet? How do I get past the guards? The worrisome thought occurs to me that this train is so old maybe there are no toilets.

The dull winter gray blends with the barren brown landscape of January in Colorado. Small pockets of snow remain, protected along the sides of the railroad tracks.

The terrible argument Mama and Tochan had the night after the lifting of the west coast ban still rings in my head. It had always seemed that my father had made right decisions and Mama had supported him. This time she was adamant. She wants to go home because Seiji will be returning from the war.

Am I doing the right thing going home? Is it safe? Should we have waited? Will our house still be there? The news of vandalism scares me, of our houses being burned and dynamited, of internees unable to cope and returning back east. Although I am finally going home, my heart is heavy and my head is filled with worries. What will I do if our house is gone? I am numbly aware of the passing telephone poles and the clickety-clack of the wheels on the tracks.

My train heads straight west into what was the "restricted zone" from where we were evicted. Terrible thoughts keep crowding into my brain. At least, we have a safe place now on the sugar beet farm. Are we better off staying in Colorado?

How will I get from the railroad station on Fifth Street to our farm? It's fifteen miles and I've always driven that stretch. I hope my Studebaker is waiting for me in our garage, but will it start after all these years? If not, I'll try the old Model T.

If nothing works, I'll walk the railroad tracks to the Mills Station Grocery Store. It will be good to see Mr. Studarus and Helen. They will be nice to me.

Remember to pick up some matches. But suppose the stove doesn't have any gas? The butane tanks will probably be empty after all this time. Better stick with bread and peanut butter and maybe a can of sardines. There might still be some of that stuff on the shelf. We left so much canned food: abalone, sardines, corned beef, salmon. I wonder if those hundred pound sacks of rice will still be there in the boys' bedroom? By now they're probably infested with worms or have been eaten by mice, or maybe somebody took them. Who would want six hundred pounds of rice?

Will there be forks and spoons and chopsticks? A can opener? A knife?

I wonder if the wild spinach is starting to grow in the walnut orchard. I will pick them for our supper. Wash them. Blanch them. Grind some sesame seeds and mix them with soy sauce and pour it over the squeezed spinach. There should still be some soy sauce left in the gallon can. Sesame seeds? Oh, well.

Will there be water? It's been almost four years! If there is no water, then what will I do? I won't be able to cook. I won't be able to clean the house. I won't be able to wash up. And I need a bath badly after two days on this sooty train.

My mind wanders and my plans don't gel. There are too many unknowns. I have only questions. And the more I think about things, the worse they seem to get. I wish desperately that Tochan were with me. He would know exactly what to do. I swallow a lump of loneliness and finally succumb to sleep, with gratitude.

I awaken as the train slowly climbs the wintry, dreary side of the Sierra Nevada mountains. We finally hit the summit and descend into California. I want to yell to the whole world, "I am home!"

Green grass covers the meadows surrounded by pine trees. Will the *ume*, the Japanese flowering plum tree in our front yard, be in bloom? It usually blooms in January, the first to herald the promise of spring. Then it's the Chinese flowering quince in the corner of our yard and Mama's daffodils everywhere. Soon the whole vineyard will be a mass of yellow with wild mustard flowers.

I shall pick the mustard greens, like Mama did every spring, and cook up a feast for the family along with *tempura* of carrots and broccoli and prawns and sweet potatoes! I will plan a welcome home party. The aroma will fill our kitchen and there will be happy chatter and story times after supper again.

I should first check in with Bill and find out the status of the farm. But something tells me maybe I shouldn't. Why did the power bills come to my father in Poston Camp II when Bill was supposed to be taking care of things? The electricity is probably cut off, which means I will have to call the Pacific Gas & Electric Company from Mills Station. That's the first thing I'll have to do. No electricity, no water, no cooking, no nothing.

At least I'll have a roof over my head. If it's cold, I can sleep in my clothes and my jacket and cover up with my Poston-Government-Issue green wool blanket.

Will Molly and Dicky come running down the road wagging their tails? Has some kind person fed them and cared for them? Dear God, I mouth, and cross my fingers, please let them be there.

I wonder if our neighbor's dog, Nuisance, is still around. I remember he had a nice doghouse by the front door, but he preferred to sleep in their old barn.

The Yamasakis lost everything and won't be coming back. Their twenty acres of grapes and strawberries and all the farm equipment had to be left.

With one stroke of our President's pen, all their hopes and dreams were wiped out.

Only a few years older than I am, Myso, the oldest, got a release from Poston Camp II to go to Chicago to find a job and a place to live for his parents and siblings. I think of him often, riding that train with a one-way ticket, twenty-five dollars in his pocket from the government, forced to travel even farther away from home, to find a job and a place for his family to live.

How sweet their Muscat grapes were! We would sneak under the fence and steal a bunch. Mama found out and begged Tochan to plant some Muscats so the children would not steal. Tochan liked to grow the succulent, dark purple Ribier table grapes, so it was only when some of his Ribier vines died that he replaced them with the sweet, yellow Muscats. In the acres of Ribiers, we would go searching for the Muscats in the late summer.

The Kitadas aren't coming back, nor the Toguchis or the Oganekus. It is a frightening thought that bankers and realtors and thieves got rich with the blessings of our government after it stripped us down to only what we could carry.

It's hard to believe that my essay in high school on "What America Means to Me" placed in the finals. Do I have any guarantee that I will not lose my birthright again? If our *hakujin* neighbors don't want us back, will we have to move inland?

Mrs. Kitada wants me to check their belongings stored in our Mayhew Church. The small church is filled up to the rafters with the furniture, stoves and pianos of four or five families. How do I crate all that stuff and ship it to them? I don't have the money, nor do they.

Immersed in unsolvable problems, I am suddenly brought back to reality by a change in rhythm of the wheels underneath. The train descends into the valley.

I am almost home.

As we roll into familiar territory, my heart beats faster with apprehension. What am I going to do? How am I going to get to the farm? I am hungry. Where am I going to eat? The train slows to a crawl and I am not ready for it to stop. Please, please, I need more time to think.

The smell of smoke from the coal-burning engine permeates my clothes and hair. I feel so dirty. How good it will be to get home and take a bath.

The train stops.

I walk across the tracks to the station and find the baggage room. A surly, middle-aged man places my suitcase on the counter, plants his elbows firmly on top and glares. I cringe inwardly but put on a brave front and smile. It comes easier now that I've done it so many times.

"Write your name and address," he demands, shoving a small piece of soiled paper towards me. I look for my pencil in my purse and write down the address of my family in Keenesburg, Colorado. He quickly takes the paper, turns around and leaves. I stretch across the counter, grab my suitcase and get out of the station as fast as I can. I am sure that he is on the phone calling the authorities, and I want to get lost in the crowd before they arrive.

Mercifully, the main street is only a few blocks away. What a relief it is to turn off from the less-traveled side street, where I stand out like a sore thumb, and onto K Street, where people are going in all directions. I hurry into the center of the crowd. For a fleeting second, I take a deep, appreciative breath, feeling safe, but I know I've got to move on.

Having consumed the last of my packed food on the train, my stomach is growling. Before catching the bus home, I decide I'd better eat. There's fifteen miles to go by bus and more miles of walking through farms. I want to get home before dark.

Walking eastward, I check each eating place. For what, I am not sure. Will they serve me? Will they be friendly? Will they at least ignore me and accept my money? The further uptown I walk, it becomes more obviously white; I know that my chances are not so good. I turn back towards the lower end of town. To avoid being conspicuous, I walk down the center of the sidewalk and try to hide my suitcase.

All kinds of people walk in and out of Hart's Cafeteria between Fourth and Fifth streets. I take my chances, noticing Chinese customers along with dark-skinned people entering. Some look scruffy. I take a deep breath, straighten myself and walk in. The line seems interminable. Finally, I get my plate of meatloaf, mashed potatoes and overcooked green beans and sit in the far corner, being careful to place my suitcase out of view. Much to my relief, everybody seems too busy to notice me.

Back onto K Street, with food in my stomach, things look better. Do I take Folsom Boulevard or Jackson Road? I am afraid to ask. Frustrated and desperate, I think of Mr. John Beskeen from the Mills Station Grocery Store, who had written to me in Poston. I walk uptown and find a phone booth.

"Where are you?" he asks. He sounds genuinely happy to hear from me.

"I'm in Sacramento. I just came in by train from Colorado."

"Do you need a ride home?" he asks kindly.

"I hate to impose, but I have no idea how to get there by bus."

"I'll come and pick you up. Where are you exactly?"

I tell him I will stand in front of Hart's Cafeteria.

As soon as I hang up the phone, all my brave defenses melt away and I want to sit down and cry. It is so good to know that there is someone who will risk being seen with me.

It seems like ages that I stand at the edge of the sidewalk, feeling very self-conscious, carrying my baggage like an immigrant.

What a welcome sight to see Mr. Beskeen's drab green Model A coupe. He opens the door from the inside and I quickly hop in and close the door. I am suddenly overcome with a tremendous sense of relief, feeling at last that I am safe. Mr. Beskeen smiles. I thank him.

He tells me that he no longer works at the Mills Station Grocery Store. John Studarus and his daughter Helen are still there, he says.

Glued to the window, I can't seem to take in the changes in my hometown fast enough. The bare winter branches of the giant trees along Capitol Avenue stand in elegant rows as always. I used to drive along Folsom Boulevard every day to Sacramento High School. This is my home. I try not to let my tears fall and keep looking out of the window on my side of the car. Mr. Beskeen looks straight ahead and says nothing.

In the town of Perkins, Mr. Beskeen takes a right onto Jackson Road. I would have gone straight east on Folsom Boulevard, but I say nothing. He must have his reasons, I presume. This is probably the bus route I would have taken. Six miles further east at Walsh Station, he takes a left on Bradshaw Road.

The Machida farm on the right side of the road looks fallow. So does the Ogawa's twenty-acre farm. Only dried up and weedy ditches remain of the once-vigorous, green strawberry fields. The Iwasa and Kobata farms look totally neglected. Down the long dirt road in the back are the Deguchi and Kawamura farms. I think it was in 1929 that the families bought one hundred and eighty acres and split them into four parcels, tilling the marginal soils, and becoming part of the top producers of the sweet and juicy Oregon Plum variety of strawberries, which were shipped out by freight car loads from Florin.

We pass Middle Jackson Road and with a start I notice that our church building is not there. I look again and all I see from the distance is a wisp of smoke rising from the ground where the church once stood. There is no sign of a wooden building having been there nor furniture or appliances ever having been stored in it. Across the road, the Kobata's farmhouse and water tower stand intact.

I don't want to even mention it to my friend, but because he had been so kind, I tell him, "Our church is gone."

He acknowledges it with a slight nod, doesn't say a word and drives on. He turns right on Old Placerville Road.

From Old Placerville Road, he turns left onto Routier Road. Mr. Beskeen maneuvers around the potholes. We used to kick the ice out of them on our way to school. Another mile and I will be home.

The rusty, barbed wire fence along the road sags. Not a shred of the huge, government posters remain. I cringe, even now, remembering the big print declaring INSTRUCTIONS TO ALL PERSONS OF JAPANESE ANCESTRY, ordering us to evacuate the area in ten days. This will all be over in time, Tochan had said almost four years ago. It doesn't seem possible that now after all these years, we are finally able to return.

My heart skips with joy, as we turn right at our mailbox onto our farm road. There is something warm and comforting about the brown dirt with its old familiar ruts. The road is damp, as if it had rained recently. No wet tracks lead out of the low muddy areas, indicating that no car or truck has been going in or out recently.

How well I know this low spot where our Model T truck would often get stuck. Gray, weathered and splintered odd shaped boards still lie on the north side of the road where they had been thrown, to be used for the next time we got stuck. How well I remember all of us pushing the truck after Tochan placed the old slabs of lumber under the wheels.

"*Ichi, ni, san*, push!" One, two, three, push!

Being the oldest to drive, Tochan delegates the wheel to me. I can still feel the exhilaration of steering the truck at full speed straight out of the mud onto dry land.

Mr. Beskeen skillfully maneuvers down the road, straddling the ruts. Four more power poles and I will be home! The barren branches of the walnut trees look thinner and scraggly. Suckers growing wild at the base of the trees hide the trunks. I can't believe it! I look again. There is a cow in the orchard looking my way. Where did it come from? With its head held up, immobile, it looks just as surprised as I am.

The water tank still stands at the end of the road. The scrubby fig trees grow wild around and over the small shed housing the irrigation pump. The large pipe and the cement tank into which the water flows are almost hidden by overgrown weeds. Mr. Beskeen turns the corner and stops in front of the old barn.

The sliding door of the barn barely hangs on a rusty hinge, with the lower corner embedded in the weeds and dirt. The protective roof, extending on the north side of the garage, no longer houses the Fordson tractor. My 1932 Studebaker is nowhere in sight. Our Model T truck, which usually went into the barn to be loaded for the following day's work, is gone. The Iwasa's big truck, which transported our bedrolls and suitcases to the evacuation point, probably never returned to our farm. Empty oil cans and automobile parts lie scattered in the overgrown weeds.

Mr. Beskeen gets out of his car and looks around. I walk down the road towards the house. Memories return of our nightly walks down this road to our hot *ofuro* bath under the water tower. At the edge of the yard, a single half-opened pink rose, stopped in its tracks by winter, tells me that the bush is still alive. It is badly in need of pruning and care. Here and there the fragrant Chinese lilies, which Mama planted everywhere, show white buds.

The Santa Rosa plum tree by the roadside looks dead. Apparently, no one has watered it. I test a branch. It is dry and brittle. The peach tree appears as if it has been dead for several years, probably from lack of water. In the back of the barn, a few seedling oranges remain at the tops of the trees. I hunger to bite into one. My mouth waters, just thinking about its sourness and fragrance.

In my silent walk down the path, I realize with a thud of sadness that Molly and Dicky have not come to greet me. They would have been here even before I stepped out of the car. Perhaps, I tell myself, they are gallivanting around and will be home later.

As I approach the house, I see from the dirt path that a large, rusty tin sheet covers my east bedroom window. I realize with a shudder that I am seeing straight through a vacant view, the view where our giant pine tree once towered elegantly, high above our house. I can't believe what I am *not* seeing. Every Christmas, Tochan would hang a red light at the top until he could no longer reach that high even with our tallest ladder. How could that tree have disappeared?

In the front yard, not a remnant remains of Mama's beautiful garden of flowers. Strewn everywhere are empty bottles and cans, parts of old cars, piles of newspapers, boxes, broken toys, an iron bed, most of these items embedded in the dead weeds.

The hardy wisteria vines, trunks gnarled, spread over the debris like unruly, tangled, long thin snakes. This will be one of my jobs, I remind myself. I will clean up this mess before Mama comes home. Tochan's trusty *kama*, the small Japanese scythe, with which I can cut the vines, should be hanging somewhere.

A rusty tin sheet covers a front window. Two more windows are partially boarded with odd lengths of old lumber. I make a mental note of the jobs which have to be done right away. Pry off the sheet metal and slabs of wood and open up all the windows. Tochan's box-making tools should be in the barn.

I should clean out the *ofuro* tub before they get here. After standing unused and dry for so many years, it will probably not even hold water. A good soaking overnight will do the trick, maybe.

My heart thrills to see that the branches of the *ume-no-ki*, the Japanese flowering plum, have grown under the eaves and onto the porch. It is still alive. The buds, though small, show tiny tips of white. By the end of January they should bloom. Tochan would gaze at it for hours in the moonlight after he delivered the children to their beds, bathed and clean. I step over the broken pieces of furniture on the front porch to enter the house.

I pull open the screen door. The top half of the rusty screen flops over my arm. Just as I am about to turn the doorknob, voices come from within.

I am stunned. Standing frozen, I listen again to make sure. Children are squabbling inside. Stepping back, I close the screen door quietly to think. Should I leave?

This had not been an option—to have to knock on my own door. My family is depending on me and waiting in Colorado to come home. I summon my courage, straighten up and knock. The partially open doorway fills with many little tow-headed children.

"Mommy! Somebody's here!" one of them yells.

A thin, young woman with wisps of blond hair falling over her harried face appears at the door. I explain to her that my family is returning and that we would like to have them find another place to live. With a heavy heart, I turn and leave.

What now? We had not been notified that a family was living in our house. I could deal with anything, I thought, but this? All I wanted to do was to start cleaning right away and call my family home. That's all—for all of us to be home again.

Numb, I walk back towards the barn, barely aware of my surroundings. What am I going to do now?

That's it! What about the barn? We lived in it while our house was being built. Why can't I do it again?

I announce to Mr. Beskeen that there is a family living in our house. He looks at me as if he is at a complete loss. What can he do with a twenty-one-year-old girl without a place to sleep? I know he had kindly intended to just drive me home and leave me there.

I tell him my plans.

"I'll be okay," I tell him.

With renewed hope, I walk to the barn and look inside the door. Cow dung, hard and soft, covers the barn floor. The south wall, where I thought I could bed down, is almost knee deep with mud and manure. Three cows huddle in the far dark corner. There is not a clean surface in the whole barn where I can even set foot.

For the first time, I feel totally defeated. I have no money for a train ticket back to Colorado. I have no place to sleep tonight.

I muster all my strength to keep from crumbling. If Mr. Beskeen had put his arm around my shoulders, I would have broken down and cried.

I try desperately to think of someone who might guide me, maybe to a shelter. Miss Cox, who had been my elementary school teacher at Edward Kelley School! It is like yesterday that I see her waving goodbye to us at the railroad tracks. Maybe, just maybe, she will need a house girl to clean and cook.

Mr. Beskeen kindly drives me to a phone at the Mills Station Grocery Store, several miles away. I am so happy to see Mr. Studarus, who gives me a friendly glance as if I had been there all along.

I call Miss Cox and I tell her of my predicament.

"Come and stay here until you find a job," she says without hesitation.

It is a long drive back into town but Mr. Beskeen does not seem to mind. We ride silently, immersed in our own thoughts. I begin to seriously worry about what is in store for my family.

Sitting in the quiet of the night, shades pulled down behind the crisp, white lace curtains, I feel safe again. After supper and washing the dishes, Miss Cox and her sister, both teachers, retire to their own rooms to prepare the next day's lessons. Bits of light shine on the polished crystal collection in the immaculate dining room and into my open door.

One more hurdle and I will be in my own room, with the breeze wafting through my open windows, falling asleep to the symphony of the frogs down in the creek. I remember the tar-papered barrack room I shared with my brothers in the Pinedale Assembly Center. I remember the stifling heat of the Poston Concentration Camp II, where we slept outside our door. Then there was the cozy dormitory room in Hillsdale, Michigan, my couch bed when I candled eggs during summer vacation, a maid's quarters in a two-story mansion. I feel my shoulders relax, thinking of the tremendous sense of relief and happiness I had falling asleep on the bench Tochan had made out of dead locust trees at the sugar beet farm.

Now here . . . my last stop before home.

The doorbell rings. Miss Cox hurries to the door while tying the sash on her robe. There are mumbled sounds of more than one person. The door closes firmly.

Miss Cox switches on every light as she walks towards the kitchen. Sue Cox appears from her room.

"What was that all about?" she asks.

"I can't believe this!" Miss Cox answers, upset and angry. "They wanted me to sign a petition!"

"For what?"

"They want to keep this area restricted."

"What does that mean?" Sue Cox asks.

She explains that this section of East Sacramento organized a delegation to go door to door to ask residents to sign a petition to keep out anybody who is not Caucasian.

I decide not to wait for the family to move out of our farmhouse. My presence is causing too much trouble. Besides I feel obligated to the sisters, even though I try to be useful. I dare not think about what discussions the delegation had before a group volunteered to rid the area of its first Jap, me.

I check the ads for a live-in maid job. It is not as easy as I had thought, even to get a job cleaning house. It is almost a week later when I pack up my one suitcase and move into the maid's quarters of a house on 45th Street, the home of a doctor and his wife. It is a temporary job, I am told. They are waiting for their maid to return from the internment camp, which is fine with me, as all I want is a roof over my head and bus fare to the farm. They pay me forty dollars a month, which will help us get started again.

To ensure that my brother Aizo will have a happy enrollment in high school, I decide to let the principal know of our return.

After my cleaning chores are done, I walk to Sacramento High School, about fifteen blocks away. What a strange feeling to be on foot along the route I drove every day in my Studebaker. At Regina's large brick house, I turn left off Folsom Boulevard. The seven blocks to T Street never seemed so long by car.

Whenever a pedestrian comes my way, my body automatically stiffens and I prepare to nod and smile. Much to my relief, I soon find out that here in Sacramento hardly anyone stares.

T Street is my favorite street in the city. To the left, elegant elm trees form an arch over the street for blocks. I turn right and walk past huge estates. When the athletic field comes into view, I become anxious. My chest tightens. What will I tell the principal? Will he be kind and understanding? Will he keep an eye on my brother? If there are any hostilities, will he stand up for him? After four years of "no Japs" on campus, how will the students react?

With trepidation, I walk into the school office.

"What can I do for you?" the secretary behind the counter asks.

"I would like to see the principal," I reply.

"He is busy right now. Is there something I can help you with?"

"I will wait," I tell her.

She looks concerned and puzzled. The clerks look up from their desks and scrutinize me. I smile. Embarrassed, they quickly look away. There is a flurry of tension as the secretary walks towards the principal's office.

I sit on a bench against the wall, where students probably sit awaiting reprimand. Though my body is erect and my head is looking straight ahead, my heart is pounding as if I am about to make an important speech. After a long wait, the secretary motions to me.

"The principal will see you."

I walk behind the front counter to his office.

He is sitting at his desk and appears nervous and agitated.

"My name is Kiyo Sato," I introduce myself. "I used to be a student here. My family is coming home and my brother will be enrolling here." I tell him the purpose of my visit as if I had rehearsed it many times.

Without responding, he stands up, walks to the side of his desk and looks at me intently. He is tall. I stand straight and smile, remembering Mama and Tochan, who do it so graciously and naturally. I feel like a cat facing an opponent, not knowing what to expect.

To my total surprise, he asks me, "What are we going to do about this?"

I am lost for an answer. My brother is coming to school and that is that, and all I am asking for is his understanding. I feel as if he is wishing that this problem would simply go away.

"Would you speak to the student body?" he asks.

Me? What would I say? There were almost eight hundred students in my graduating class. How many students will I be facing? Wouldn't it stir up unnecessary feelings? Couldn't we just quietly go to classes?

"If you think it would help," I hear myself responding, "I will be glad to."

It is not the truth, of course. I dread having to talk at a school assembly in the first place, but not knowing what to say is the worst part. Do I tell them that we have finally been released, that we are free to return here, that we ask for their understanding?

Back at 45th Street, I find myself in my room, barely remembering my walk back. So engrossed was I, thinking about my conversation with the principal, that I didn't see the trees or hear the birds. After fifteen blocks I still didn't know what to say. There didn't seem to be any intelligent thing to tell the students. Instead of being one in a crowd of hundreds of students in the huge auditorium, I would be standing, alone, on the cavernous, empty stage. My legs feel weak just thinking about it.

I might tell them of my three-and-a-half-year journey of "wandering in the wilderness" and how it feels to be finally coming home.

After a quick toast and juice, I hurry upstairs to clean the bathroom. I want to get my job done quickly in order to check out our farm. At the kitchen table the lady of the house reads the paper over her cup of coffee. The good doctor is already gone.

The crisp, midmorning air quickens my steps along the two-block walk to the bus stop. On Folsom Boulevard, I catch the bus heading east. Through the bus window, my town does not look as it did driving my Studebaker. I feel like a visitor.

At Perkins, to my dismay, the bus turns onto Jackson Road, which means I may have a five-mile walk. I get off at Walsh Station and walk north on Bradshaw. After four years of neglect and rain, the beds and ditches of the strawberry fields are flattened. A few dried and scraggly plants remain, with roots exposed from erosion, their tips barely touching the earth for sustenance.

Having heard that the Kawamuras had returned from Poston Camp II, I decide to walk a mile down the dirt road to see them. Under the watchful eye of the Fairbairns, the houses and barns belonging to the Machidas,

Ogawas, Kawamuras and Deguchis stand intact. The burned Mayhew Baptist Church was only a half a mile away.

I find Mrs. Kawamura squatting in her front yard, cooking.

"*Yoh kite kureta.*" How good of you to come, she says with such gratitude.

She knows about our burned church.

"*Shikata ga nai ne,*" she says, a reassuring phrase I have heard over and over again, reminding oneself not to waste one's time wallowing in anger, but to go on, that this is just a curve in the journey of life.

Into what appears to be a five-gallon oil can cut out in front, she feeds twigs and grape brushes into the fire. On top sits a large soot-blackened pot. The boiling rice rattles the lid and dribbles white foam down the sides of the pot. The aroma of the steaming white rice reminds me of home. Squatting beside her as she feeds the fire, I listen to news about their neighbors.

The Deguchis will be home any day now, she tells me. They live across the road. She repeats over and over how good it is to be home. The Kawamuras, too, found nothing left but an empty house and shed. Windows had to be replaced.

"Stay and eat with us. The boys will be in for lunch soon," she tells me. "Come inside."

She allows the fire to die down and lets the embers continue to steam the rice.

In the barren kitchen, the long, unpainted, wooden homemade table is set with a mismatched collection of rice bowls, plates, teacups and chopsticks. A large pan of *okazu* with vegetables and hamburger meat already cooked sits in the center. Soy sauce and *koko* of pickled cabbage are already on the table. She tells me that her sons made the table and the two long benches.

James and Jack, both a few years older than I am, wash their sweaty faces and soiled hands at the outside faucet. Mrs. Kawamura brings in the pot of rice and loosens the grains with a moistened, bamboo spatula.

The boys barely acknowledge my presence. "Hi," they say matter of factly, and sit down. The younger children and Mr. Kawamura appear from somewhere and sit down quietly and eat, as Mrs. Kawamura serves each one a steaming bowl of rice.

"Sit down, sit down," she gently urges, handing me a bowl of rice. James slides the pan of *okazu* towards me. I help myself. Mrs. Kawamura finally sits down to eat.

I am so hungry that my politeness dissipates when I watch the family devour the food with gusto.

"Eat, eat," Mrs. Kawamura urges.

Nobody talks, unlike our family, where everybody talks. And as quickly as they appeared, the boys leave.

Although January is a bit late, they are preparing the ground for strawberry planting.

I help clear the table. Mrs. Kawamura chats happily while washing the dishes in a small basin of soapy cold water. I wipe them and place them on the end of the table for the next meal. Soon, I hope we will be doing the same.

"*Arigatoh gozaimashita*." Thank you so much, I tell her, grasping her hand with both of mine, and bid her goodbye.

"*Mata kite ne*." Please come again, she says, almost pleading, her small dark eyes piercing where words do not.

She takes her white, rice-sack cloth bonnet from the nail on the wall and heads for the fields to continue the planting.

From the Kawamura farm, I head north walking through a fallow field, and crawl through a barbed wire fence onto a dirt road. The Furuikes' water tower and farmhouse stand intact. On the opposite side of the road, the Sakumas' vineyard is overgrown with unpruned vines, curling upwards and then down, crawling in the dry tall weeds after years of neglect. By the side of the grove of tall eucalyptus trees, their tiny house and shed look dark, forlorn and abandoned, roofs and yard thickly carpeted with dry eucalyptus leaves and long shreds of brittle bark.

The strawberry fields, which belonged to the Toguchi, Oganeku, Matsumoto and Kitada families, lie dead and silent. They look as if they have reverted back to their original state, fallow and non-productive. Hopeless, quiet anger wells in my chest, knowing that most of our neighbors lost their properties and will not be coming back, all the years of hard work gone, under orders of our President. It doesn't seem possible that a few years ago our farms were vigorously producing and the area was known as the "Strawberry Capital of the World," shipping by freight car loads top quality strawberries to all parts of the country.

Shattered dreams lie mute on the eroded, barren rows.

With the closing of the ten concentration camps, what will our old neighbors, now without land, do? Where will they go? How will they support their families? Why couldn't they have been allowed to keep a part of their farms?

Another mile to go, and I will be home. I cross my fingers that the occupants have left and I can freely enter our house to stay there to start cleaning up for my family's return. I shall prepare a great homecoming!

Crawling under the fence and walking along the edges of the gravel pits, I take a shortcut towards the barn. The abandoned pits are no longer deep and threatening. Giant, ugly holes replace the hillside where we used to hunt for mushrooms, empty lard buckets in hand, bundled up for the cold and foggy mornings. In the spring, golden California poppies would carpet the slopes a brilliant yellow-orange. Spots of tall bluebells bloomed on the lower slopes and Indian Paint Brushes turned the flat areas into mixed shades of red and green. The four-mile walk passes by, filled with memories.

A half a mile through the property of the Teichert Gravel Company brings me to the south edge of our twenty acres, of which only ten acres now belong to us. Someone now owns the orange grove and the walnut and almond orchard east of the barn and adjacent to the railroad tracks. "If you don't sell, it will be seized for wartime use," a realtor had written Tochan while we were incarcerated in Poston. I hear later that it was sold to the Teichert Gravel Company.

Apparently plans for expansion didn't pan out. The trees that Tochan planted and nurtured still stand.

I feel like an explorer, surveying our farm from higher ground. To my left, the boysenberry vines grow wild in every direction, not having been pruned or trained to grow along the wires stretched along the posts. The posts no longer stand upright, having succumbed to the winter rains and eroding soil. The vines should be trained along the horizontal wires now. Otherwise it will be too late for the next harvest.

The only signs left of a strawberry field once being here are the straight, shallow rows of undulations, which were once deep ditches. A few plants remain among the weeds. Fuzzy green grass grows on the road separating the fields. The ruts left by our old Model T farm truck remind me of the time I drove a hundred empty crates to the pickers and stepped on the wrong pedals, ending up with all four wheels in the ditches, with boxes scattering everywhere! I remember holding onto the steering wheel with total embarrassment when Bautista, Valentino, Juan and Ceriaco, the pickers, came running from their rows and lifted the truck back onto the road.

The carpet of winter grass feels soft and comfortable under my feet. The crisp January air enfolds me like it always had done.

This is my earth. I am home.

From the distance, I see several children playing in the front yard and my heart sinks. This changes all my plans for moving in and preparing for my family's return. Should I talk to them again? My better sense tells me that I had better leave well enough alone. With our church and many houses in our area already burned down, I had better keep quiet.

I quickly walk to the back of the barn. The children do not see me. I cut across the road through Mrs. Abe's strawberry field and hurry into their almond orchard, hoping that no one sees me.

Walking deeper into the orchard, I feel protected by the old tree trunks standing like sentinels around me. When we were growing up, I remember the aura of mystery about the large barn and house hidden in the orchard. At the end of the day Mrs. Abe walked into the almond orchard and disappeared. Sometimes she had candies for us. Often her plaintive Japanese songs wafted our way with the breeze as she tended to her strawberry plants.

It looks like someone is living in Abe-san's farmhouse. A shiny, dark sedan is parked on the south side. I don't want to face any hostility. I decide to cut straight through the orchard towards Routier Road.

Mrs. Abe's crudely built lean-to for shading the crates of strawberries, lies collapsed and embedded in the damp earth. I look northward towards her house. Other than a badly needed coat of paint the house seems intact. White curtains cover the windows. Something tells me to change my course. I owe this much to the Abe family, to at least check out their house.

With trepidation, I climb up the front stairs. My heart pumps faster. My hands become cold and clammy just like the time that policeman followed me down Folsom Boulevard. Go ahead, a small voice tells me, before you lose your nerve. Knock.

You're taking a chance, I tell myself. You'd better turn around and run for the road while you can still get away. I knock and stand glued, listening to the heavy footsteps of a man coming from the back of the house, where the kitchen is located.

A middle-aged Caucasian man with a mustache opens the door.

"Hello," he says with a look of surprise. Just the tone of his voice makes me feel that I am in safe company.

"Come in, come in," he urges, with such friendliness that I immediately find myself becoming suspicious.

"I'm Kiyo Sato from the next ranch," I tell him.

He is Captain Fitzgerald and is stationed at Mather Field. He has apparently been here since we left.

He tells me, "Your dogs would not eat or drink anything."

I listen with an aching heart as he describes how Molly and Dicky looked for us.

"Every day they came back and searched madly around the house and around the barn and all over your property. Then they disappeared. The next morning they came again and frantically looked all over for you people. They wouldn't stop to eat or drink, even when I tried to put the food right under their noses. They didn't stay at your house."

"Where did they go?" I ask, knowing full well that he does not know. Where did they go? Did they follow our scent to the train tracks and lose us when we boarded? Where did they sleep at night? I take a deep breath to keep the tears from welling up into my eyes.

"You people left in May. I tried to pet them but they ignored me. Near the end of June they had lost so much weight and still they wouldn't eat. I tried to coax them once but the German shepherd growled, so I left them alone. By then there was no flesh left, only skin covering their bodies."

Our dogs had not abandoned us, even when we were abandoned by our classmates, and even by our President. We had left two helpless members of our family to fend for themselves. How many pets, I wonder, had roamed in search of their families and died of grief after our incarceration?

"During the few weeks in July they were so weak that they had difficulty walking and still they kept looking. And then they never returned. I'm sorry."

My tears can no longer be dammed up.

"To change the subject," the Captain says kindly, "did you hear that one of our planes ran into your house?"

"No!" I exclaim in disbelief.

"I never did find out how it happened, but the plane destroyed the corner bedroom and filled the basement with high octane fuel."

"So that's why the pine tree is gone." The beautiful gnarled wisteria is probably gone, too. I had not checked that side of the house.

"A family was living in your house. Their son had just left the bedroom for the kitchen seconds before the impact. It's a miracle that the whole place didn't explode."

The family didn't move out, he tells me, even with the basement full of gasoline.

"I went there and scooped out buckets of that fuel for my car. You should've seen my car go!"

According to Captain Fitzgerald, repairs were done immediately. If not for the disappearance of our elegant, giant pine tree, I would have difficulty believing his story.

SPRING, 1945.

I am in a state of panic! The morning mail brings a letter from Colorado saying that my family is coming home. Mama and my six brothers and sisters will be in Sacramento tomorrow by train! What am I going to do?

They can't stay with me. They can't stay at the farm. It's been over a month and the tenants are still there. And I don't have money to put my family up in a hotel. What am I going to do?

Tochan writes that he and Aizo are loading up their 1936 Chevrolet with food and blankets and will be leaving soon. The gas tank is filled. At the Keenesburg gas station the owner would not take their ration tickets, saying that Tochan will need them along the way.

Cat, a pet, will come with them, he writes. He has made himself the twelfth member of our family since our relocation to the sugar beet farm.

I tell Dr. McDonnell, my employer, my predicament.

"Let's go look for a place," he says, to my surprise and gratitude.

"When? They're going to be here tomorrow!"

"Now," he replies without hesitation.

We hop into his car and ride west to the lower end of town where Japanese immigrant families lived before the evacuation. Fourth Street, where *Issei* businesses flourished and the *sakura*, the Japanese flowering cherry trees bloomed, is no longer swept clean. Papers and trash blow in the breeze and gather along the vacant storefronts. Winos idle here and there.

We stop on Third Street, in front of an old, two-story house. He finds a tenant and inquires. I learn later that many of his patients are from this part of town.

The Japanese tenants are coming back, he is told, but until then the apartment upstairs is vacant.

We climb up the unpainted, weatherworn wooden stairs along the outside wall, holding on to the 2 x 2 wooden railing. At the top I look down with a worrisome chill, seeing the barely anchored pieces of steps floating downward. Down below are remnants of a long-forgotten vegetable garden.

We enter a small, screened area with a cement laundry tub, and go into a kitchen with a small oilcloth-covered table in the corner. Through the door, a long dark hallway opens onto small rooms on both sides. The place could have been a rooming house for immigrant laborers.

"What do you think?" The doctor asks me.

"This will be just fine," I tell him. I am concerned about the rickety steps my little brothers and sisters will have to climb, but it is no time to worry about that. I am so grateful that my family will have a roof over their heads that I don't even think to ask about the rent. I later find out that Mr. Osada is asking only sixty cents per day.

After days on the sooty, old train, the children emerge looking neat and combed, even with white shirts wrinkled and smudged. They have slept in the ladies' bathroom, Kazu tells me, on the side benches, and Sylvia gave Mama her seat. The boys sat on the floor between the coaches.

"You know what?" Masashi says, holding my hand and vying for my attention as we walk to the baggage room. "We went right through the mountain."

"The tunnel?"

"Yeah! It was dark." Masashi, now almost six, is still a boy full of curiosity.

The six of them follow me while Dr. McDonnell helps Mama with her armload of coats and sweaters.

Kozo, fourteen and the oldest coming by train, brings up the rear, carrying the *furoshiki* with leftover food and more jackets. Is this how Mama managed to feed the family for two days, I wonder? They couldn't afford to go to the dining car.

"Mama had a seat in the daytime," Kazu tells me. A kind old man gave his place to her. "Sylvia let Mama sit in her chair at night." Whoever Sylvia is, I silently thank her for making Mama's difficult trip a bit easier.

Kozo, Naoshi and Kazu ride with Mrs. McDonnell in her white Cadillac. I worry that the smudges and smell from the train's coal smoke will rub off on the white upholstery. Mama and I and the little ones go with Dr. McDonnell in his everyday car.

At the apartment, Masashi climbs the stairs with glee. I hold my breath as he stands at the top, grinning widely, arms akimbo, looking down upon the rest of us. Tomoko navigates carefully up the steps, holding on to the unsteady guardrail.

The children scatter down the long hallway, poking their heads into each room and staking out their territory. I untie the *furoshiki* and spread out the leftovers while Mama heats some water. Stale peanut butter and jelly sandwiches. Carrots and celery sticks and apples, crackers and raisins and dried fruits. Inside the *zyubako* lacquer box are a couple of pieces of teriyaki chicken and in the lower section I am delighted to find small rice balls wrapped in *nori* seaweed. What a feast it is for me. I have not had Mama's food for so long.

I drop a stale rice ball into a bowl of hot water. *Ochazuke* tea and rice without the tea and without the *koko* pickles. Still, how good it tastes slurping down the softened rice, retrieving the salted, red pickled plum from the center to eat in small bits. Each warm swallow comforts my stomach.

We will all be together again as soon as Tochan, Aizo and Cat get here.

⸺

"Your father is on the phone!" Mrs. McDonnell calls to me from the foot of the stairs.

I drop my cleaning rag on the floor of the upstairs bathroom and rush to the phone in the master bedroom.

"We drove to the farm and found the family still living there," he tells me. He is calling from the Mills Station Grocery Store. "Where is Mama?"

I tell him to pick me up on Folsom Boulevard opposite the East Lawn Cemetery and I will guide him to the apartment. It will take him about half an hour to get there, which gives me enough time to finish my cleaning and walk two blocks to Folsom Boulevard.

My hands scrub the sink and toilet bowl at top speed. In fifteen minutes I rush out the door, hardly able to contain my happiness. My father and my brother are now home.

I recognize our old, faded blue Chevrolet coming down Folsom Boulevard. There is barely space for me to sit in the back seat after pushing some stuff over.

"Hi," Aizo says.

"Which way?" Tochan asks.

"Go straight ahead to Third Street."

Cat snoozes behind me in the rear window.

A dirty gallon jug rolls under my feet.

"What's this?" I ask.

"It's water from the Great Salt Lake in Utah," Tochan says. "I wanted all of you to have a taste of it." Even in times like this, Tochan is forever the teacher.

Aizo wasn't too happy about the long walk on the salty sand before they reached enough water to fill the jug. "We walked on salt for about a mile," he tells me.

"And then we had to stop in Auburn just to see a sign!"

"How come?" I ask.

"There was this sign Tochan read about that said No Japs Allowed. Tochan wanted to see it for himself, so we parked a few blocks away from that street and walked. I didn't want to go but Tochan went so I followed him."

The sign was there in the barbershop window, Aizo says. Satisfied to have seen it, they walked back to their automobile.

"And we almost fell into a canyon," Aizo continues. "It was snowing in the Rocky Mountains and we slid and turned completely around on the mountain road," he says. Shivers run down my spine as I visualize the car going off the road and falling into the canyon. Nobody would have found them. From what he tells me, I am even more relieved that they have safely returned to Sacramento.

Playing on the sidewalk, Masashi spots us coming. Flailing his arms and jumping up and down, he yells at the top of his lungs. Soon helping hands appear from everywhere, unloading blankets, canned food and clothing. Masashi coaxes Cat from the back window and carries him into the dirt yard.

The principal hasn't called me about speaking to the student body. It's just as well. I'm nervous just thinking about it.

It's been a rough trip these last three years, trying to keep up with schooling with so much moving. Sacramento to Pinedale Assembly Center for a couple of months, to Poston Camp II in Arizona, to the sugar beet farm in Colorado, and now back to Sacramento. At each new location it is understood that *tomorrow* we go to school. *Today* we find out where and how to get there and Mama and I wash and iron school clothes.

Tomorrow arrives. We get up early.

Lunches in hand, washed and combed, six of us pile into our Chevrolet. Tochan drops Aizo off at Sacramento High School. Aizo does not know that I have spoken to the principal, but he must be worried. A knot forms in my chest; I want to tell him it's going to be all right. I remember the many times I've had to face an unknown enemy and how scary it was. He gets out of the car and stands for a moment, looking straight ahead down the long pavement to the front door. As we drive away, I wonder what is in store for him when the principal himself is afraid to have Aizo in school. I hope that he will pass for Chinese.

Kozo appears excited about junior high school. Always one to take things in stride, he does not seem particularly worried, for which I am relieved. He is fifteen. He will go to Kit Carson Junior High School, the same school I went to before the war, driving my Studebaker twelve miles from our farm to town.

I get out of the car on 45th Street in the old and rich part of Sacramento. The rest ride on to the country to be dropped off at Edward Kelley School. Miss Cox no longer teaches there. She was fired, I hear later.

When I arrive back at the mansion, the good doctor is already gone. Madame is in the kitchen, reading the morning newspaper, sipping her usual cup of coffee.

I work non-stop in order to finish by noon. After cleaning up in the kitchen and picking up downstairs, I clean the upstairs, strip the bed, and do the laundry. I am grateful to have this job, as it is the only income we can depend on right now.

⁓

I catch the bus on Folsom Boulevard and head for the lower end of town, eager to hear of the day's happenings. Half a block away, Masashi comes running, happy to see me. He looks like an unwashed orphan child.

"You are a mess!" I tell him, taking him by the hand. "What have you been doing?" I know Mama would have a fit if she caught him walking down the sidewalk looking like this.

"I made some mountains and rivers and tunnels. I'll show you."

"Where?"

"In the backyard. You will like it."

When we reach the house, he proudly shows me the maze of mountains with rivers flowing around them. Small pieces of wood form bridges.

"Take off your overalls and let's wash your feet. I have an idea. How about a paper boat for your river?"

"Okay!" he says excitedly. A happy, naked boy scampers up the steps.

I am worried. Aizo hasn't returned home from school yet. All the children returned from school long ago.

It is almost suppertime when I hear him come up the steps, not too enthusiastically, as if he is carrying a heavy load.

"Where have you been?" I question him.

"School."

"What took you so long?"

"I didn't want to take the bus. I walked."

"That's at least thirty blocks, Aizo!"

"Yeah."

He doesn't seem to want to talk and tries to leave the kitchen.

"Why didn't you take the bus home?"

"I wanted to walk," he replies and heads for the hallway.

"Aizo! How come?" I insist.

He sees that I'm not going to let up on him.

"Okay," he replies, finally resigned to my questioning. "The principal told me if I got beat up, they weren't responsible. I didn't want to ride the bus and then have to walk with them."

"How terrible!"

I really don't know what to say to my brother, who is now old enough to know what is going on around him, and that some of it is ugly. He must still surely bear the scars of the secret baptism performed in Colorado at Reverend Duncan's Baptist Church when the congregation didn't want them and their cousins.

I wish I could spare him hurt. Having had a conversation with his principal, my hope is that he will feel better in some of his classes.

Mama is pleased that Aizo leaves very early for school. I don't tell her why.

· 14 ·

WITH ONLY
A SHOVEL AGAIN

Moh ichido

Meh o dase

Koyashi sore yaru zo

   – JOHN SHINJI SATO

Sprout again,

One more time!

Here's a handful of manure

   –TRUDY SATO, TRANSLATOR

ALONE, TOCHAN ARRIVES at the farm and easily backs the Chevrolet half-way into the barn, as he has done so many times before. Coming from the sunny outdoors, it takes a moment to adjust to the dark interior of the barn. Only jagged pieces of the 60-watt light bulb hang by the door.

A barren spot remains where our farm truck had been parked, loaded with empty crates and ready for the next day's harvest. A rat scurries to the back, leaving a thin trail of dust, and disappears behind a pile of old sacks. Empty oil cans and odd pieces of pipes remain on the wide shelves. Pruning shears are gone. The long saw, the short handled hoes, shovels and pitchfork are nowhere in the barn. No tools remain.

Cows standing in mud and dung stare curiously from the far corner, chewing and drooling.

Around the barn, only weeds grow where the farm equipment had been: the disk, the garden cultivator, the Fordson tractor and the plow. The Studebaker is no longer sheltered in its small garage. Oil drums, open and empty, roll in the grass.

The nail feeder, dusty and leaning on its hinges, still holds rows of three-penny nails, ready to be pulled ten at a time by skillful fingers, to make shooks into crates. The large wooden keg of nails, purchased for the oncoming strawberry season, lies on its side with a mound of dust-covered nails. The old box-making stand remains intact with the heavy iron rail in place. Bundles of shook ordered for the coming crop show no signs of ever having been used. The tall, neat piles of boxes Tochan had prepared for Bill before leaving lean over with the weight of time, and tell eloquently of dreams rudely interrupted.

Tochan opens the trunk. His favorite shovel lies at the bottom, covered with small tools placed there in Keenesburg, Colorado. With both hands, he picks up his pruning shears and holds them for a moment, remembering the many handwritten letters he had sent to the War Relocation Authority, requesting this important working tool from home before the family's release from Poston Camp II. After accumulating a one-inch stack of typewritten government letters, his pruning shears had finally arrived. He carefully leans them against the rear bumper.

One by one, he places the tools back in the barn, a few of which he had smuggled inside the bedrolls almost four years ago. He pulls out his shovel and begins by scraping the barn floor of cow dung, working in his knee-high green rubber boots. With his well-worn hammer, he mends an old broken lug box, into which he gathers the cow manure, and carries it through the back door of the barn. Steadily, box after box, he deposits the contents at the base of each of his orange trees, feeling their hungry roots reach out with the next rain.

Just at sunset, he walks into the walnut orchard with his pruning shears and his *kama*. He slashes off the young suckers growing from the base of his tree with the *kama*. Then with his sharp pruning shears, he cuts off the two- and three-year-old branches, revealing finally the walnut tree he had grafted, standing straight and tall.

Tomorrow he will trim another tree.

Tochan sits down wearily and removes his green, muddy rubber boots.

"*Tai hen desu ne*." It is not so easy, is it? Mama empathizes.

"I took the cow manure from the barn to the orange trees. The trees look as if they are barely alive. We may lose some of them."

I remember how Mama and Tochan had worked all night during a bad freeze to save the young trees, wrapping them with burlap sacks. I can still remember Mama in the morning, her frozen nose peeking out from the layers of old wool plaid rags wrapped around her head.

Tochan talks on as if he is planning out loud. Mama listens.

Without a wheelbarrow it takes time to haul the manure.

"There must be an old wheel somewhere. There's plenty of old lumber I can use to build one."

"The walnut trees," he reports, "have been sapped of energy by the suckers. Some of the suckers are too thick and had to be sawed."

He tells Mama that the squirrels have been harvesting the almonds and putting them away in holes inside the barn, leaving almond shells everywhere.

"We don't have the tractor. I will see if the Fairbairn brothers can plow an acre or two for us to start our strawberry field."

The *ofuro* bathtub is dried up and won't hold water, so he will have to build another one.

"What do you think about a shower?" he asks Mama.

Mama agrees. I haven't heard her disagree with anything that Tochan says, except for that awful argument about coming home.

"The pump works and that's good. We have plenty of water."

That pleases Mama.

Tomoko wanders in. "Tochan, did you see Molly and Dicky?" she asks.

"No."

That's all he says. Tears threaten to well up in my eyes, thinking of Captain Fitzgerald's account of their grief that killed them.

He continues: "Tomorrow I will prepare a plot to plant vegetables. When the soil is warmer, we can put in cucumbers and tomatoes, maybe peppers and *nasu*, if we can find the seeds." The long Japanese eggplants may have disappeared, but he thinks someone returning from camp might have seeds.

⁓

"The people have moved," Tochan announces wearily one night. "The children were not playing outside today while I was working in the orchard, so I went to check the house before I left."

"Yay!" Masashi yells. "Can we go home now?"

"Not yet. There's a lot of work to be done before we can move in. Six windows are broken and boarded and need to be replaced. The stove and the butane tanks are gone. I don't know how the family managed to survive in the house. We have a few broken chairs and several iron beds. The kitchen table and bench are still there, and the piano."

I wonder why our piano has been spared.

"I checked the attic. Someone's been up there and opened up all our stored boxes. The pots and pans and dishes are gone. I found a few books and photographs scattered on the floor."

He pulls out a small, thin book from his pocket, carefully wiping the dust from its soiled covers. It is Robert Service's *Spell of the Yukon*. How well I remember the "abysmal loneliness" from that book.

"After the children leave for school tomorrow, Mama, we can start cleaning. I will finish clearing the overgrowth around the pump house and work on the main irrigation ditch."

"I wonder if my new boots are still on the roof," Kozo says, like he is talking to himself. Even after three years, he has not forgotten that he had placed his washed boots outside the attic window to dry quickly for the trip. In the chaos of loading up and catching our nervous dogs, he had forgotten the new boots.

"On Saturday and Sunday we can all go home and clean up the yard."

Tochan does not talk about the awful mess I had seen when I came home three months ago—Mama's beautiful garden piled up with old car parts, newspapers and magazines, bottles, cans, parts of our iron beds embedded in Bermuda grass and tall dead weeds. What a job it is going to be!

An air of excitement fills our apartment.

"I'm going to pack my things," announces Masashi.

"We're not going yet!" big brother tells him.

It's hard to believe that my little brother was only three years old when we left.

It is cleanup day at the farm.

Excitement fills the front yard. Tochan finds an old wooden sled he had made to level the creek in 1930. He pulls it with the Chevrolet from the side of the barn to the house, followed by excited children.

"Throw everything on here."

Big and little hands throw car parts, bottles, boxes, broken toys and tires on the sled. In no time there is no more room. They follow the load to the back of the barn, yelling, and picking up and throwing back onto the sled what has slid off. While the children load and unload, Tochan cuts the wisteria vines, spreading like hundreds of snakes tangled in the Bermuda grass, unearthing more junk.

Mama cleans the kitchen while I tackle the parlor. Much to her delight, Mama finds her old bristly *tawashi* brush under the sink. I chuckle, thinking just the sight of Mama and her *tawashi* in hand would scare any germ away. And the smell of Clorox!

We scrub the boys' bedroom. We scrub and scrub and scrub until Mama finally gives up and pushes a water hose through the window.

"Let's let the floor soak for a while," she suggests, "and let the droppings soften up."

The day passes by much too soon.

Tochan calls through the kitchen window.

"Five o'clock! Mama, I'd better take you home to cook." Mama looks at me. It almost sounds like home. One of us always starts cooking supper at five.

"Kiyo-chan," Mama says, "will you go? I want to finish cleaning this kitchen and the boys' room. All you have to do is cook the rice and the *okazu*."

I can do that easily enough, vegetables with chicken seasoned with *shoyu* and sugar. Besides, Mama cleans better. She suggests I take the little ones back to the apartment with me and have them bathe.

"I don't wanna go!" Masashi insists.

"I want to stay, too!" whines Tomoko.

"You will go with me," Tochan says. "Kazu, you will help your sister." She scrunches her mouth and says nothing. She knows that her father's words are final. "Naoshi, you help your brothers." Naoshi doesn't mind either way.

"Tomorrow, maybe we can all stay," Tochan assures the children.

⌒

Early Sunday morning, Tochan's "transportation service" begins after breakfast. Mama is the first to load up her ubiquitous, rice-sacking *furoshiki,* not one, but three large ones, all tied up and filled with rice balls with *nori* and *umeboshi* salted plum, boiled eggs, chicken teriyaki, salted cabbage *tsukemono*, peanut butter and jelly sandwiches, a box of Graham crackers, apples and carrots and milk and a thermos of hot green tea. I don't think Mama slept much.

Everybody wants to go on the first trip of the day.

We look like Evacuation Day in 1942, carrying our suitcases filled with clothes. Only this time we head towards home.

The mail-order pants and shirts, which the boys wore when we left three and a half years ago, are long gone. I decide I'd better wash the dirty clothes from yesterday before leaving and take them home to dry on our long, wire clothes lines.

It doesn't seem possible that even in the few months of apartment living, we've accumulated so much stuff. Kozo and Aizo carry boxes down the swaying wooden steps to the sidewalk. How many trips to the farm is it going to take us, I wonder, in one car? Mama and the big boys go first.

The old '36 Chevrolet, loaded to the gills, reminds me of the families from Oklahoma escaping the dust storms with all their belongings strapped to their trucks.

We are going home.

⁓

"Mama, can we have *tempura* for supper?" I suggest, thinking it would make our first supper at home special.

"Do we have what we need?" Mama asks.

"We have plenty of Wesson oil. There's squash, there's potatoes, carrots, onions. Flour, eggs. No shrimp." I take an inventory out loud. Too bad, no shrimp, not even fresh fish. We have plenty of rice.

"How are you going to cook it outside?" Mama asks.

"Oh, no! I didn't think about that!" I exclaim, all plans for a great homecoming dinner shattered. Cooking *tempura* over an open fire would be a mess, maybe even dangerous, with bits of ashes landing on the surface of the oil.

"Shall we open up cans of corned beef or salmon then?"

"*Dotchi demo ii.*" Either one's fine, she says, continuing to scrub around the sink.

Just outside the back door of the kitchen, Tochan has a "stove" for us, a cutout five-gallon oilcan. Beside it lies a pile of twigs the children have gathered. I wash a big pot of rice and place it on the wires stretched across the stove's top, and start the fire below.

Slowly the heavy pot heats up and the lid begins to jiggle, and white aromatic bubbles exude down the sides of the pot. As if led by the scent, like Molly and Dicky, Tomoko and Masashi appear around the corner.

"Can I do that?" Tomoko asks.

"Sure. We need a good fire for the rice to boil for a while. Don't let it die down."

I go back to the kitchen to prepare the rest of the meal: cold, canned salmon, canned corn, *sunomono* with shredded carrots and *daikon* seasoned with Mama's sweet vinegar.

The fire roars under the rice pot and the drippings sizzle as they hit the flames. Another few minutes and the liquid will totally evaporate, resulting in partially cooked, burnt rice.

"Hey! We need to slow down now." I pull out the flaming twigs. "We need to go real easy now for about half an hour." Cooking like this is not like turning the knob on our gas stove and knowing that it'll stay on low heat.

Tomoko and Masashi leave, the excitement of feeding the fire and seeing the flames gone. I set the rice pot on the ground and restart the fire to heat the kettle of water for the tea.

With a *tawashi*, Mama vigorously scrubs the top of the wooden kitchen table Tochan had made years ago. Worn out pieces of oilcloth still remain tacked to the sides, caked over with food. The cheerful, flowered oilcloth table cover is gone.

I make a mental note: two yards of oilcloth from Mills Station Grocery Store plus stew meat. Tomorrow I'll start early for a pot of good curry stew.

Nine of us sit around the table, four on the long bench against the wall. I find an orange crate. Aizo and I sit at opposite ends. Mama, Tochan and Naoshi sit along the other side. Tochan bows his head, we do the same. He asks God to watch over Seiji in Europe, fighting with the 442nd Regimental Combat Team, and Sanji in Michigan finishing high school. He thanks God for our home.

The prayer is short, his voice controlled. I hear a slight quiver as he ends with the Amen, and I realize for the first time that my father is not the Rock of Gibraltar, that he, too, hurts inside.

The rice bowls keep coming to my end for refills, just like old times. I take care of the rice and Mama sees to the rest of the food. Everybody takes turns talking and listening, except for Mama.

"Story, Tochan?" Masashi asks, as soon as Tochan puts down his teacup warming against his cheek. He remembers the signal even after almost four years.

The instant Tochan agrees, Masashi's body slithers under the table, but with some difficulty. He is no longer a small three-year-old crawling under the table to reach his father's lap.

In a small village in Japan a farmer works on his tiny plot, tilling the soil and planting the rice one by one.

"One day," he says, "I will save enough to buy an ox. If I have an ox, I can do more work by using a plow. I can pull heavy loads. And I can grow more rice."

"Why doesn't he buy a tractor?" Masashi asks.

"This is a long time ago," Tochan explains. "Do you remember Charlie, our white horse? Charlie pulled my plow before we had our tractor."

When the rice is ready to be harvested, the farmer takes his kama, *the small hand scythe, and cuts a handful at a time, straightening his body only to walk to the edge of his plot to empty the full basket on his back. The stalks dry in the warm sun, on a large* tatami *mat, which he makes from rice straw.*

"What's *tatami*, Tochan?"

"*Tatami* is a floor covering made with rice straw. Every house has *tatami* mats. Every part of the rice plant becomes something useful," Tochan explains.

"Is the *kama* the thing you carry around, Tochan?" curious Masashi interrupts.

"That's the same *kama*," Tochan explains. "I used it when I was a boy in Japan. My mother cut the rice stalks with the *kama*. Now I can buy the *kama* right here in Sacramento."

Every night, the farmer sits on the tatami *mat by his hibachi warmer with a pile of rice straw beside him. He weaves the straw into* zori *slippers. From a worn* out yukata *robe cloth,* he rolls the straps to hold the foot onto the zori. Late into the night he works in the dim light, until the pile of straw is gone.

For many years he tills and plants and takes his sacks of rice and zoris to market until there is finally enough money to buy an ox.

It is a proud day when he goes to market with his earnings, and returns home leading a beautiful, strong ox, which he ties to a tree in his yard.

Neighbors come by to see the ox and to congratulate him.

"How good," they say, that finally he is the proud owner of a healthy ox. They lovingly pat the ox's rump as they view it from all sides.

"What a fine ox," they say.

"Yes. Now I can plow my field."

"You will be able to grow more rice," a neighbor says.

"Yes," replies the farmer. "I will plant more rice and you may borrow my ox and plant more rice."

"You will be a rich man."

"Yes, and my ox will carry my load to the village."

He ties his ox where it will have plenty of green grass to eat. He sets out a bucket of water.

Weary and happy, he retires to his farmhouse, thinking of the work he and his ox will be able to do tomorrow. Finally, he will not have to labor so hard.

"And I will share my good fortune with my neighbors."

The farmer goes to sleep looking forward to the next day when he and his ox will till the soil together.

He awakens early, anxious to start the day. He goes out to look at his ox.

"Eh?" He looks with surprise when he sees his ox lying on his back. "Stand up," he coaxes but the ox does not move.

He tries to lift its head. It is too heavy to move. The ox's eyes are open but not seeing.

He walks around his ox and pulls on its leg. The leg is stiff.

"Komatta nah," he sighs. "Now what am I going to do?" He sits on the ground beside his ox with his chin cupped in his hands.

His ox is dead.

"Oooh," the children empathize.

"Then, what did he do?" Kozo asks.

"Did Charlie die?"

"Let him finish the story," Aizo interjects impatiently.

One by one the neighbors gather around the dead ox.

"You have worked so hard to buy this ox," they say.

"Now what will you do?"

"It will be many years before you can buy another ox."

Word spreads in the small village of the farmer's terrible loss. One by one, the neighbors stop by with words of condolence.

"I am so sorry."

"You have worked so hard."

"And for so many long years."

"We wish we could be of help."

They bring offerings of food.

The villagers help the farmer dig a large hole near the tree to bury the ox.

"I am fortunate," the farmer tells his neighbors. "It is the ox that died and not I. I could have been the one who died this morning."

"Instead," he continues, "I am able to work as I have always done and I have many good neighbors. I am truly a fortunate man."

Like Molly bringing in a dead jackrabbit to us, Tochan hauls in an old, dirty, rusted two-burner kerosene stove with no legs, which looks like it has been embedded in dirt forever.

"Where did you get that?" I ask.

"In the garbage ditch behind the barn."

There is a silent rule that we are not to go there. There are broken glass panes and bottles, wires, rusty nails protruding through old boards strewn over piles of broken car parts, discarded metal headboards and furniture. My brothers sneak over there and find treasures like skate wheels to make scooters.

"Does it work?" I ask Tochan, as he begins to dismantle the stove. It is covered with petrified dirt, I swear, as if it will never get clean. I would scrub it first but Tochan pays no attention to the looks of it. He places his mouth on the end of the metal tube and blows. Air does not go through. He takes a long wire and pushes it through until it is cleaned out. Meticulously, he does this with each connecting tube.

With debris caked into every pore, I don't see how the burners will ever work. As I go in and out the back door I can't see much progress, with small screws and more parts strewn about.

It is the middle of the afternoon when I hear Tochan call "Mama! Mama!" I run through the kitchen door. It is so unlike Tochan to yell for Mama.

Standing triumphantly, arms on his hips, he looks upon his stove. Smokey, orange flames spew out from some of the holes.

"I will soak the burners in gasoline and clean out all the openings. Tonight you can cook on this, Mama."

"*Yokatta ne*," That is so good, Mama says, gratefully.

But there's something about cooking rice outdoors. I like the open fire and the comfortable aroma of rice cooking. Best of all, of course, I don't have to clean the stove of the boiled-over drippings.

Tochan comes into the kitchen, which he rarely does, after he returns from the *furo* with the children, who are now asleep. I slide half-made sandwiches aside to make room at the table.

This is not his usual routine. Each night, while Mama and I clean up and fix school lunches, Tochan pulls down the lid of his old desk where he keeps his bills and letters and farm papers in the cubbyholes. In the past, he would practice on his old Remington typewriter, which is gone now. I remember falling asleep to his repetitive, monotonous spelling practice. O-R-T-H-O-D-O-X. ORTHODOX. ORTHODOX.

"*Ocha?*" Tea, Mama asks. She looks at him expectantly.

"Ah," he answers.

"The camps are closing and everybody has to get out by the end of the year," Tochan tells us. "I just heard that the Inouyes have no place to go. With nine young children and only one able adult, no one wants them. Mr. Inouye is not well, I hear."

I can see that Tochan had given this a great deal of thought. I remember Mrs. Inouye well.

"Come, come!" she would invite us on our way home from school, in her loud, boisterous voice. The ice cold Kool-Aid on hot days made the rest of our one and a half mile walk not so long. Sometimes she would have soda crackers for us. The Inouyes worked as tenant farmers on the Robinson property for as long as we'd been walking to Edward Kelley School, almost three miles from home. They were our halfway stop.

Reports are that thousands of people who cannot get jobs are now left in the ten camps. Those are the too old and the too young, who have been imprisoned for almost four years.

Many young men who are old enough to help their families are in the United States Army. Others are working on sugar beet farms in Colorado and Idaho, and at Seabrook Farms in New Jersey. Factories, schools, dry cleaners, construction— wherever there is any kind of a job—the young *Nisei* go, with twenty-five dollars and a one-way ticket given to them by the government.

They find jobs and places to live for their families. It does not matter what they do as long as they and their families can survive. They bed down in temporary hostels set up in vacant Japanese churches and any available shelter, and look for work. For large families, there is no choice but to work as contract laborers and hope that their earnings will feed their children.

Our neighbor, the Yamasakis, won't be able to return home. The realtor tells me that their twenty-acre property was foreclosed as if it was no big deal, their vineyard of Muscat grapes gone with the "blessings" of our government. How could my country do this to its own people?

How could President Roosevelt have signed an order to banish us into concentration camps, 120,000 people, with no regard for their properties? The bank had no right to seize their land, Tochan says, when they were forced to leave by the government.

Myso Yamasaki, the eldest, went to Chicago with twenty-five dollars, found a job and relocated his family there. There was Yukio, my classmate Michiko, Yoneko and the parents. Our dogs died of grief but their dog, Nuisance, found them in Chicago and was written up in *Reader's Digest*.

The Kitadas lost all their belongings in our church fire. I hear that Frank went to Denver and moved his sisters and parents there to work in a dry cleaning shop. He's only a few years older than I am. What would I have done in his shoes, if we had lost all our property? I would surely not have gotten to college. He is like so many young *Niseis*, forced to take on family responsibilities.

How could a great country do this to us, as if we were less than animals? Even animals get more human understanding. It's been "*muga-muchyuu*," as Mama would say often, describing that moment when one is on the verge of drowning, flapping and kicking with fury to stay afloat.

"The Inouyes have ten children," Tochan goes on. "The oldest, Kanji, is working somewhere out of camp. Where can they go?"

Tochan says. "What do you think, Mama? Can we manage with nine more children here?"

That's eleven more bodies! Eleven! I can't believe that Mama and Tochan are even considering this when we are barely surviving ourselves!

Mama doesn't hesitate when Tochan explains the plight of the Inouyes. She never does when it means helping someone in need. There's always room for one more. But eleven! Where do we put them?

"There's plenty of farm work around here. Farmers are looking for laborers. Mrs. Inouye and the older boys can go with us to work." Tochan says.

"But where are they going to sleep, Tochan?" I ask, finally.

"We can manage," is all he says, as if plans are all in order.

~

JUNE, 1945.

"My father is making a kitchen for you," Masashi tells six-year-old Tomoji Inouye, his buddy now.

"That's not a kitchen. That's a mess hall," Tomoji matter-of-factly replies.

"No, it isn't! It's a kitchen."

"It's a mess hall," Tomoji insists.

The boys argue back and forth while watching Tochan put in a sink along one wall of the old workers' cabin. He panels the inside walls with new one-by-twelve lumber with lots of knotholes. He extends the electric line off the main house line. Water pipes are installed for the kitchen area and to the *furo* bath, which he constructed by the side of the cabin for their family's use.

Most of the supplies come from surplus sales at nearby Camp Kohler. Even so, I wonder how my parents manage. Having quit my maid job to help on the farm, I no longer have forty dollars at the end of each month to give them.

Mama and I scrub and clean the three workers' rooms in the barn for sleeping and for storage of their baggage. With nineteen people, our farm looks like a mini-Poston camp. Only we are free!

~

I've never seen my father look so weary. Tochan sits at the kitchen table, holding his warm teacup to his cheek while Mama and I do the usual after-supper dishes.

"Mama, what do you think? The Inouye family should not feel obligated to us for having them here. If they were to pay a few dollars a month it may alleviate their sense of obligation."

Mama agrees. The Japanese have a word for it: *Ohn*. It means having to pay someone back for favors done and sometimes the sense of obligation continues a lifetime. Tochan wants to avoid that.

There are many things we should have left in Japan, Tochan would say about the superstitions and social beliefs he grew up with. Americans are *assari shite iru*, he would say. That is, just a "thank you" would suffice.

"They need to save towards having their own place one day," Tochan continues. "Do you think charging them five dollars a month might help them not to feel obligated?"

The suggested five dollars a month seems too much for Mrs. Inouye.

"*Muri mo nai.*" It's understandable, Mama says, empathizing as a mother of a large family.

With no more discussion, Tochan pays the extra water and electricity bills each month as if the two families were his own.

~

Early Saturday morning, the screen door squeaks and there is a knock on the door.

"*Sato-san, sumanai ga . . .*" I hate to impose, says Mr. Yamamoto.

He and his wife have returned just yesterday from Poston Camp II, he tells Tochan. He is Tony's father. Tony, their only child, is in the United States Army. He was the envy of the children in our neighborhood, the only boy who had a shiny, brand new bicycle.

I remember Mr. Yamamoto when he came to our house four years ago just before we had to leave, to ask my father to "borrow" his money for safekeeping. He had six hundred and fifty dollars in cash in his hand, a sum of money no *Issei* around had ever seen, and no one was allowed to take. Tochan kindly refused.

"We don't know where we are going, Yamamoto-san," Tochan had told him. "And if I use your money, I may not be able to pay you back."

He is stopping by now to let us know they are back, I think.

"Sato-san, I need your help," he tells my father.

He pulls out an old piece of paper from his wallet and carefully unfolds it.

"This is where I buried the money, in the orchard across Folsom Boulevard," he explains to Tochan, in Japanese. As they were tenant farmers then, he needs to get permission to dig on the property. As father is bilingual, Mr. Yamamoto asks him to talk to the property owner.

They pick up two shovels from the barn and drive off in the old Chevrolet.

It is not until after supper is over that Tochan shared what transpired on their treasure hunt.

We drove into the orchard and to the main house. The owner was busy in the shed, taking care of old boxes, getting ready for plum picking.

"Sure, sure. Dig anyplace," he told us, so we drove through the orchard to the biggest oak tree on the property.

I think the oak tree must be at least one hundred years old. It would take all our arms to get around it.

Mr. Yamamoto's map was on a piece of paper from an old school tablet. It was worn out along the folds and the penciled lines and notes were barely legible.

"Nine feet this way," he told me. I measured off nine feet with my tape. "And then twelve feet this way," which is northward. We started digging at the spot. The hard ground yielded begrudgingly. We dug and we dug and we dug.

The hole was now at least two feet in diameter. Several Mexican laborers stopped to watch quietly.

"Somebody stole it," Yamamoto-san said finally, sticking his shovel in the pile of dirt.

"I don't think so," I told him. "See this ground? It doesn't look like it has been dug before. A section of soil dug four years ago would not be so consistently hard."

I looked at his map again. He was right, nine feet one way and twelve feet another way. I turn the map sideways: Nine feet going north, and twelve feet going west?

"Yamamoto-san, let's try it this way." I said.

"All right," he said, not really convinced.

By now, we were surrounded by more workers, who talked animatedly in Spanish.

"Que pasa? Que pasa?" they keep saying to each other.

We kept digging, a shovelful from my end and then a shovelful from Yamamoto-san, just like making mochizuki ground rice at New Year's. You remember how Okamura-san, Ojisan and I would pound the small mound of rice in the wooden usu in perfect rhythm? Well, the two of us dug that way for quite a long while and then Ching! We hit metal!

Mr. Yamamoto was ecstatic. "At-ta! At-ta!" he yells. You see, he had placed the money inside a piece of metal pipe and tightly screwed up both ends and buried it.

He dusted the dirt off and tried to unscrew it but after four years, it was rusted and would not loosen. I placed it on the ground and hit it hard with my shovel several times. It would not turn. We both hit it at both ends. He picked it up. The screw turned and Yamamoto-san pulled out all the money intact.

"Olé!"

"Caramba!"

Triumphant yells from the onlookers fill the orchard.

Mr. Yamamoto passed out a one-dollar bill to each of the spectators. He offered me ten dollars but I refused it. It is his money. His family's survival depends on the contents of the pipe until he finds a place to live and work.

⁓

Yale School of Nursing requests a report of my physical condition. Finally my application is being processed. It is not a "We have a policy" letter right off the bat. They are already in receipt of my academic report, which includes the last requirements for my Bachelor of Science degree, earned by correspondence while I was at the Colorado beet farm.

Having been rejected by the Johns Hopkins University and Western Reserve University schools of nursing because of my ancestry, I had not placed much hope in Yale and had been exploring other avenues. When scholarship offers come from Washington University in St. Louis and from Columbia University in New York in Social Work, I stash the letters away, still hoping that nursing will open up.

Yale University has sent me a medical form to fill out. It costs me ten dollars to have a doctor fill out a single page to report that I am in excellent health. With renewed hope, I send it off. There will be no medical reason to reject me. I am healthy. And if my academic record hadn't been acceptable, I figure, they would not have sent me the medical form. Finally, I will start on my career path.

Months pass with no word.

Prune picking is backbreaking, but it's a job the whole family can do. Besides, Johnny Horn's prune orchard is only a mile away and he sounded relieved when Tochan contracted to pick his prunes. Picking ripe prunes off the ground is a messy job. They mix with dirt and form a gluey paste which sticks to our shoes and pants and shirts. Our buckets have layers of permanent dark brown coating.

Every morning, we walk down Routier Road, each carrying his or her own bucket. Even Masashi has his small lard can bucket. Mama has the lunch and I carry the jug of water. Aizo and Kozo work as adult laborers at another orchard, being strong enough to carry a sixteen-foot ladder.

Occasionally, we run into Mr. and Mrs. Furuike, who walk three miles to their jobs. Their car and truck were gone when they returned home. They have begun again, like so many of us, with only what they were allowed to take with them four years ago, grateful to have a place to return to. Quietly the *Issei* and *Nisei* find jobs. It doesn't matter what kind of work they do, as long as the family can have enough to eat and survive.

"Lunchtime," Mama announces from under a prune tree, already cleared, where we had left the gallon of water and *furoshiki* of food. About the only thing good about prune picking is lunchtime.

Mama has a large old towel already soaked for wiping our sticky hands of prune juice and dirt. She unties the ends of the rice-sacking *furoshiki* and spreads the cloth on the ground and lifts the lid of the three-tiered, lacquer *zyubako*. She separates the tiers, *onigiri* rice balls with *umeboshi*, salted plums in the center of each, wrapped in strips of *nori* seaweed in one; chicken teriyaki in another; and cucumber and tomato slices in the third box. For *oyatsu*, our mid-afternoon snack, which Mama never forgets, there are big Baby Ruth bars cut in half. My brothers and sisters have acres of ground under their feet, the sunshine above and the love of family all around.

We sit on our overturned buckets and help ourselves, Kazu, Naoshi, Tomoko and Masashi feel like an important, contributing part of the family with each little bucket they fill and empty into a lug box.

At the end of the day, my knees hurt and I feel filthy. Mama goes all day squatting and moving her hands like a machine. There's nothing "triumphant" about prune picking except for lunchtime and quitting time. As we pick up our things to leave, I survey the field with a sense of satisfaction, seeing the acreage we cleared today, and look forward to a warm *ofuro* bath to soak my aching muscles.

"They want more pickers," Aizo mentions at the supper table. "Maybe you can get on."

"Me?"

I am surprised that my brother thinks that I can handle that heavy job, carrying a ladder and harvesting a tree at a time.

The peaches are ripening rapidly in the hot, summer sun and they are short of pickers.

"*Kitaeteru*," Tochan would say proudly of my tall and agile younger brothers, that they have muscle strength from having worked hard. I do, too, but I am only a little over five feet tall.

"You can try it," Kozo encourages me.

The next morning, Tochan drives the three of us to the orchard off

Folsom Boulevard. Mama walks later to Johnny Horn's prune orchard with Masashi, Tomoko, Naoshi and Kazu. Tochan returns home to his unending tasks of reviving the walnut orchard and planting and irrigating strawberries, tomatoes and cucumbers for quick crops for family use and income.

Sometimes it takes him half a day to trim one walnut tree of overgrown branches and suckers, using his pruning shears and saw to cut four years of growth.

The peach pickers go from one tree to the next, clambering up and down their ladders, emptying their buckets of peaches into lug boxes. My brothers show me how to anchor the pole of my ladder inside the tree where I can reach the most fruit. My bucket fills quickly as I step up the rungs and pluck the ripe peaches on both sides. With my fourth trip down, I need to relocate my ladder. I pull the center pole and fold it against the ladder and lose my balance trying to move the ladder from out of the heavy growth of branches to reposition it.

The pickers are way ahead when finally I finish my tree and go on to my next one in my row. My arm barely reaches around the center of the horizontal ladder, which is heavier at the end with the longer steps. I look for my brother who is nowhere in sight. Holding my ladder horizontally under my right arm and the bucket in the other, occasionally losing my balance on the hard dirt clods and ditches hidden by weeds, I manage to reach my next tree.

The setting up becomes easier. My bucket fills up quickly. I reach the top and pause, discovering for the first time a sea of green treetops as far as I can see, feeling like a triumphant Balboa standing on a ridge and "discovering" the Pacific Ocean.

With sure steps I hop up and down, enjoying my new sense of confidence. Five trees ahead, someone moves into my row to help me catch up with the crew.

⁓

Another job, packing pears, helps with the family's survival.

"Here come the inspectors!" someone whispers.

A ripple of commotion starts at the far end of the Earl Fruit Company packing shed. The constant chatter of the packing ladies at the front of the shed ceases. The footsteps on the wooden planks come nearer to our station.

The inspectors come by often. I don't see why. We do good work and they never find anything on us. We help each other. No one goofs off. In fact, the inspectors themselves cause problems. They make us nervous.

"*Ojisan*, here comes the inspector," I announce to the *Issei* man working next to me at the far end of the shed. Four of us go through the piles of boxes brought in from the field and pull out the culls, pears that are blemished, too small or rotting. Only top quality fruit is carried to the front of the shed to be sized, wrapped and packed by the women. The rest goes out the back to be thrown out in the orchard.

As the inspectors slowly walk down the aisle, occasionally checking a lug, all eyes quietly focus on their work. In the silence, I hear strange thumping noises. Pears come rolling by my feet.

"*Ojisan!* You forgot your box!" I exclaim. He had forgotten to replace his filled cull box with an empty one. I rush to the front to get one for him.

"*Arigatoh. Arigatoh.*" Thank you, thank you, he says with short bows and we laugh together, breaking the tension.

"*Toshi tottara dame da na-a.*" When one gets old it's not so good, he says. I like working with the *Issei* men. Time goes by fast, chatting about anything that comes to mind—the internment camps, farming, jobs. I look forward to coming to my section each morning to be with the four *Issei* cullers, who treat me with respect and offer help whenever I need it. The inspectors must realize by now that they will not find a more industrious and honest group of workers. And to think only four years ago, hundreds of *Issei* men were corralled by the FBI as "spies" and thrown into the Justice Department prisons. Those who used to manage their own family farms now work as laborers, starting all over again.

I am picking hops.

"Hey! I need another vine!" I yell, pulling off the last of the hop flowers from the long vine.

Naoshi and Masashi, followed by their newly acquired playmates from Mexico, come running to my row and hang onto the long, hop vine, strung twenty feet high. It takes strength to cut the twine strung across the wires at the top. Whenever I need another vine of hop flowers, I yell for help. Children appear from everywhere, hang onto a vine and pull, running out of the way as the "beanstalk" falls.

Hop flowers, like cotton, weigh almost nothing, like white puffs of air. It takes forever to fill up my large sack. I drag it from vine to vine and finally at midmorning, I carry my full sack to the weigh-in truck with a great feeling of accomplishment.

At the end of the day, Tochan drives into the ranch with boxes of tomatoes he's grown, packed into the front and back seats and trunk of his '36 Chevrolet. The Mexican families gather around, delighted to buy tomatoes for twenty-five cents a lug.

"*No tengo dinero, ahora.*" I don't have money now, a father tells him. Tochan leaves the lug of tomatoes anyway, knowing how difficult it can be to feed a large family.

I have received an offer of a scholarship from Columbia University at their New School of Social Work.

Faced with the daunting task of survival for our family, I decide I need to stay home and help us get back on our feet, at least for another year or two. At the supper table, I mention my plans, expecting a grateful response from my parents. Their totally unexpected response floors me. I had thought that they would be happy to have me at home.

"Your job is to get an education," they tell me in no uncertain terms. "You will study nursing if that is what you want." During and after our four tumultuous years of internment and relocation, schooling continues unbroken for all of us.

Mama gives me the stern look. Tochan speaks.

"You will go to school," he states firmly. "We can manage fine. Accept the scholarship."

Not having heard from Yale School of Nursing, I then decide that I must accept the scholarship from Columbia University.

Somehow we manage the cost of a train ticket. My well-traveled suitcase and I again head east, free and alone, my *furoshiki* of food beside me. Unlike the train of four years ago that transported us to the assembly center, this train is clean. In place of unsmiling, bayonet-wielding soldiers standing guard at both ends of my coach, neatly uniformed Negro porters busily see to the comfort of their passengers.

Wyoming. Desolate and dry. If I were to get off here and take a bus going south, I would pass by our cabin with the windmill, our home for almost two years on the sugar beet farm.

The terrain changes from the bare winter hills to undulating, fallow expanses of Nebraska and Kansas and on to Illinois. It is through here that I rode to get to Michigan, alone, at age nineteen, watching with a tinge of sadness the long shadows around the cozy farmhouses disappear into darkness.

It is not until the houses begin to crowd around me that I worry about what's ahead, and then the dirty, industrial buildings, which go on forever.

New York City. What a huge city! Reality sinks in. How do I get from where I am to where I am supposed to go?

The train crawls on forever, slowly sapping my resolve, and fear oozes in. I remember Tochan's words when he gets ready to tackle a big job. *Zazen o kunde!* I straighten my back, take a deep breath, and center my mind like a *samurai* raising his sword.

With my suitcase in one hand and books in the other, I ring the doorbell on the sixteenth floor. The promised job did not pan out and this was a new listing in the registrar's office. I will be taking care of two children for ten dollars a week and room and board. An unsmiling young woman opens the door and hurries me inside.

"Come this way," she says, as we quickly pass through the spacious living room, the dining room and into an untidy bedroom with toys strewn everywhere.

"You can put your things here." She points to the top of a bureau.

Two little girls, about four and six-years-old, run in and bounce on the beds. They look at me intently, as if to size me up.

"That's your bed," the mother says, pointing to the third single bed along the wall, its thin, striped cotton cover hastily pulled over it.

Just as quickly, the mother leaves without telling me the children's names, as if she has to tend to something important, fixing dinner, I surmise.

As I open my suitcase to unpack, the girls look on curiously.

"Are you going to be our nanny?"

"What's your name?"

"Can you take us outside?"

I open a drawer and find it stuffed with children's clothes. To my dismay, there is not a single empty drawer. In the crowded closet I look for a hanger. There is no choice but to keep my belongings inside my suitcase.

I straighten the cover on my bed and find the sheets wrinkled as if someone had been sleeping in it.

"Help me pick this up," I suggest. The girls sit Indian style on their beds, defying my suggestion. They don't move.

I wait for the lady of the house to return with further instructions. It is dinnertime. I saunter out of the bedroom. The girls follow me. I see myself in the huge, mahogany cupboard mirror as we walk past the large dining table.

Though the kitchen is spacious, it is devoid of any kind of food, with not even a fruit bowl. Parents are nowhere in sight. Have they gone out, I wonder? What am I supposed to do?

I realize soon enough that dinner is not going to be served and that I have two hungry little girls to feed, to entertain and to put to bed.

"What shall we have for supper?" I ask.

"I want peanut butter and jelly sandwich."

Simple enough.

I find a can of spaghetti on a cupboard shelf and eat it cold.

From early Saturday morning until late Saturday night, I see to the needs of the girls. Their mother appears long enough to tell me that I can take them to a square a few blocks from the apartment complex. We go sixteen floors down by elevator, and walk to a small area of lawn with a swing and a slide, which the children enjoy.

Sunday is the repetition of Saturday. The children awaken early, demanding my attention. I feel sad that the children have not had a single, family mealtime. In the dimly lit living room, I have seen the back of a man, who was apparently not their father.

After sleepless nights I decide that this is a job for a full time governess. I had come to New York to go to school, and with this schedule there is no time to study.

On Monday morning I tell my employer of my plans to leave. She pays me $2.48 and returns my ration book with the week's ration coupons removed.

I move in to the Margaret Louisa YWCA and get a job at the front desk.

Fieldwork in New York City with Columbia University's New School of Social Work exposes me to a totally different way of life. I am assigned to do a home visit to an elderly couple living in a small apartment. A twenty-one-year-old student listens to two people unable to work because of severe medical problems and age. Existing on fifteen dollars a month welfare allotment, they have difficulty meeting their medical and nutritional needs. They are prisoners in a big city. All I can do is listen.

Back at the office, I report my observations and am advised that there is no reason why they should not get along fine on their allowance and that it is my responsibility as a social worker to help them do so. Several months later, to my relief, New York City increases the welfare allotment, but for that elderly couple it is far from adequate.

I do well in my courses but my fieldwork supervisor is not happy with my performance and gives me a final grade of "Incomplete."

I decide to try again for nursing and write to Yale, Johns Hopkins and Western Reserve, stating this time that my brother (with the 442nd Regimental Combat Team in Europe) and other young people are fighting to uphold democratic principles and that I cannot understand that an institution of their standing would have a policy that excludes me from applying.

I receive three application forms with no letter and choose Western Reserve University. I plan to enroll in the fall.

Needing money to go home after my quarter in Social Work is over, I find a job at Reuben Donnelley & Company, correcting thousands of contest entry forms cut out from magazines. In a tiny cubicle, my job is to check 2" x 4" pieces of paper for eight hours every day, then go underground and ride the subway for forty blocks and emerge at the YWCA to my evening desk job and room. With enough earned for a train ticket, I head for home, and for the first time in my life, I must face what I'm sure will be my father's deep disappointment in me.

I enroll at Western Reserve University under the Cadet Nurse Corps Program, working towards a Master's in Nursing. From January to June of 1947 I work at the WRU University Hospitals.

For a new experience, I return home via Canada. A restaurant in Victoria refuses to serve me. The many empty tables are all reserved, I am told.

After my graduate semester in Public Health Nursing at WRU in the fall of 1950, I drive back in the most terrible ice storm in January, 1951. I receive orders to report to Shepard AFB, Texas, with a commission as First Lieutenant.

I, a total greenhorn, am assigned to take charge of the officers' ward. Several months later, I request overseas duty and am sent to Clark Air Force Base in the Philippines.

· 15 ·

I'm Too Old to Fight

Waga shigo mo
Ama no kawa ari
Natsu no yu

– JOHN SHINJI SATO

After I am gone
The Milky Way will still shine
On summer nights

– TRUDY SATO, TRANSLATION

"*Kotoshi da na, Mama.*" This is the year, Mama, Tochan states contemplatively as he sips his morning coffee.

"Eh," she agrees.

The long awaited year finally arrives. It doesn't seem possible that forty years have passed since Tochan decided that America was to be his home and his children's home, even when its laws prevented him from ever becoming one of its citizens.

Only white immigrants were accorded the privilege to apply for naturalization. "Someday the law will change," Tochan would often tell us. He seemed to sense that the Founding Fathers that he admired so much would not allow for a faulty democracy to continue, that one day the system would correct itself.

Tochan reaches for *The Secret Place*, a Baptist devotional, which he reads and translates for Mama every morning.

"Read this," he encourages Mama, pointing to a short passage. Mama pronounces each word carefully.

"Very good."

Then it is a short lesson in United States history.

"Who is the President of the United States?"

"President Dwight Eisenhower," Mama answers.

"Who is the Vice President?" Tochan quizzes her, question after question, on all aspects of United States history, which Mama answers correctly. After many years of coaching after breakfast, Mama has become better-informed than her children.

After a long struggle with the Alien Land Law, the Exclusion Act, the

Anti-Miscegenation Law and the terrible impact of Executive Order 9066, which destroyed the *Issei* farms, the McCarran-Walter Act passed in 1952, allowing for the naturalization of immigrants from Japan. The politicians take all the credit, posing with the President and getting commemorative pens. They don't realize that it was soldiers like my brother who finally turned the tide of prejudice by putting their lives on the line to prove their loyalty. How many sons had to die before their parents could be accorded equal status?

"Mama, you need to be able to read English if you are going to vote."

Mama enrolls in an English class at the Fremont Adult School, three evenings a week. Tochan takes a class in Civics and Government. They drive twelve miles each way after supper, and after a long day's work. On Tuesday and Thursday evenings they study.

"I think we should be ready soon for our naturalization application," Tochan assures Mama.

Only my youngest brother, David Masashi, now lives at home. Letters come from Hawaii, Korea and Japan where three of the children are stationed with the US Army and the US Air Force. After his stint with the 442nd Regimental Combat Team in Europe, Steve Seiji graduated as a Civil Engineer and now works with the US Army Corps of Engineers, overseeing dam projects. This takes him traveling to all parts of the state and overseas. Don Sanji attends Humboldt State College in Arcata, California, after having served with the US Military Intelligence Service in Japan. He studies towards a teaching credential. George Kozo serves in Korea with the Air Force and later plans to enroll at California Polytech in Agriculture.

Since I am assigned to a hospital in the Philippines, I stop in Hawaii to see Ronald Aizo, who is stationed at Schofield Barracks. Peter Naoshi serves stateside during his time with the US Air Force.

Kay Kazu writes frequently from San Francisco, where she is enrolled at the University of California School of Nursing. Marian Tomoko works in a home in town as a house girl while attending Sacramento Junior College.

Except for David Masashi, whose birth certificate gives him two names, each of the children has added an American name. I stick with Kiyo.

Each morning after breakfast Tochan pulls out another letter from his homemade wooden box to read again to Mama.

⁓

"How'd it go today?" David asks at the supper table.

"Fine. Fine," Tochan beams.

For almost two years, they have attended classes. Mama can read English now.

She had tried to keep up with each one of her nine children, but her tired body and mind could not concentrate. It was not until her last child was in college that Mama could finally study without dozing over her book.

Today they went for their citizenship examinations. They had prepared well for this day.

"Mama did better on the test than I did," Tochan says with great pride. "She missed only one. I missed four." He is proud that his student did better than he did.

"After all, I taught her," he says.

⁓

The small farmhouse Mama and Tochan built by lantern light in 1932 now has necessary additions, an ironing room and a small den, which Tochan shares with a large freezer, and an old student desk where he keeps his irrigation schedule, writes checks and composes his *haiku*. On the shelf sits a bottle of Manischewitz Concord grape wine, which he enjoys after the day's work. An old violin leans in the corner with a wobbly music stand on which he has his favorite songs, some of which are still written on pieces of cardboard he salvaged in Poston Camp II.

Outside the back door, near the tall bamboo grove, a cabin houses the *ofuro* bath-shower with cement laundry tubs attached to the outside wall, next to the old wringer washing machine. A distance away, stands the "boy house," which was built for Seiji, Sanji, Aizo and Kozo. Now the small rooms are filled with the boys' belongings: military uniforms left by the five brothers and a sister, which Mama stores carefully, books from their college days, old lamps, a desk and odds and ends.

The internment years fade away like a bad dream.

~

MARY TOMOMI SATO
JOHN SHINJI SATO

The long-awaited trip to the courthouse in Sacramento goes well. Mama adds "Mary" to her name as a naturalized American. "Mary is a beautiful name," Tochan says. It is the name of Jesus's mother.

Tochan chooses "John," a common American name.

"*Korede anshin da na*, Mama," Tochan reiterates, as if to seal their naturalization with permanence. It is a relief, he says, to finally have this done.

Mama and Tochan quietly return home. Mama removes her white pillbox hat with the short veil and her pink cotton-blend suit. She puts on her workday clothes of beige khaki pants and an oversized man's shirt.

"*Yokatta na*." It's been good, Tochan comments, not without a sense of relief, as he takes off his Sunday suit and places it on their bed. As always, he expects Mama to check it for soiled spots, press it and hang it up in their closet.

No one would understand but the two of them, not even their children, who upon birth were given the right of citizenship, who did not have the long years of waiting to finally be accorded equal status in a country they long ago adopted.

~

From Clark Air Force Base in the Philippines, I am transferred to FEAMCOM Hospital in Tachikawa, Japan. I find out that it is less than a day's train trip to Onjuku, where Tochan and my uncle Riichi were born.

I look up cousin Hannah, who works with the US civil service in Tokyo, and we embark on our exciting search for our fathers' relatives.

"Kisarazu!" the conductor announces loudly.

"I remember that," I tell Hannah. "Tochan used to mention it. It's the next big town."

We ride for hours through small villages and rice paddies and finally reach Onjuku, hardly a town, with a few shops attached to houses.

I remember the mountain road. It is exactly as Tochan had described. Anytime, I imagine a *kitsune*, a wily fox dressed in a beautiful kimono, will appear to lead one down the wrong road. Two more curves around the mountainside and there should be Tochan and Ojisan's boyhood home.

At the small thatched-roof farmhouse, we meet Ichiji-san, the eldest of the three brothers, who leads us through the dirt floor cooking area into the immaculate *tatami* room where a tiny, frail person lays bent on a *futon*.

"*Okaasan!*" Mother! Ichiji-san yells close to her ear. "*Shinji to Riichi no kodomo da yo.*" It's Shinji and Riichi's children.

She doesn't seem to hear.

Okamura-san, a neighbor, repeats it in an even louder voice.

I touch her bony hand.

"Eh?" she says very faintly, and squeezes my hand with an amazing strength and will not let it go. I sit by her cradling her bony fingers with both my hands. How hard these hands have worked; how deeply this small body has worried and worked to keep her family intact! How desperate was she, the mother who would tell her young son: "*Koko e kaette kuru na, Shinji,*" trusting that hope for her son's future lay in America. Don't come back here, she had whispered, her heart aching that it would be the last time that she would ever see her son.

"*Korede anshin shita,*" she says so softly that I have to bend down my head to hers. "*Moh shinde itte mo ii.*" Now I am ready to die, she says. And adds, With this I am relieved. Tears well as I think that this small body, devoid of flesh now, barely covered with skin, still cradles the deep love for her sons.

She dies quietly the following day.

~

My time with the Air Force is up, and I must decide to extend my time or leave. It is not easy to leave this large family of friends wherever I go. I have not had to worry about food or shelter.

It's been a good trip. "Stay in. You'll be a Chief Nurse," I'm told. And then what? But with four brothers who served in the military as enlisted men, I find the "caste" system uncomfortable.

Even with promises of a bright future with the United States Air Force Nurse Corps, I decide that there is more to life than being a Captain and perhaps even a Chief Nurse.

I apply for a discharge and happily head for home. In June I sail on the *SS Sullivan* from Japan to San Francisco.

⁓

ON THE FARM, SACRAMENTO, CALIFORNIA.

The soft sound of a walnut falling from the giant tree above breaks the quiet of Saturday morning. Under the huge umbrella of the fifty-year-old Franquette, one of the first varieties of English walnuts Tochan had grafted, I gather nuts from the heavy layer, nuts which my brothers knocked down the day before. Airplanes from Mather Field rest on weekends, a welcome respite when often one has to stop talking in mid-sentence when the engines warm up and fly overhead. This morning I hear the birds. I hear the quiet. Tochan and my sisters work under their trees nearby, leaving swaths of clean paths as they slide along the old heavy lugs behind them.

Another falling walnut . . . how good it is to be able to hear the sound of a walnut gently falling to the soft ground, another and then another.

One falls on my shoulder. From the corner of my eye, I see that it is not a walnut, but a clod of dirt, probably stuck on the branch, from one of my brother's boots, I surmise.

Dirt clods shower in from the north. Surprised, I look up.

A group of boys approach my tree slowly, picking up and throwing clods. They appear to be about twelve- and thirteen-years-old.

Now what? Tochan, Kay and Marian seem to be ignoring them. Will they leave if they are ignored?

The wall of boys comes closer and closer, and the clods hit me more often.

Lately, plagued by burglaries and vandalism, Tochan has placed a lock on the barn door. A ladder left against a tree during lunchtime disappeared. One morning Tochan found the windshield on the farm truck totally shattered.

Should I ignore the gang and see how close they will come? Pretending to be busy, I keep looking from the corner of my eye. When the leader moves forward, the others follow. Emboldened, they throw showers of clods my way. When it looks like they are not about to stop, I slowly stand up and straighten up, rubbing my lower back. I look around, trying to appear non-confrontational, only curious.

From beneath my old, floppy straw hat, my gaze meets theirs. I deliberately step carefully around my lug, giving my audience time to leave. When I see them still standing, arms at their sides, intently watching me, I decide to take my chances and take a slow step forward, and then another. The boys, some bigger and some smaller than I am, stand still, almost in defiance, as if to say "try me." Maybe it is curiosity that keeps them still, as the small oriental body, well protected from the sun with long-sleeved, faded work shirt, baggy pants and yellow Playtex gloves, slowly walks towards the group of boys. I feel the worried eyes of my sisters silently telling me to get back.

If they attack with a barrage of dirt clods, I plan to fall dead. I know that if I retreat, it will only refuel their resolve to move forward.

Walking with slow, determined steps, I come face to face with the boys and stand in front of the one who appears to be the leader. I look up and acknowledge his presence and then scan the others, trying to remember their faces.

"Hi. Where do you boys go to school?" I ask.

"Lincoln Village," several answer. Others are visitors from outside the district.

"Do you know that my father planted every one of these trees from walnuts way before you were born?

"I helped him when I was your age," I continue. "Your fathers go to work and support you, right? My father does the same. He and my mother work hard to feed and clothe us and we children help them on our days off."

"Is that your father?" one asks.

"Yes. Would your father like it if some boys climbed over your fence into your back yard? This is my father's property and he would appreciate it if you didn't come into it."

The boys listen not knowing exactly what to make of me. A timid voice in the back says "Sorry."

"I know you are good boys," I tell them.

The boy I am facing drops his dirt clod. I hear the soft sounds of clods dropping in the back. Slowly they turn around and leave.

1956. SACRAMENTO, CALIFORNIA.

"I need to go to the box factory this morning," Tochan tells Mama, as he picks up his hat and goes out the front door after breakfast. Lim's Box Factory in Sacramento sells used boxes for berries and grapes.

Mama is still washing dishes when she hears the screen door open. Tochan has not been gone five minutes.

"*Nani ka wasure mashita?*" Has he forgotten something, Mama asks, as she pours hot water from the kettle into the teapot and adds a pinch of green tea leaves from the airtight Japanese tea can.

Tochan sits down, picks up his teacup, places it against his cheek and closes his eyes. Mama waits. She knows this is his thinking time.

"Our road is gone," he says.

He had driven the blue pickup truck down the road a short distance when he suddenly realized that there was no road ahead, only an expanse of freshly bulldozed dirt. Looking down, he found that he had stopped just in time to avoid a three-foot drop. Troubled, but relieved that he had escaped without injury, he backed his pickup up the road and drove it back into the barn.

Without his access road, there is no way to get to the grocery store. There is no way to get the crops to the shipper in Florin. How will David drive to his classes at State College?

Mama listens as Tochan describes his dilemma.

"Mama," Tochan finally says, putting his teacup down. "There's the Teichert Gravel road on the other side of the fence. I think I will cut a road onto it. We will have to build a sturdy enough bridge over our main irrigation ditch so that the Berry Growers' Association truck can get through without getting stuck."

Mama is worried. Will it mean more trouble for them?

"I don't think so," Tochan says. "Mr. Teichert is a good man."

So it is settled. Mama picks up her floppy, broad-brimmed straw hat from the back entryway, puts on her long-sleeved work shirt and follows her husband. Along the way, they pick up discarded nine-by-twelve boards from behind the barn.

Tochan snips the barbed wire fence and removes several stakes for an opening wide enough to accommodate a truck. Mama returns with a shovel and begins to dam the sides of the main ditch, which might collapse under the wheels of their pickup truck. By shovelfuls Mama carries the extra dirt, creating reinforcement for the irrigation ditch.

It is almost noon when Tochan successfully drives his truck over the bridge. "Get in, Mama. Let's check the rest of the road," he says.

With a sense of satisfaction, they drive slowly along the abandoned gravel road along the edge of the cavernous old pit. On the north side of the barbed wire fence grow youngberries and strawberries, grapes and walnuts. Their farmhouse in the center of their land lies surrounded by a replanted Japanese Black pine tree, several pomegranate trees, ume-no-ki, crabapple, Asian pear, plum trees, several peach trees, a Zabon graft from Japan and many orange trees. A tall grove of bamboo canes, which are used to knock down walnuts, grows on the north side of the house.

Tochan stops. A bridge over a drainage creek appears too dangerous to cross. It has some boards missing.

"Let's get more nine-by-twelves," Tochan suggests, as he slowly and skillfully backs up.

Large four-inch nails secure the boards to what appears to be railroad ties crossing the creek. Having supported hundreds of pieces of heavy machinery in its time, the bridge appears still serviceable, except for the few rotted boards. Tochan finally drives his pickup truck over the newly-repaired bridge, remembering with regal satisfaction his often told story of the deacon and the deaconess riding in their one-hoss shay.

This bridge, he recalls, caused him to lose a whole field of strawberries when the Teichert Gravel Company bulldozed the natural drainage. Rain, which would have nourished the young plants, only stood in the flooded fields to rot the roots. When finally they listened to Tochan's complaints and reopened the drainage, thousands of plants were beyond reviving, plants that they had carefully placed into the redrained soil one by one.

The long, bumpy half-mile road ends at Routier Road. A barbed-wire gate extends across their path, firmly secured by heavy wire. Trash left by nightly trespassers lies in the weeds. With difficulty, Tochan unwinds the long wire holding the gate to the field post, and slides the gate open. Triumphantly, they drive onto Routier Road.

"*Yoku yatta monda,*" Tochan remarks, thinking back to the many challenges they had faced together and conquered. We did well, he muses.

In the distance, they see Masashi David's Volkswagen returning home from college, weaving through the walnut orchard, finding a way to get back to the farmhouse.

Tochan tries to engage the services of a lawyer, but to no avail. He finds out that Kanji-san's almond orchard was purchased by a prominent politician. Tochan decides to watch and wait. So far he had only lost his access. In the meantime he is grateful to have the gravel pit road to get on and off the farm, and to have the Association truck pick up his berries.

Happy times prevail. Children continue school. Five sons and a daughter return home safely from military service. Each of us pursue our own goals. I marry and adopt children. No matter where each of us goes, we know that the farm will be there with Mama and Tochan glad to see us.

1975.

When my husband decides to leave us, all the difficult times I have had seem of no consequence, compared to the present. Whenever our children are out of sight, I break down and cry. Our house is barren. The large, white Herman Miller table, which I loved as our dining table, is now in my husband's conference room. With high hopes, we had put the best we owned in our design office. We had borrowed money for our exciting new venture. With a commitment to adopt four children, divorce had never entered my mind.

I start to pick up the pieces. Feeling better, I enroll in a home repairs class to prepare our house to sell. Paint, tile the bathroom and change the front fascia. After having returned from a five-year job assignment out of state, the property is a total disaster requiring many loads by hired truck to remove the trash.

At work one afternoon, I catch myself momentarily losing consciousness. It is a frightening wake-up call. I sit quietly with my head in my hands. You can't let yourself get sick, I tell myself. You've got to take care of your children.

It is a tough decision. I swallow my pride, quietly accept the accusations of poor parenting, and ask my husband to help me with the children. Our oldest teenage son, almost seventeen, seems happy to go with his father.

I decide to move into the best school district in our county. As luck would have it, it is the district where Don and David, my two brothers, teach. And it is not too far from my parents' farm. With my brother David's help, we find a small, two-bedroom apartment. The girls, seven and seventeen, sleep in one room, and Paul, fifteen, has the smaller bedroom. I have the studio couch in the front room.

I am devastated, just when I thought we would start to get on with life. Cia refuses to attend the high school only a block away.

"There's no music!" she says. She is first chair on the violin at Luther Burbank High School.

"If you can figure a way to get there, Honey, I'll try to get a permit for you," I tell her. I know it is impossible for me to drive her halfway across the county, get to my job, and then pick her up.

To my amazement and pride, she finds a way, with several changes by bus, leaving early in the morning before some of us are out of bed. It is late afternoon when she returns carrying her books and violin.

A flurry of activities across the road lately indicates that the rear portion of the Kanji Abe property might have a new owner. For years it lay fallow, the stunted almond trees with fewer and fewer pink blossoms each spring reminding us of our neighbor's shattered dreams.

The sale of his forty acres to a prominent councilman was to have sent his children to school and to have made life a bit easier for him and his wife. Instead, with the sale not concluded, Kanji took his case to court and was awarded two duplexes and the abandoned rear property. Because he was unable to pay the accumulated back taxes, Kanji's parcel was claimed by the state and sold. A discouraged man, nonetheless he found a job as dishwasher at the university medical center to support his family of five.

~

"If that is to become a subdivision," I speculate, "why not name one of its streets after Mama?"

"Sounds like a good idea," the family agrees.

"How about Tomomi Street?"

So it is settled, and I embark on the task of petition signing by property owners within 500 feet of our twenty acres as required by law.

~

APRIL 24, 1975.

Not without trepidation, I knock on the door of a large, pretentious home off Folsom Lake. From the top of the steps, a spectacular view of the lake spreads out below.

"Come in, come in." An affable middle-aged man invites me into the high-ceilinged, spacious living room.

I tell him the reason for my visit.

"Where is the property?" he asks.

"Near Mather Field," I answer, surprised that he does not know exactly where his property is located.

He walks off into what appears to be his office and returns with several large rolls of project maps under his arms.

"Come here," he beckons, leading me to a long table in the next room where he spreads out the project maps.

"Is this it?" he asks.

I recognize Routier Road to the west and Ellenwood Avenue at the bottom of the map between the Sato and the Abe properties.

"That's it," I agree.

He tells me that he is a Christian and a Baptist, possibly alluding to our Mayhew Baptist Church on the corner of Routier Road and Ellenwood Avenue. Immediately, my defensive shoulders relax, knowing that he will sign my petition and I will be on my way.

"I think it will be all right but let me call the project engineer to make sure," he tells me.

He goes to the phone in his office. I don't see him but I can hear him loudly and clearly as if he were speaking to be heard.

"A lady with a sweet gesture to honor her parents is here. She wants to name one of the streets in our subdivision after her mother. I think it's a nice thing to do. Do you have any problem with that?"

They have a long conversation regarding other projects, which gives me time.

Not without feeling a bit guilty, I study the map with care, looking carefully at all the houses and streets being planned on the sixteen acres. I have a wide choice and Tomomi Street, I decide, should be an important street, which radiates out from the Sato property, not one which is in the back end of their subdivision.

I notice that our farmhouse and the barn are clearly designated on the south edge of the map.

I blink and look again. Where are our irrigation pump and the water tank? Upon closer scrutiny, I recognize an outline of what appears to be the irrigation pump in the middle of their main street! And to the side of it, on the street, I recognize the water tank. There is no doubt: the irrigation pump sits on their main street, including the pneumatic tank and part of the shed.

Who sketched in the irrigation system? Didn't he question it? Or is it like the Poston latrine plan, where no one gave a thought to the children, and cut out only big round holes? I study the map twice, three times, four times, not able to believe what I am seeing, grateful that he is taking his time on the phone.

When he returns, I explain in my quiet, controlled voice that our irrigation pump is in the middle of their street. He looks at the map, looks up and states coldly, "Your father can move it."

"That will be very difficult to do," I tell him.

"Then he could run a pipe," he says.

I tell him that we probably could not afford to do that.

"That's too bad," he retorts, his friendly, Christian demeanor turning cold.

Seeing that a decent conversation is not possible, I leave, thanking him for his time.

I drive the twenty-three mile trip back to the farm in a daze. Now what? Will Tochan be forced out of farming like so many other Japanese farmers along the American River?

My clipboard with the unsigned petition lies on the front seat. Tomomi Street fades away and I am thrust into a territory I know nothing about. Our family's survival is at stake.

⌒

"I'm too old to fight," Tochan says, leaning on his shovel upon hearing my report of my visit. "I just want to keep on doing what I am doing."

"Don't worry. We'll fight for you," I assure him, although I have no idea where to begin or what it entails. Tochan tells me that lately strange stakes have appeared in his walnut orchard but that he has received no notification regarding any plans by the county.

It is almost five o'clock on Friday. I hurry to phone the county office.

"That map is being heard Monday morning by the Subdivision Review Board," I am advised.

"Next week? Why weren't we notified?" I ask aghast, trying to hide the anger in my voice. "Our property is adjacent to the planned subdivision!"

"The meeting is scheduled for April 29th at ten o'clock," the secretary efficiently answers.

I find out that two months prior to submission of the parcel map, zoning for the 75-acre parcel to the south bordering our farm had been changed to R-2, Residential. Now only a strip of forty acres remains AR-1, Agricultural. Those forty acres belong to my father and his brother, neatly trapped by residential and surface mining zoning and Mather Field to the east.

What had caused the demise of so many family farms now hits us. Where is the government for the people? It seems we are victims of a giant conspiracy, with county government totally ignoring the small family farms.

There is no time to waste and certainly there is no use in arguing.

APRIL 29, 1975.

On the morning of the 29th, Steve takes time off from the United States Army Corps of Engineers and accompanies me to the hearing. We sit against the wall, behind a large conference table of dignitaries.

The project engineer presents the plans for the proposed subdivision. He explains that there is an existing subdivision to the west, and that his map will be an extension of the county's housing plan. With mostly single dwelling homes being planned, he states that their project will be an upgrade to the existing area. He describes our property as an eyesore where a "poor dirt farmer" grows a few things. There are no known adverse effects to their proposal, he assures the Board.

My hands begin to perspire. No adverse effects? They are destroying my father's life and that is not an "adverse effect?"

"Any other comment?" the chairman asks.

I stand. I hope my voice will be steady.

"My name is Kiyo Sato-Viacrucis. I represent my father John Shinji Sato, who farms twenty acres to the south of the said map. It has been producing walnuts, Ribier grapes and a variety of berries for forty-five years."

I go on to explain that the irrigation system has been in place since 1930. It is now under the main street of the said subdivision map. Without it, I explain to the Subdivision Review Board, my father's twenty-acre farm can no longer survive.

"During the peak of the season, our farm sends out over one hundred crates of strawberries, raspberries and boysenberries per day. In the fall we harvest table grapes and walnuts."

The Subdivision Review Board approves the map upon condition that the boundary problem is settled.

Steve and I leave the chambers unaware of the problems we have left in our wake. With their well-laid plans foiled, what will the developers do?

"Let's stop and ask for a transmittal," Steve suggests.

"What's that?"

"Minutes of the proceedings."

"Sounds good."

"And we'd better find out about the Environmental Impact Report, too."

I've never heard of the often-mentioned EIR upon which our fate seems to lie. Working with the Army Corps of Engineers, supervising dam projects, Steve has read many of those reports.

On our way out we stop by the office to ask that a transmittal and a copy of the EIR be sent to us.

I take a deep breath, relieved that at least we have stopped the developers dead in their tracks. No doubt they had planned on an easy approval this morning, expecting no opposition from the "farmer to the south" who was totally unaware of his impending fate.

We must now fight for water and Tochan's survival.

"Hey! Check this!" exclaims Don, reading the Environmental Impact Report prepared by the county. "They call our property 'vacant!' Vacant!" he almost yells. "Where'd they get that kind of information?"

With the copies of the Environmental Impact Report I had made for each of my brothers and sisters spread out on the kitchen table, the family gathers at the farm to study the county's assessment of Tochan's property.

"Read this! It says the property to the south is vacant and that "the soil is marginal and has supported only a narrow range of crops!"

"It used to be marginal," explains George, the soil analyst working for the State Department of Water Resources. "You're too young to remember, but in 1930 when Tochan bought this land, this was an open field with a creek running through the middle. But now?" He shakes his head. "All they have to do is see this place and know that it's neither marginal nor vacant. Tochan worked this into prime agricultural land. Where have those guys been for forty-five years? Look at the walnut trees! Look at the vineyard! I can't believe it, and they get paid for writing this?"

"Check this. What they describe as a 'swale' on their subdivision map is our main irrigation ditch. I can't believe this." David shakes his head as he reads on.

"Did you read the copy of the transmittal?" I ask. "Listen to this. Everybody who made a statement during the Subdivision Review Board hearing was recognized by name except for me. I am the 'daughter of the farmer to the south.' Tochan's name as the owner of the property isn't even mentioned! And I made it very clear that I was representing John Shinji Sato, the property owner to the south."

Pete, leaning his chair against the refrigerator, flips the pages muttering now and then under his breath, "No kidding."

"Mark the passages you don't agree with," I suggest to everyone, "and write your comments in the margins."

"I can't believe it! What a lot of good-sounding lies." David the youngest, studying for a teaching credential, reads with a critical eye.

The family no longer fits around the kitchen table. Steve, cramped at the window counter, underlines and writes on page after page. He addresses the problems of irrigation, drainage, public access and other factors inadequately explained, reassessed from an engineer's point of view.

All afternoon the team dissects, discusses and writes.

"Wow! Who's going to put all this together?" I ask, holding the stack of papers.

"You are." No one disagrees.

As a single parent of three teenagers and a toddler working as a school nurse, my only time is late at night after the children are in bed. With papers spread out in a small trailer parked in my driveway, I write and rewrite and cut and paste every night, glad to have a place where I can leave the papers until I come back.

When finally I clip together the thirteen pages of the corrections and the additions, I ask my brothers and sisters to meet me at the farm.

"Looks good," Steve comments. "When's the Planning Commission hearing?"

"May 19th. How about reporting?"

"No, you do it."

"But you know what you are talking about, Steve. I don't know anything about engineering."

"That's all right. You've got it all down on paper. Besides you're a better speaker."

MAY 19, 1975.

An imposing figure enters the county chambers just as the meeting is about to begin, and motions to me. I follow him into the hallway and found myself surrounded by big, Caucasian men. I recognize the property owner. Later I found out that the others were the consulting engineer, the realtor and probably a lawyer.

"If you don't go along with our plans, we're going to sue you," one of them tells me.

I look at them with an even, soft gaze, concealing rapid heartbeats about to fibrillate.

"This is a democracy," I tell them calmly, meeting them eye-to-eye. "You can state your opinion and I will state mine and I will go by whatever the county decides." I leave them and walk back into the hearing chamber.

My palms are sweating, awaiting my turn on the agenda. It suddenly occurs to me that the men had hoped to scare me from appearing before the Planning Commission. This would allow them a clear route to developing their subdivision with no opposition. The gravity of the situation hits me. They will go to any extreme to carry out their plans.

The hearing progresses quickly. I observe that citizens who are not familiar with county protocol are brutally interrupted. They are not kindly or patiently treated. It is not a "government for the people," as I had learned in school. There is no time for compassion, no time to help those in need of an explanation. I am relieved to have done my homework with my brothers.

I nervously wait for my turn to speak, worried that I may not understand the "county language" and the agenda and miss my opportunity.

The spokesman for the Subdivision map presents the plan with professional suavity, as if he had done it many times before. How can I, who have never spoken at a county hearing, be believable? Will they take me, the "daughter of the farmer to the south," seriously?

I walk up to the podium with my clipboard of notes and face the six members of the Planning Commission seated behind the long, semicircular table with a microphone for each commissioner. Flanking me, in the rear of the gallery, sit a row of Oriental faces, obviously part of the Sato clan. I am scared but proud to be a part of this intelligent appearing, nicely dressed group representing Tochan, "a dirt farmer."

The commissioners listen intently to my lengthy report. No one reminds me that my five minutes are up. Item by item, I challenge their EIR with corrections and suggestions. They ask many questions. I am able to answer them intelligently, having been well-tutored by my brothers.

I address the obstruction of natural drainage flow. Once before, I say, Mr. Sato had lost a field of strawberries when the Teichert Gravel Company dammed up the flow to the south. We ask that the natural drainage not be obliterated or obstructed.

The subdivision map is approved on the condition that the boundary line between the two properties is settled.

Relieved with the short reprieve, I leave the chambers with mixed emotions, knowing that this is only temporary, aware that I leave behind a few angry people.

As I walk towards the elevator, an older couple hurriedly follows me.

When they enter the elevator, I acknowledge their presence with a nod and smile, recognizing them as one of the presenters who had problems regarding their property in the foothills. The Commission was neither helpful nor kindly to them.

I am taken aback when the man asks me, "Would you represent us?"

"I wish I could help you," I tell them, "but I am not a lawyer."

They walk out of the elevator, appearing totally defeated.

"In my next life," I promise myself, "I'm going to study law."

At the kitchen table, analyzing the EIR, I remember one of us telling Tochan, "You have everything in your family except a lawyer. We need a lawyer, Tochan."

"I'm glad none of you are lawyers," he quips. "They are all crooked."

Late at night, there is an ominous knock on my door. A special delivery messenger hands me a document, legal papers claiming rights to the property in dispute and all improvements, which include the irrigation system and the access road on the Sato property.

"The benchmark is gone," Tochan announces solemnly. It had been in place near the railroad tracks since the land was purchased in 1930. We know that a benchmark is a sacred surveying landmark, not to be moved.

Tochan is also served with a lawsuit.

"I think we better not make waves," George suggests solemnly.

"This may cause more problems than it's worth," Steve says.

"It might get dangerous."

"They might really cause us trouble."

Several of my brothers agree that we should keep our mouths shut.

"They'll get their way no matter what."

I have fears of being killed in a strange automobile accident.

"Look at all the farmers who were forced to sell. Maybe we should sell and move."

Pursued by developers, the *Issei* and *Nisei* truck farmers fall like dominoes along the fertile American River. Some opt to prematurely give up their lifelong pursuit, sell and move into town. Others buy plots of land across the river in the less populated West Sacramento.

Tochan says, "All I want is to continue doing what I am doing. I enjoy what I am doing. If I sell, I only have money in my pocket."

But Tochan cannot farm without water. The family cannot live here. Without water, the land will revert back to its original, fallow state. To dig another well and develop a new irrigation system is out of the question. Against my brothers' warnings and concerns, I decide to leap the last hurdle before the County Board of Supervisors.

The wait is an agonizing time of discussions and sleepless nights of worry. If they can serve me, and then my father, with a lawsuit, what will prevent them from mysteriously causing an accident to shut me up?

I prepare, nonetheless, remembering how Mama and Tochan have gone through hell for us. At seventy-nine, Tochan will accept life's challenges with grace and dignity as he has always done, even in incarceration, but only over my dead body will I allow the developers to trample roughshod over my father.

I receive a message through my brother's attorney friend that if I agree to "go along with their plans" and do not speak at the hearings, they will withdraw the lawsuit.

JULY 9, 1975.

I have a plan.

On the morning of the hearing before the Sacramento County Board of Supervisors, I fill my old briefcase with the largest walnuts from the last harvest.

At the hearing, with confidence gained from my previous experiences before the county, I introduce myself as "representing John Shinji Sato, the adjacent property owner to the subdivision map under consideration."

Fully aware of the fact that my small five-foot two inch stature does not command the same respect as the handsome, tall, male Caucasian testifying before me, I hold myself erect and face the Board sitting a level higher in their black, swivel chairs. With the lack of respect afforded my father and me at the previous hearings, and the memories of evacuation and internment still raw in my mind, I know that this is not going to be easy.

This is Tochan's last stand.

"Your Environmental Impact Report states that the Twenty-acre Sato property is vacant," I begin, with all the steadiness of voice that I can muster. I open my briefcase and pick up three large walnuts, which barely fit into the palm of my hand.

"These are what grow on land you describe as 'vacant and marginal soils.'"

I take my time to give to each member of the Board three giant walnuts. A Supervisor reaches for the gavel and cracks one open, much to the surprise and delight of those in the austere chambers.

They listen intently for almost thirty minutes as I dissect their Environmental Impact Report, uncovering, item by item, the gross errors and incompetence of their employees. I offer corrections suggested by my brothers, knowing that I have the input of top experts, an engineer and a soil analyst, working for the federal and state governments. They listen intently.

The Supervisors vote unanimously in my father's favor and place two conditions on the developer's plan: to settle the boundary and to build a buffer fence between the two properties.

The project engineer is aghast and stumbles for words. "We've already spent five thousand dollars on this plan," he complains.

A county employee stops me in the hall. "You know what? I've never seen a property owner win against those guys before," he says.

Exiting from the county building, I stand numb at the top of the steps, staring at the humanity passing by. Having traveled in high gear for so long and now at a stop, I don't know in which direction to move.

Finally Tochan is safe, but for how long?

⁓

JULY 10, 1975.

News articles appear the next morning. "BOARD SAYS NUTS TO LOCAL SUB-DIVISION," a columnist writes in the *Sacramento Union*.

"Supervisor Melarkey shatters a giant walnut with the gavel passed on by Chairperson Smoley. The Supervisors' chambers looked like the Nutcracker Suite."

"Her eloquent plea that a subdivision threatened her father's nut and fruit farm helped the Supervisors to reverse earlier approval of the subdivision."

The *Sacramento Bee* writes that "she found walnuts to be effective ammunition against the proposed subdivision."

⁓

On the bed of the old red farm truck, grandchildren build houses with the empty boxes, handing them to the pickers whenever needed. The "water boy" happily carries the jug to the thirsty workers with a bag of Auntie Kay's cookies.

"How about some over here?" calls Uncle George. Scott, just turned nine, sits along a ditch, feeling important as his uncle tilts the jug for a stream of cold water.

Noon arrives none too soon, a welcome relief and a chance to straighten up.

"Lunchtime!" Marian calls from the farmhouse.

"Bring them all in!" Tochan calls.

"Mine's about full," I yell.

The partials are packed into several lugs and everyone scrambles to fill up the last box.

"Forty. We did well. Thank you," Tochan says, as the boys stack the lugs to be taken to the barn for protection from the hot sun.

When the truck engine starts, children come running from all directions. With their dusty, sandaled feet dangling down the sides of the truck bed, bodies bump against each other. Their wide, happy smiles tell me that no moment is more precious, as weary adults walk behind them, carrying jackets, water jug and leftover cookies.

With the help of his sons, the truck is again loaded with empty boxes for the afternoon's picking.

"How about a beer?" George asks me.

"Sounds good."

George and I sit under the shade of the wisteria arbor, drinking ice-cold beer, glad for the respite from the hot midday sun. The wisteria, retrained again after the family's four-year absence during the war, now provides beauty and protection for family gatherings around the picnic table below.

As the kitchen table no longer can seat the family, children spread outdoors onto tatami mats out on the lawn.

When the master of the house leaves at one o'clock, with his faithful Taro at his heels, it signals the harvest crew that work begins again, except for the kitchen helpers whose chores never seem to end.

It promises to be another warm day in late August. Heavy clusters of deep purple Ribier grapes hang beneath the shade of the vines, the result of many years of nurturing since the family's return from internment.

"These are pretty good grapes," Don says, and his compliments are few.

"Yeah. It's fun to pick them. There's hardly any clipping to do," Kay comments, holding up a huge bunch from the next vine. "Look at this one!"

With her tiny figure hidden beneath a huge vine, Mama fills a thirty-pound lug without moving. She reminds us, "Only pick what we would like to eat ourselves." She is still the champion picker.

"You need another box, Mama?" George calls out. The boys see to it that Mama does not have to carry out the heavy lugs.

One after another, sons and daughters and grandchildren bring in their filled boxes, keeping Tochan busy leveling the clusters and nailing the covers, a sharp contrast to the silent hammer of years before.

The birds sing. The sun shines. The earth produces. A quiet gratitude flows on this land.

· 16 ·

MAMA'S LAST GIFT:
HOW TO DIE

Kan-puu ya

Kaki hadaka naru

Jyu-ni gatsu

–JOHN SHINJI SATO

Cold winter wind

Naked persimmons

Of December

–TRUDY SATO, TRANSLATOR

MAMA'S ALLERGIES SEEM to be worsening. She sneezes and coughs and blows into her rag handkerchief more often. Her doctor prescribes stronger medications, which do not help her. Kay, who takes her to the doctor, worries that the symptoms do not abate and that the drugs only slow her down. Mama would never think of stopping to rest.

"How about an X-ray?" Kay, a nurse now, suggests.

The results are devastating! Possible lung cancer. We refuse to believe it. Not Mama! She had been active all her life and had not even touched a cigarette. We are angry with the doctor. Why didn't he listen to her instead of writing her prescriptions for stronger and stronger doses of allergy drugs? Didn't he see that her coughing was becoming worse with each visit?

Mama is hospitalized for further tests. We cannot believe what we are told. Both of her lungs are diseased with cancer. Only one-fourth of her lung space is functioning, the doctor tells us. How did she manage to keep up with us in the vineyard? She has six to eight weeks, her doctor says. We listen, numb. Then the questions slowly come.

"What do we do now?"

"What is the treatment?"

"Will she stay in the hospital?"

"Is it possible to operate?"

"What is her prognosis? What does six to eight weeks mean?"

Almost constantly one of us is at her bedside, seeing that her needs are met. I drop in at lunchtime whenever I am working in a school nearby. Sometimes George sits with Mama, taking his lunch hour from the Department of Water Resources downtown. Steve drops by if he is not supervising a project out of town with the US Army Corps of Engineers. With the many children and spouses and their children, Mama is never without somebody watching over her.

"You have a nice family," a nurse says.

⁓

I remember Tochan's story of long ago, *Oba Sute Yama*, a classic Japanese legend. What a terrible title, I thought . . . a mountain where one throws away old women! How appropriate this old Japanese legend is now.

A young son sees that his mother is growing old. Soon it will be time. He begins to weave a basket. Each night he sits by the hibachi. The large base of the basket is done. The sides begin to curve upward. Seated on the tatami floor, his mother quietly watches. She knows that each night means that she is closer to the day when she must leave her house and plot where she and her husband had toiled for many long years. Now as custom dictates, she is under the care of her oldest son and his wife.

The sides of the basket begin to form. She notes that the front of the basket remains open. The back lengthens. It will not be long before the sides will curve upwards and close at the top.

With an old cotton cloth he forms the shoulder straps to carry the basket. It is ready.

Tomorrow, she knows, is the day.

In the early morning he brings the basket and places it beside her. "*Dozo*," he motions as he places the *zabuton* pillow inside. She obediently steps inside and sits with her legs folded under her. The basket fits well. Its top will protect her from the rain and snow. Her small, frail body is easily carried on his back.

Soon the dirt path along the rice paddy ends. The incline becomes rocky. Small patches of snow appear here and there. Hours pass, it is a slow, difficult climb.

The mountain slope appears ahead dotted with old women sitting quietly and waiting.

He finds a spot and takes the basket off his shoulders. She steps out, takes her *zabuton*, places it on the cold ground and sits on it.

"*Sayonara*," she bows to her son, thanking him for his care.

He takes leave.

"Wait," she calls, "you are forgetting the basket!"

"I will not need it," he responds.

"You may need it when you are old," she says.

He hesitates, then stands still.

He turns back.

"*Dozo*." Please. He motions to his mother to get in.

They walk back the way they came.

On Saturday, Mama is all smiles when her teenage granddaughters, Cia and Cindy, visit.

"How are you, Grandma?" they ask. Her standard response is always "Fine," with a wide smile.

"Mom, is it okay to take Grandma for a walk?" Cia asks.

"I don't see why not. I'm sure it's all right in the wheelchair."

"I can walk," Grandma insists.

"Wheelchair," the nurse says. "And remember, she cannot go off the floor," she adds.

The girls exchange side-glances.

With a blanket over Grandma's knees, we are out into the hallway, Cindy, Cia, my sisters Kay and Marian, and me.

We can hardly keep up with the two girls, both seventeen, who are pushing the wheelchair at full speed. Mama appears calm. I worry that they might spill her head first into the hall. Cindy checks a doorway.

"Nope," she says and Cia pushes on.

She peeks into another doorway. Like a burglar about to make a hit, she looks around, hand on a doorknob.

"Okay," she says, and opens the door wide. Cia quickly pushes the wheelchair through the door. We follow.

To my horror, it is the fire escape.

"No! No! No! You can't do that!" I tell them in a loud whisper, thinking they were going to take her down the fire escape if they can't take her down the elevator.

"Hi, Grandma!" A tumultuous greeting wells up from three stories below when Grandma appears at the fire escape platform. Bending from her chair, she waves with the happiest smile to her grandchildren, who are too young to visit upstairs, gathered below in the small courtyard. For the moment there is only joy. There is no pain, no sadness. Cia and Cindy stand on both sides of Grandma like proud and victorious royal soldiers.

It is a foggy, gray morning. As soon as Paul and Tanya leave for school, I leave for work. On my way, I drop in at the farm to check in on Mama to see how she is tolerating the medications and her chemotherapy treatments.

Mama is not in her bedroom.

At the kitchen table, Tochan is writing in his daily journal.

"Where's Mama?"

"Outside."

"Outside?! What's she doing out there? It's cold!"

I rush out the back door and find her bundled up in her warm robe, standing by the incinerator, burning trash.

"Mama, what are you doing?" I ask.

She appears embarrassed, as if caught in the act. She is burning the bag of soiled tissues which collected during the night.

"I didn't want anybody to touch it," she says.

"It's all right, Mama. Cancer doesn't spread that way," I tell her. "Don't worry about it. We'll take care of it."

I don't know that I convinced her. She shuffles back into the house, hugging her robe.

Mama eats the cold, toasted English muffin Tochan had fixed. Having never cooked in his life, he doesn't understand that toast should be served warm but Mama eats it with gratitude. Steve makes the coffee before he leaves. I have a cup of coffee with them and leave, feeling better that all is progressing as well as expected.

～

"Kiyo-chan," Mama scolds me in her weak voice trying to sound strong. "Go and get some sleep." I sleep outside her door now, on the couch. I listen to her cough as I have done when my children had coughs. With each cough I can hear the fluids gradually creep up in her lungs. When the cough brings up mucus, I go to her bedside and encourage her to lower her head and chest over the side of the bed while I gently tap her small back. Her pretty, pink gown is damp and sticky.

Sleeping next to her, Tochan sleeps soundly. He refuses to move to the next room. For over fifty years they have slept together. My sister and I tactfully suggest that Mama might rest better alone, but at the end of his workday and a hot bath, he slips in beside Mama as always.

"*Tochan mo tai hen da ne,*" she whispers quietly. It is hard for him too, she says, knowing that without her help, work does not progress well.

～

Mama continues to cough. She meticulously wipes her sputum with tissues and deposits them in the plastic bag beside her. Her coughs become gags.

"*Sumanai desu kere domo.*" I am so sorry but I need to go to the bathroom, she says apologetically.

Her body is so small and frail that I could almost carry her. She holds my arm as we walk to the bathroom. Even though she scolds me for doing too much, I have a feeling that she is grateful to have my arm to hold on to.

As soon as we reach the bathroom, she collapses by the toilet and begins to vomit as if she had been holding it off, her arms embracing the bowl. As I gently stroke her shoulders, I feel totally helpless and tears fall.

"Dear God," I plead, "please let her get well and let her enjoy a few more years. She has worked so hard for us." I desperately bargain with God.

Her vomiting continues forever, it seems. Mama puts her head down and allows her lungs to drain. She doesn't quarrel with God as I do. Why, oh why, I question, if you are a good God, why do you allow so much suffering? It seems an eternity to me before she finally lifts her head, pulls herself up to the sink and washes her face and hands. She gargles and rinses her mouth. Feeling better, we walk back to the bedroom. She gratefully sinks onto her bed.

"Thank you," Mama says, barely audibly. After a few breaths, she continues, "You have children to take care of. They have only you to depend on. I know where I am going so you need not worry about me. Go and get some rest."

She fumbles under her pillow. She places her small fist in my hand and drops a crumpled twenty-dollar bill.

"Mama!" I exclaim. "I don't want that!"

She looks at me with anger in her eyes. I had not seen that before. She pushes the money into my palms and I know that the only way to soften that anger is to accept her gift.

Steve cashes her Social Security checks, with which she remembers the grandchildren.

I control my tears, tuck her in and leave the room.

It is not until the sky begins to lighten that Mama's cough awakens me. She is in great distress with the accumulated fluids in her lungs. I rush in and help her with postural drainage. From her small body, it is hard to understand how so much stuff can be coughed up.

"Thank you," Mama says every time. For what, I want to tell her, but all I can do is stroke her back, this little body which has toiled so long for the nine of us without ever a complaint.

I said to her once, "How do you manage to keep working so hard, Mama?"

"When I get tired," she said, "and I don't think I have another ounce of energy left, I just cling to God's hem."

⁓

Tochan is gone when Mama and I return from a long session in the bathroom of morning ablutions after the drainage. I give her a sponge bath in bed. Clean pajamas, a pretty bed jacket from her daughter-in-law, her hair combed and Mama is ready for breakfast.

"Hi, Grandma," Tanya, seven years old, who has slept in my old bedroom, brings a tiny bouquet of flowers she found growing in the lawn.

"Thank you," Mama says with the happiest smile. There is no sign of the suffering she has endured during the night. Her breathing is regular and I hope again that she might reverse the ravages of the disease.

⁓

"The persimmons are ripe, Marian. Do you think we can take her to see it?" I ask her.

Mama rests under the wisteria arbor in the chaise lounge, wearing her floppy, white hat. Marian cares for her while the rest of us work the walnut husker by the barn. Beside her, on the lawn, are a box of tissues and a paper bag lined with a plastic bag for her frequent spasms of coughing. On the side table she has a pitcher of water and a small plastic cup, which she is able to hold up to her mouth.

"Sure. I don't see why not. I'll get the wheelchair."

Mama is delighted. We lift her on to the child-sized wheelchair we have rented. She weighs no more than eighty pounds. Mama had always been about one hundred and fifteen pounds, slightly plump for her four feet nine inches. Marian places the box of tissues and a bag on Mama's lap.

Outside the garden, the yard is gravelly and bumpy. Marian pulls the wheelchair and I push. Mama looks at every little thing as if for the first time: the pink rosebush, the Santa Rosa plum tree, the walnut trees. She notices the seedling oranges still remaining at the top of a tree they had worked so hard to save after the war, and the Zabon Tochan had grafted. We bump along the road towards the barn.

"Grandma! Grandma!" the children yell, running towards us. Grandchildren appear from all sides.

"Can I push?" Scott asks.

"Sure."

Small hands reach in front of mine.

Walnuts are offered and placed on Grandma's lap. "Thank you," Mama says smiling radiantly.

"Here, Grandma." Tanya finds a dandelion.

"Thank you," she says. Little hands want to give Grandma something. A leaf from her grandson David, a rock picked up as we wheel along, a feather. Like one of Tochan's stories, we look like Momotaro, the Peach Boy, gathering his *kerai* warriors along the way to conquer the *oni*, the monster.

Mama removes her floppy hat and carefully places all the little treasures in it. We go by the noisy husking machine.

"Hi, Mama!" The workers wave to her.

Four persons work at the conveyor belt, picking out culls, their hands moving like machines, hardly giving enough time to lift up their hands and wave. Two fellows carry away filled boxes from the end of the belt to the sled. On the platform, Tochan empties boxes of walnuts into the tank from where the walnuts roll off onto the belt. George carries the heavy boxes to the tank and hands the empties to grandchildren, who scurry like busy little ants piling the empty boxes back onto the old farm truck.

"You're looking pretty good, Mama," Kay tells her, leaving her post at the conveyor belt, depending on other hands to do double time to cover her, which is so unlike her.

We gather more *kerai* followers and by the time we reach the persimmon tree down the road Mama is surrounded by sons and daughters and children. Bodily, chair and all, strong arms carry her over the rough dirt clods. They set her down beneath the drooping branches, which are loaded with large, orange colored persimmons. She holds a branch in both her hands and looks at it as if for the first time . . . or perhaps, for the last time. Her lap fills with persimmons picked by little hands, some still green.

"Please God," I plead silently. "We will do anything if you will let us have her for one more year, or two. Give her time to enjoy her family."

For countless years, the persimmon tree has signaled the coming of fall. There's the early morning chill, the first crisp bite of the Fuyu persimmon, and then the bright colored leaves.

Mama looks up slowly.

"See that one?" she says.

We all look up to where she is pointing, almost at the top of the tree.

"That's the one that will taste the best," she tells us.

Mama is beginning to lose her faculties, I think to myself. The tree is loaded with ripe persimmons and she wants one that is beyond reach. Besides, if it is the one I think it is, it has a hole in it.

"A bird has pecked at it and they know what is good," Mama says.

Already Pete is halfway up the tree.

"You can't reach that. It's too high, Pete," I yell, fearing that he might slip.

"You wanna bet?" he counters.

In no time, he reaches the top and forces the big branch to bend towards him.

"I got it!" he says and plucks the orange-red persimmon and throws it to me. I catch it carefully in the cradle of my hands.

Mama holds the semi-soft fruit as if it were a treasure of some sort. With her finger she carefully digs around the hole where the bird had pecked and discards the discolored, soft flesh. She wipes her fingers with tissue. She bites into the fruit. She takes another bite and then another.

I look at my sisters. They are both looking at her. Mama could hardly swallow her *okayu* rice gruel this morning. The knot in my chest is about to break out into tears, so I look away. At this moment only God knows my gratitude, and maybe my sisters.

EARLY SPRING, 1977.

As I drive into the farmyard mid Saturday morning with my children, I notice someone bent over in the far end of the vineyard. Mama's illness has interrupted Tochan's yearly pruning schedule, I figure, and poor Dad, we haven't given any thought to what he has had to now do alone. It is a cold, drizzly February day.

I go to Mama's room. She is not in bed. She is not in the bathroom. Not in the kitchen. She is not by the incinerator.

I am frantic. "Have you seen Grandma?" I ask the children.

"No." They are playing with Taro, the German Shepherd dog grandchildren Mark, Ellen and Jodi rescued from the pound.

I walk into the vineyard to ask Tochan. To my total disbelief I find Mama, bandana tied over her head, picking wild mustard greens!

"Mama!" is all I can say. Beside her are already three large plastic bags filled with the tender greens we look forward to each season before the yellow flowers cover the vineyard. She parboils them, cools and squeezes the water, cuts them in two-inch lengths and drizzles over them ground sesame seed sauce. Each year since childhood the mustard greens heralded springtime and nourished our bodies after winter.

I help Mama carry the bags. The woman who carried thirty-five pound lugs of Ribier grapes with ease so many times a day now finds her own body a burden to carry over the ditches and the dirt clods.

I say nothing. My heart is filled to bursting. This tiny person, who left her homeland for love of a man, who gave love totally to her nine children and everybody else in her path, who didn't have time to master the English language, is even in her last days picking mustard greens for her children.

Gratefully she lies down in her bed as I quietly remove her shoes and work clothes.

As I take care of Mama during the night, Tanya, my youngest, sleeps in my childhood bedroom. Back at our apartment, Cia sees that she and her brother get to school.

While I help Mama brush her teeth and wash her face, I hear Tanya chatting happily with her grandfather as he fixes their breakfast. He then drives her to her elementary school five miles away.

Each morning, Kay comes to take care of Mama after she sends her four boys to school and her husband to work. I give her the night report as Mama and I have breakfast. As a recent graduate of the University of California School of Nursing, she keeps us apprised of the latest information on medications such as Choledyl, Methrotrexate, Arlidin, etc.

We record in our notebook what Mama has taken and at what time, including food.

In mid-afternoon, Kay leaves to be with her family returning from school and work, and my sister Marian, after seeing to the needs of her son and husband, checks in at the farm to care for Mama until Steve comes home from work.

Steve, who cooks every dinner after he comes home from his job as assistant chief with the Corps of Engineers, writes down what she has eaten, who has visited, etc.

After my job of school nursing, my children and I spend time together at our apartment. At eight, Tanya and I pack up and leave for the farm, leaving Cia and Paul doing their homework.

⌒

We observe sadly that the amber-colored Depression glass coffee cup, a dozen of which we have had forever and used for hot cocoa, coffee and tea, now is held with both of Mama's hands. Mama's strength slowly diminishes, no matter how hard we try.

"Let's find the prettiest and lightest tea cup for Grandma," I suggest to Tanya when we finish our shopping.

"Okay," she agrees cheerfully, hopping along holding my hand.

In the china department there is a mesmerizing collection of cups and saucers, the likes of which I had never seen before. Tanya goes from table to table.

"How about this one, Mommy?" she exclaims going from one set to another.

"Remember, it has to be light, Honey."

"Look at these tiny cups, Mommy! Lots of them! Are they play cups?" she asks.

"Those are demitasse cups. 'Demi' means half in French and 'tasse' means cup. It's for drinking coffee that's stronger than ours. I think one of them would be perfect for Grandma. You pick out one for her."

From the display she chooses a maroon scroll design on a cylinder shaped cup, and only $14.95, to my relief. I can't believe the price tags on these tiny, exquisite cups and saucers.

Tanya can hardly wait to get back to the farm. Mama is sitting up, looking pretty in her pink bed jacket, a gift from her daughter-in-law. She opens her package so slowly as her granddaughter looks on with anticipation. She is delighted, of course.

"Grandma, would you like some tea?" asks Tanya.

"Yes, thank you," she says softly, her happy smile telling more than she is able to say.

⌒

It is Saturday night. The farmhouse buzzes with activity. Hunkered over a *shogi* board, David, nine-years-old, challenges his Grandpa with Japanese chess.

"I used to just let them play with me but now I have to pay attention," Tochan tells me with pride. His sons and now his grandsons drop by often and challenge "the master."

I hear lively conversation in the kitchen while my sister and I care for Mama.

"*Suma nai kere domo*," Mama says apologetically. "I need to go to the bathroom but I don't think I can walk that far." For Mama to ask for help means another step backwards. Until now her small body, barely seventy pounds now, has clung to one of us. Suddenly we realize that we had not thought about a bedpan. We look at each other—both nurses!

I rush to the kitchen.

"Guys, Mama needs to be carried to the bathroom." Everybody stands up.

"Just two of you will be fine."

They lift her and carry her easily to the bathroom and return her to bed.

"*Arigatoh*," Mama says. "*Tondemo nai koto ni natte shimatta*," she says apologetically as she leans back on her pillow. She wonders how she had become such a terrible burden on everyone.

Now what am I going to do during the night without my brothers' help? Diapers? Rubber sheet? Tired and ready for bed myself, I grumble why God made it so much easier for males. They can pee in any can.

"I'll call Thrifty Drugs and see if they're open," Kay says.

She returns discouraged. "There's no place open. You'd think there'd be an all night drug store somewhere in this town."

We pad the bed with several layers of draw sheet over a rubber sheet. Having been a bed wetter until eleven or so, I remember Mama wrapping a flannel blanket several times around my waist. "This will keep you warm until you wake up," she would say. She did not want my sleep disturbed.

Just as we are ready to turn out the light, Steve walks in.

"Here. I hope this works."

He hands me a small bedpan, just the right size for Mama's bottom.

Bedpans are usually of cold metal. This one, to my delight, has soft half-inch thick foam around it.

"Where did you get this?" I ask.

He has a sly grin. I turn it over.

"Isn't this Taro's dog dish?" I exclaim.

It is the best-engineered, custom-made bedpan, made of a doughnut-shaped plywood rim covered with foam. It is not the most practical, but by far it's the most comfortable. It will see us through the night.

⌒

Doctor's appointments become progressively more difficult to keep. It is painful to see Mama having to sit upright in her wheelchair for long hours. Her spine is weak. Her head droops to one side from fatigue. She has uncontrollable bouts of coughing. Waiting patients look at us with pity, but the office staff appears uncaring. If I were the nurse or the doctor, I would see to the needs of the seriously ill patients immediately. We are to wait our turn even if Mama were to die right there. Regardless, we are determined to care for Mama at home. Mama never complains. She worries that we are taking so much time away from our own families.

I feel for the aged patients who do not receive the compassionate care they need. It is a sad commentary that patients are to become ill between the hours of nine to five, and on weekends take an aspirin and wait until Monday. It saddens me that medicine is no longer a service—it's a business and patients are to get ill during business hours.

My sisters and I decide that Mama cannot tolerate sitting upright in a wheelchair for long periods. She is totally exhausted after each visit. We need to make our medical visits more comfortable for her.

"How about a stretcher?"

"Where do we get one?"

"Medical supply house, maybe?"

"We could make one."

I call every possible lead. Finally I find one available from the Red Cross. To my relief, the nurse does not think me odd to request the use of a stretcher.

Mama is a trouper. My sisters and I keep her as comfortable as possible at the radiology lab and wherever else it is necessary for her to go and wait.

⁓

It is almost the end of June, almost ten months since her diagnosis. I sit by her bedside as she leans back on two pillows, ready for lunch. Her grandchildren's colorful artwork and notes cover the walls of her small bedroom. Meals are served on place mats designed by little hands and laminated by Auntie Kay. Numerous gifts of flowers and plants cascade from a wrought iron stand in the corner of her bedroom. Never a day goes by without her children, spouses, grandchildren, neighbors and friends dropping in to see her.

"I didn't want to die during Christmas," she tells me slowly and softly, "and spoil your holidays, so I got over Christmas. Then I didn't want to die near Easter and spoil your vacation days, and so I got over Easter, and I am still here," she tells me, as if she can hardly believe it herself.

One could not tell above the bedcovers that her body weighs only sixty pounds, that my sisters and I have bathed and rubbed every inch of her body to guard against bedsores, that we have kept the intestinal tract and colon functioning, that she has become our child in body, while teaching us the dignity of the spirit.

I remember the day when she could no longer manipulate her chopsticks. We knew then that we needed to accept the inevitable. *Shikata ga nai*, we were reminded, to not stubbornly fight against the odds, to acccept, something we had learned during the war.

⁓

"I wish I could die like your mother," Mrs. Ogawa, our neighbor and good family friend confides to me. She is Mama's age. "Your mother is very fortunate to have all of you."

I lie in bed thinking about what Mrs. Ogawa has told me. It's the other way around. We are fortunate to have had Mama, and for all these eighty-two years. I should not quarrel with God and ask for more time.

⁓

"Your mother will be more comfortable in the hospital with continuous oxygen," the doctor advises us.

It is a difficult decision for the family. We do not want her to suffer any more, and yet we want her to be able to die in her own home. All the children discuss the pros and cons. Finally the consensus is that we need to make her last days as comfortable as possible. I can see that Tochan is not too happy with the final vote. I am torn. Mama is willing to do what is best. I know that Mama is thinking that hospital care will make it easier for the rest of us.

In the hospital she is connected to a nasal oxygen tube. Her color improves. Although only fifty-five pounds are left on her body, her face is round and smooth, not gaunt. Only when she sleeps are there tight wrinkles on her forehead, indicating that her body is suffering.

"*Kurushii.*" A soft cry of agony.

I clearly remember when she said it, as if no one was around to hear. What is worse than to be alive and not be able to breathe? It is worse than the sufferings of Job. It is as if one's chest is slowly crushed and one cannot expand it.

All day, the children and their families come and go, watching and waiting. Mama appears to be in a coma. She tugs at her nasal tube. It dislodges. I tape it more securely on her upper lip. She does not hear me.

After work, the walls of her room are lined with visitors, quietly talking. We know it won't be long, as Mama had been in a coma all day.

Unexpectedly, Mama lifts her head off the pillow, surprising everyone. Her eyes open wide. She looks at each one of us, with longer glances towards her grandchildren. It is like a miracle, like a resurrection! There is total silence and awe.

"Thank you very much," Mama says, slowly and clearly. Then she falls back on her pillow and closes her eyes, never to open them again.

At dawn she quietly takes her last breath. I kiss her forehead and tell her, "*Shinpai shinai de Kamisama no tokoro ni itte.*" Don't worry about us and go to your God.

I think of a dream she told me. "A beautiful basket bathed in bright, white light came down from heaven and I stepped into it."

WEDNESDAY, JULY 6, 1977. SACRAMENTO, CALIFORNIA.
SACRAMENTO MEMORIAL LAWN VIEWING ROOM.

How empty and artificial it is here, alone with Mama in her coffin. The ornate and superficial surroundings are almost sinful. Even the flowers, which Mama loved so, have lost their beauty from forced arranging and commercialism. I wish I could place a rose from her garden in her hands.

Only the quiet is beautiful.

Mama would not be happy seeing herself in a ruffled, satin-lined coffin, but she would understand that such is society and such are human needs.

Mama's soft, gentle, loving look is gone. The undertaker has changed her hairdo completely. Her thin, gray hair is carelessly combed downward making her look gaunt, giving her the appearance of a lost, old woman, stripped of dignity. I remove the bun and hairpins from my hair. I brush Mama's hair upward into the usual way and roll her hair around the bun just above the small satin pillow. Her body is no longer soft and giving. It is difficult to lift her head. My small, black net holds her hair in place. She looks more like Mama, with a gentle look.

Mama would tell me not to worry, that all this is not necessary, that I should go and see to our guests. But I know that my sisters are there, and they will see to everybody's needs.

I remove the scarf from Mama's neck.

"She looks too bundled up and warm," Tochan had mentioned.

It is July. Mama wears her favorite pink suit from Okinawa, where she and Tochan had spent their happiest months with Steve, who was assigned there on a project with the US Corps of Engineers.

"Thank you, Mama," I whisper quietly. As I grow older, I understand that death is not something to fear. This is the body that loved us so completely, until her very last breath. She leaves in each one of us a part of her beautiful soul for which we should be eternally grateful.

This is the body we nursed and massaged and turned and powdered and bedpanned and loved until her last breath. This is the body that taught us how to die with dignity.

I kiss her forehead and leave.

⁓

Long before I was able to understand death, my father took me to the funeral of a young boy who had died after a tonsillectomy. I still see him in the coffin, his skin so like porcelain, his hands and face so young and pretty. I was about twelve, the boy's age, sitting beside my father with complete trust. This was his way of gently introducing me to dying.

My father gave a white envelope with money, as did everyone who came. On the outside he had written, "With Deepest Sympathy." Instead of flowers, the Japanese practice of giving *koden* gift money helped the family with funeral expenses.

Usually Tochan is asked to speak at funerals. That day, I sat besides Tochan, feeling good that my father now felt that I was old enough to attend a funeral. At the end of the long Buddhist service, the people filed by the casket paying their respects with a bow. I did the same.

"*Shikataga nai ne*," It cannot be helped, I heard them comfort each other as they bowed and left.

⁓

Mama's funeral is a true celebration of her life. Nine children and their families take part in a service of gratitude in a small country church overflowing with more than four hundred friends.

"A beautiful lady died this week," a reporter writes in the local newspaper. "She left a living legacy."

Years later Tochan would quote from a *haiku* poet. "The dew on the grass would cease to be beautiful if it stayed forever," he said. Only after Mama died did it all come together for me.

"If we have been given eighty years on this earth, we should be grateful," Tochan reminded us.

· 17 ·

AND THE SEEDS SWELL

Hana chirite

Itsu fukuramishi

Sakura no mi

– JOHN SHINJI SATO

Petals fall

When did they swell

The seeds of the sakura

– TRUDY SATO, TRANSLATOR

"It's taken me fifty years to grow good grapes," Tochan muses, taking a bite from a large, deep purple grape, almost the size of a half dollar. He throws the remaining half on the ground.

"Good sugar content," he says, satisfied. He nails the cover on the full lug and piles it on the back of the flatbed truck.

"Here, Grandpa." One of his grandchildren hands him a box from the truck bed, where the three of them have built a "house."

As their parents and cousins bring in their filled boxes, the children scramble to be the first to hand out an empty one, feeling like an important part of a working family.

At the end of the day, his sons and sons-in-law reload the lugs of Ribier grapes from the old farm truck onto the blue pickup truck, a more dependable vehicle. They secure the load with heavy rope, skillfully tightened with cinch knots. Where and when we learned to tie down stacks of boxes so securely that they would never lean or shift, none of us remembers. It all seems just a part of growing up . . . little things like washing each other's backs . . . like working together . . . like sharing . . . like loving each other.

As the rest of us trudge back to the farmhouse, Tochan delivers the day's harvest to General Produce, a wholesale house fifteen miles away in Sacramento. His supper will have to wait.

As he turns past the barn, he stops for joggers.

"They don't look happy," he observes. "And they don't seem to see the trees or hear the birds." He breathes a prayer of gratitude that he enjoys his exercise every day.

On the freeway, with the wind in his face and the hum of his tires hitting the road, he has time to contemplate. His mother's last words surface again.

"Don't come back here, Shinji."

They were the desperate words of a mother who could not feed her children. They were the words of a mother's deep love that sustained and directed him even across the vast ocean.

Unlike his father, he saw America not as a land of gold, but as a country of hope. As he learned to read, he was awed by the minds of the men who came together to write the Constitution to govern a new country, and who worked diligently for the common good.

One day, he dreamed, he would be a part of this great country. He would have a plot of land. He would nurture its soil. He would have a family. He would serve where necessary.

The Alien Land Law, the Oriental Exclusion Act and the Anti-Miscegenation Law challenged his dreams for a better future. Even after the devastating Executive Order 9066, when all dreams were wiped out, he had kept the faith. He understood the slow process of human growth and forgave the mistakes even as he suffered.

"A person who never suffers has no chance to become strong in mind and body," he tells his children.

"One day," he said, "the law will change and I will become a citizen."

He never doubted that America, too, would grow.

He knew the Preamble by heart:

We the People of the United States, in Order to form a more perfect Union, establish Justice, ensure domestic Tranquility, provide for the common defence, promote the general Welfare, and secure the Blessings of Liberty to ourselves and our Posterity, do ordain and establish this Constitution for the United States of America.

When the Constitution was ignored, America crumbled into disaster resulting in the shameful and cruel internment of 120,000 citizens and their parents.

In the end, it was our Constitution and its amendments, which our children studied to redress grievances, which resulted in our country's apology to its incarcerated people of Japanese descent still surviving.

⁓

Quietly the seeds swell . . .

Kiyo a nurse, Seiji a civil engineer, Sanji a teacher/principal, Aizo an aerospace engineer, Kozo a soil scientist, Kazu a nurse, Naoshi a teacher, Tomoko a secretary, Masashi a teacher.

Five sons serve in the military, in Korea, in Hawaii, with the 442nd Regimental Combat Team, the segregated *Nisei* unit in Europe. A daughter serves as a captain in the Air Force Nurse Corps.

Love grows and encompasses . . .

Filipino-American . . . Norwegian-American . . . Japanese-American . . . Caucasian . . . graphic designer . . . homemaker . . . teacher . . . office assistant . . . draftsman estimator . . . medical transcriber . . . grounds maintenance supervisor . . . administrator . . .

And the grandchildren climb the trees and eat the fruit and work on the farm.

They become . . .

Bank operations manager . . . chef . . . computer technician . . . project manager . . . assessor . . . telecommunications technician . . . lawyer . . . writer . . . homemaker . . . designer . . . accountant . . . business recruiter . . . physical therapist . . . business executive . . . electrical designer . . . engineer . . . software consultant . . . Ph.D. . . . technical writer . . . loan processor . . . songwriter . . . mathematician . . . youth citizenship coordinator . . .

And they marry . . .

Supervisor . . . marketing coordinator . . . research analyst . . . photographer . . . assessor . . . lawyer . . . accountant . . . analyst . . . physical therapist . . . HTML specialist . . . property manager . . . lawyer . . . kinesiologist . . . interior designer . . .

And they beget children . . .

Stacey . . . Rochelle . . . Kyle . . . Mikayla . . . Masashi . . . Alex . . . Aiden . . . Bryson . . . Ripple . . . Piper . . . Grey . . . Preston . . . Wesley . . . John . . . Aaron . . . Mia. . . Timothy . . . Alyssa . . . Stephanie . . . Lawrence . . . Julian . . . Derrick . . .

And they continue to bloom, inspired by the love of two immigrants who set foot on American soil ninety years ago with a dream. With hard work, the twenty acres of land produce well and sustain children for three generations.

Their progeny is no longer discernible by race.

—

"The world will become like our family, all mixed up," Tochan says proudly of his many multi-ethnic biological and adopted grandchildren.

"And the world will be a better place."

He thanks his mother for her sacrifice and for her foresight.

He breathes a prayer of gratitude for Mama, with whom he had met so many difficult challenges.

He thanks God for the privilege of tilling the small plot in this vast America.

He thanks God for his nine children. "I only want nine good citizens," he says.

He thanks God for his grandchildren, who love the farm.

He feels the exhilaration which comes with being in rhythm with life and nature.

He begins to understand the *satori*, a deep sense of knowing that comes with age, when all the pieces fall into place, and one becomes comfortable with life and death.

—

Late for a meeting, I rush down the stairs of the city parking lot and almost stumble, trying to avoid a yellow object on the ground floor. Through a crack in the cement floor, a tiny dandelion blooms with all its brilliance. Its leaves, trampled upon, tell of its struggle to survive.

The dandelion sent down its roots and found sustenance.

I gaze downwards; time stops. Tochan's oft-quoted *haiku* surfaces. Where it came from I am not sure. Was it Tochan's *haiku* or was it from a classic *haiku* poet?

Tanpopo ya
Iku hi fumarete
Kyoh no hana

Dandelion,
You've been stepped upon—for how long?
Today you bloom.

· POSTSCRIPT ·
A LETTER TO TOCHAN

Dear Tochan,

At 85, you told me: "I would like to die in my vineyard."

I would often find you sitting in the shade of your fifty-year old Ribier grape-vine, shovel held upright in one hand, watching the flow of the irrigation water, looking so at peace with your surroundings. Were you composing a haiku?

I am 85 now, in the decade in which you and Mama left. You were 87; Mama was 82. "If one lives for 80 years," you said, "one should be grateful."

Your funeral, like Mama's, was a time of gratitude, with all of us hugging and thanking the hundreds of friends who gathered at the small country Baptist Church, built on your brother's land.

After you left, it became increasingly difficult to farm. You remember what a struggle it was, even when you were with us, with a subdivision on one side and industrial zoning to the south. We were plagued by burglaries and vandalism. By a vote of 8 to 1, it was decided to sell the property, and you would know that I was the single dissenter, wanting to have the ground for our children and grandchildren to stomp on. Not practical, we decided.

The developers assured us that their plans included the many trees on the farm, the walnut trees, the Japanese Black Pine, ume-no-ki, the elegant, gnarled wisteria vine and so many more. Each one would enhance someone's front yard. Pete and I made a list of all the varieties of trees you and Mama planted, and including veg-etables, we counted over ninety!

One day, Preston, your great-grandson, and I decided to drive by our farm. I wished I hadn't the minute I saw before me a huge expanse of what might look like

Mars—twenty acres of flat, reddish brown dirt with not a single tree standing, emptiness from here, clear through to the gravel pit!

One might think that that ended an era. Not so. I am sitting at my white break-fast table with a cup of coffee, savoring the Ribier grapes, which my brothers bring me every season from their back yards.

Boysenberries grow in Kay's back yard. Her boysenberry jam is to die for! She retired from nursing, but you would think she's now a geriatric nurse, seeing to the needs of people around her, including me. Her garden is like Mama's, forever beauti-ful and productive. I often find armloads of chrysanthemums and gladioli, and even a tree peony, at my front door.

You grafted so many varieties of English walnuts, persimmons, flowering peaches and zabon, the Japanese grapefruit. Don's zabon tree grows high above his house. What a spectacular sight to see, the giant zabon hanging all over the tree! Kay, Marian, George and Pete all have persimmon trees. Each one has a different flavor and sugar content. So much depends on the years of experience of feeding, watering, and the soil.

All your children grow vegetables in their back yards. Every spring Pete grows a garden for me, with Japanese cucumbers and Japanese eggplants, tomatoes, okra and jalapeños. What an indescribable pleasure it is to crunch into a first crisp cucumber! Marian and Kay's takana brings back the piquant flavor of Mama's tsukemono. How good they were, the salted down nappa, turnips, cabbage, and even watermelon rinds. You wouldn't believe it, but stores are finally beginning to offer an organic section. We grew up organic from the 1930's, thanks to you and Mama.

Pete stopped by the other day, looking like the cat that ate the canary. He handed me a foot-long tororo-imo that he grew. How can a skinny potato be so heavenly delicious when grated and poured over a bowl of hot rice dribbled with soy sauce?

Remember the mustard greens? Our vineyard is gone, so Pete drove me to the southern part of our county, where he had found an unplowed edge of a farm with beautiful wild mustard growing. We picked enough for everyone!

You would be proud to know that three of your sons retired from teaching. You were their master teacher. A mother said to me, "My son is waiting to be in Mr. Sato's class."

All of your children are retired now, except for me. George served with the California State Department of Water Resources, addressing the water needs of our state. You will be happy to know that his oranges are an improvement over ours at the farm. Maybe it's the river soil. He feels guilty, he told me, for living in a house built on Class A soil. What will California become, with our productive valley soil growing more and more houses and lawns, and being overtaken by agribusiness? Tragically, family farms, the backbone of our country, are becoming extinct.

I took your great-grandsons to experience what was left of the original farm, next to the railroad tracks, which you lost in 1942 while in Poston. We sat under one of the few almond trees left, eating our peanut butter and jelly sandwiches, while we felt the same gentle breeze of fifty years ago. We walked on the fertile ground, now mostly weed-covered. This is the ten-acre parcel which, under threat of seizure for wartime use, you were forced to sell for $175 per acre. Upon your return, you irrigated, pruned and plowed the neglected trees, located the owner and shared half the crop of almonds and walnuts for many years.

Years ago you said in passing, as if for no one's ears, "David is a great man." His courage shows as he adapts to his relentless diabetes and dialysis. David has the most beautiful **ume-no-ki** in his front yard, just like the one you planted at the farm. Every January he cuts generous branches of the fragrant blossoms for me to take to your cemetery. I love to place them in your and Mama's urns and those of your neighbors, the Ogawas, the Kobatas, our aunt and uncle, and now Steve. Next to Mama, strangely, a marker for Yabumoto-san appeared, as if he belonged there. Was he the young man Mama saw off to war in the middle of the night in Poston? He had no family and lived in the bachelors' barracks. The cemetery comes alive with the **ume-no-hana** that the Issei love.

I expected Ronald to be the writer, as he has always had a creative bent, but it is his son Michael who translated your diary of 1942. Thank you for leaving us over forty years of your journals. Ronald taught high school for several years and left that to work for Lockheed as a biochemical engineer, working on challenging projects. In his retirement, his passion is singing opera! Does that surprise you? Probably not. You took a few violin lessons in camp. That surprised me.

Before multiple myeloma disabled him, Don adopted a two-mile stretch of the American River, picking up trash with his kayak, bringing in old tires and sacks of garbage. You took us swimming and shad fishing there, remember? We held a beautiful memorial service for Don by the river, where so many students and teachers spoke of his dedication to children.

When Steve left us, I found on his kitchen table a generic will, with hurriedly written notations designating his eight siblings and thirty-four nieces and nephews as heirs. It was rejected as a legal document. Eight of us agreed on Steve's intent and his niece and nephew, Jodi and Scott, filed the papers. None of us knew that Steve was a rich bachelor. The aging attorney said, "In my whole career, I never worked with a family like yours."

I would meet Steve at El Chico, the neighborhood bar and restaurant, and we would talk, the only time he spoke about the war and his experiences with the 442nd Regimental Combat Team in Europe. He loved to cook. He'd call me at the office. "Want to come for an abalone dinner?" He had found fresh abalone. Grated ginger in a pretty Japanese dish, soup in a lacquer bowl, cocktails. Not a detail was missed. "How did you learn to cook, Steve?" I asked him. "Watched Mama," he said.

When I was a single parent and broke, Steve loaned me $2,000 to print my working tool, the Blackbird Vision Screening System, which I had devised to screen the vision of three- and four-year-old children. Would you believe, Blackbird won a grand prize award of $2,000 from the RN Foundation for Excellence in Nursing for being the most innovative? You said to me then, "One day your idea is going to be useful internationally."

Your granddaughters, Jodi and Lisa, who attended schools where David and Don taught, asked me to speak to their classes shortly after you left. Because of the growing number of requests, I organized a speakers' bureau with our VFW Post. That was over twenty years ago. At our peak we filled over seventy-five requests to speak during the school year. With a grant from the California Civil Liberties Public Education Program, we developed a slide presentation, Lessons From Our Lifetime: The Internment of Americans of Japanese Descent and the United States Constitution," which is being used by other Nisei veterans' posts. Our work keeps growing. Several years ago, we were recognized by the Sacramento Magazine as "The Best Public Servants Over Seventy." Now we are in our eighties. Our group has dwindled from fifteen to four.

My one regret is that you were gone when our President sent us a letter of apology. We also received a check for $20,000. By then the Isseis, who had suffered greatly, had died. Only 65,000 internees were still living. I wouldn't doubt that you already knew that the Civil Rights Act would eventually come about in America.

You and Mama are so much a part of us that it's as if you never left. I hope my children and grandchildren will feel the same about my leaving this life, and that they will be able to carry on with gratitude in their hearts for those who have lived *before them, and to live* isamashiku, *as you would say, valiantly and with courage, no matter what adversities they face.*

Kodomo-no-tame-ni, *you and Mama said so often, for the sake of the children. I have a little knot deep inside of me which surfaces now and then, reminding me that a part of me is not acceptable. How clearly I remember the words of my classmate, "You don't seem to remember you're not white." I wonder if this is what led me to adopt my children—that injured connection, that common thread of social rejection? We know that a child born with a darker skin faces challenges that a white-skinned child may never experience.*

Mama helped us to understand the universal need of children for love. We know that every child thrives on unconditional love, and yet we find it so difficult to give it. Rejection, no matter how small, pierces childrens' souls forever.

As with all humanity, challenges continue, strengthening us as we move on. We face the loss of a child, problems of addiction, teenage anger, cancer, diabetes and dialysis. You gave us the tools of patience and love and you helped us to understand the art of shikataga nai, *to accept what cannot be changed. You created a place where every child is born to the welcoming arms of many. No child is alone. No child is unwanted.*

Here on earth, seeds that you and Mama planted continue to bloom . . . Violet Kimiko . . . and our most recent birth, Thelonius Shinji . . .and more . . . Julian . . .August . . .

Our love and deepest gratitude,
Kiyo

· ACKNOWLEDGMENTS ·

READERS WHOSE INPUT was invaluable are those "who'd been there," my brothers and sisters—Steve Sato, Ronald Sato, Don Sato, George Sato, Kay Yomogida, David Sato, Peter Sato, Marian Sakakihara—with all of whom it has been a great privilege to grow up.

My daughters Cia Vancil and Tanya Duncan offered input through the eyes of third generation readers, as did many nieces. Michael Sato, my nephew, read and translated his grandfather's diary, giving me further insight into my father.

My deep appreciation goes to Clare Dusek, history teacher at El Dorado High School in Placerville, California, who has for fifteen years requested a VFW presentation, allowing us to speak to three- to four-hundred students each year on the topic of internment and the Constitution. It has become more and more apparent that much is left untold in the classroom. Clare's critique and encouragement spurred me on. I hope this book will offer a deeper understanding of the peoples who made America.

I owe much to my writing teachers from many years back—Ethel Bangert, Bud Gardner, and Duane Newcomb. Kay Gay of Elkhart, Indiana, offered to help me write this "important book" twenty-five years ago! Susan McHale and Bob McCloskey, instructors at the McClaskey Adult Center of the Sacramento Unified School District, facilitated the process not only with their computer expertise, but also with their editorial critiques. Mike Fallon, retired from the *Sacramento Union* newspaper, reviewed several chapters with the eye of an editor.

Bill Hosokawa, a journalist and retired editor of the *Denver Post*, author of many scholarly works, including *Nisei, the Quiet Americans*, read my manuscript with the eyes of a fellow *Nisei* and offered many helpful, meaningful directions, for which I am deeply grateful.

Steve La Rosa, the filmmaker who produced *Stories From America's Concentration Camps* for our VFW Nisei Post 8985, and *Gaman* for PBS, reviewed my manuscript with compassionate understanding.

I have a mentor and "guardian consultant." I wake up wondering how this intelligent, knowledgeable, kind human being dropped right in front of me and not elsewhere? Dr. Ken Umbach, a fellow member of the California Writers Club, read my manuscript and took me under his wing. He proceeded on a relentless and tireless one-man crusade to see *my story* published. He wrote queries and synopses and contacted Dr. Kevin Starr, retired chief of the state library system, agents, writers, artists, friends. He printed bound copies and passed them on to readers, prodded me on, etc., and finally found a perfect publisher, Barry Schoenborn of Willow Valley Press in Nevada City, California, who published this memoir under the title *Dandelion Through The Crack* in 2007.

A special note of thanks is owed to Dr. Starr, whose kindness and generosity in reading and commenting on the manuscript has been pivotal to its success.

Thanks also to Barry Schoenborn and to his fine staff, including Patty Boyte, Chuck Petch, and Jim Collins. And to Barry's friend, Lynda Straus. Each of them contributed to this book's success. Likewise, my thanks go to Ken Umbach's friends, coworkers, and business associates who read the manuscript and provided real evidence that my story resonated with men and women of widely ranging age. They formed an informal "asynchronous focus group," as Ken phrased it, and were wonderfully supportive. And, too, my thanks to Ken's lovely and vivacious wife, Rosa Umbach, who has been a wonderful friend and supporter in this project and beyond.

I am especially grateful to Kim and John Chlang of Bradshaw Donuts for allowing me to write in the early morning hours over a cup of coffee and donut holes. They, too, have a story to tell of their long and arduous trek from Cambodia and their remarkable resettlement in America in just fifteen years.

It is with deep love for my precious children—Cia, Jon, Paul and Tanya—that I leave this, perhaps their legacy for survival. My father said of our children by adoption, "You and Gene could not have done any better." They, too, survived incredible odds and now stand tall and proud.

In my ninth decade of life, I am privileged to be able to tell this story of all those who encompassed my life—parents, siblings, spouses, my children, nieces, nephews, their children, our friends, and even our "enemies" who forced my growth.

I have been blessed with many friends and colleagues who have quietly endorsed my writing this story. They are my "Dandelion family."

And now we embark upon a new journey, *Kiyo's Story*, with Laura Hruska of Soho Press. I thank Laura for taking this leap of faith and proceeding full steam ahead with the transition from *Dandelion Through the Crack* to *Kiyo's Story*.

KIYO SATO